A COUNTRY SCHOOL HOUSE.

SCHOOL ECONOMY.

A TREATISE

ON THE

PREPARATION, ORGANIZATION, EMPLOYMENTS, GOVERNMENT, AND AUTHORITIES OF SCHOOLS.

BY

JAMES PYLE WICKERSHAM, LL.D.,

STATE SUPERINTENDENT OF PUBLIC INSTRUCTION OF PENNSYLVANIA, LATE PRINCIPAL OF THE PENNSYLVANIA STATE NORMAL SCHOOL, AND AUTHOR OF "METHODS OF INSTRUCTION," ETC.

"Doce ut discas."—SCHOOLMEN.

"All who have meditated on the art of governing mankind, have been convinced that the fate of empires depends on the education of youth."—ARISTOTLE.

PHILADELPHIA:
J. B. LIPPINCOTT & CO.

To the Pupils,

who have so eagerly treasured up his words in the lecture-room, and so faithfully followed his precepts in the practice of their profession; whose gratitude has been his richest reward in the past, and whose kind remembrance he is most anxious to secure for the future;

This Volume,

in which they will not fail to find much that will remind them of old classmates and by-gone times, is respectfully dedicated by their teacher and friend,

THE AUTHOR.

PREFACE.

All that relates to the Theory of Teaching or to its Practice may be embraced under the four following heads:—

1. School Economy.
2. Methods of Instruction.
3. Methods of Culture.
4. The History of Education.

Under the head of School Economy could be considered the preparation for, and the organization of, the school, and the conditions of its efficient working; under that of Methods of Instruction, an investigation could be made into the nature of knowledge and the methods of imparting it; under that of Methods of Culture, the physical and mental constitution of man could be examined, and an effort could be made to arrive at the best means of developing and strengthening it; and under that of the History of Education, there could be related the success or the failure, the causes and effects, of the various educational systems and efforts which have characterized the past.

The preceding classification of the object-matter of Teaching was made after several years of careful study, and an experience in teaching of almost a quarter of a century.

In the summer of 1855, about one hundred and fifty teachers, of the county of Lancaster, in the State of Pennsylvania, assembled to receive professional instruction, during three months, at the little town of Millersville. The author was then Superintendent of Common Schools for the county, and became *ex officio* Principal of the school thus established. In the discharge of his duty as Professor of the Theory and Practice of Teaching, he delivered a series of lectures; and these form the nucleus about which he has continued to collect additional matter, as diligently as his other duties would permit, until the present time. Elected Principal of the Normal School in 1856, he has delivered twice a year, in the form of lectures to his classes in Teaching, the matter thus collected; and he has allowed no such opportunities to pass without turning them to advantage by reviewing opinions and testing theories. That his views now approximate the truth appears from the skilful school-work of several thousand of his pupils who have become teachers.

When the idea of publishing a book was first entertained, only one volume was contemplated; afterwards, two; then, three; and now the material on hand has taken shape as indicated on the preceding page. The printing of this volume will be ventured upon as an experiment, and its reception by the Profession may determine the fate of the rest. At the best, some years must elapse before all of them can be prepared. The matter intended for the volume on "Methods of Instruction" is now almost ready for the press; but that intended for the volume on "Methods of Culture" exists only in the form of outlines of lectures, and that intended for the volume on the "History of Education" lies scattered about in notes, references, and fragmentary remarks.

In preparing the lectures which constitute the ground-work of the present volume, use was made of all the books relating to Education and Teaching that could be procured in this country, and numerous English, French, and German works were consulted. The names of very few authors, however, will be found in this volume; and it is much regretted that the credit due him cannot now be given to each. The lectures were at first arranged without any reference to their publication; they were delivered many times, with additions and amendments, until the whole became so connected together that it has been found impossible to unravel the web thus woven and point out the place whence each thread was taken. But, though many marks of quotation are not used, it must not be supposed that the author desires to erect a superstructure for himself by taking forcible possession of the materials prepared by others; and, in order to avoid all controversy, if indeed any one should care to dispute about the matter, he is willing that every thing contained in this book which was published prior to its date may be considered as borrowed; but to claimants is left the difficult task of dividing the allotment for themselves. This is the more readily done, because little is cared as to who first stated an isolated fact or discovered a disconnected principle. This work aims to embody what is known in the department of education of which it treats, into a system; it professes to be a practical treatise based on scientific principles; and as such its merit must be judged. It would have been easy to fill the book with accounts of particular methods and special cases,—with descriptions of funny school-scenes and relations of amusing anecdotes; but it is thought that the time has gone by when it was proper to introduce such things into our graver professional literature. No work upon Teaching can now be welcomed by the thinking teacher whose methods of treating the subject are not scientific in their nature. So much that is superficial has been spoken and written upon Education, that it has almost come to be doubted by some, whether there can be found concerning it any broad, general principles that may be used to unite its facts into a coherent whole. As treated of in the present volume, Teaching is more an art than a science; but it is an art based either upon the observation of facts or the apprehension of principles. The second and third volumes of the series will treat more strictly of Teaching as a science.

Readers of this book, it is hoped, will be found not only among teachers and school-officers, but among the unprofessional friends of education. Every parent will find matter in it with which he ought to acquaint himself. But the author has no disposition to conceal the fact that he has written mainly for teachers. His own class of student-teachers has been constantly before his mind, and he has earnestly endeavored to supply their wants and the wants of others situated like them. It is thought that the matter of the book is so arranged that it may be profitably used in the regular recitations of the Normal School and the Teachers' Institute.

Finally, if his book fail to accomplish its purpose, the author will not consider his time misspent if what he has written shall aid in opening the way for another to perfect the work he has labored to begin. Education has its principles, and is a science. These principles can be arranged into a system. TEACHING will be recognized as a learned profession, and TEACHER will become an honored title among men: to wish to be remembered as one who contributed to these ends is, surely, not an unworthy ambition.

J. P. W.

STATE NORMAL SCHOOL, October, 1868.

CONTENTS.

CHAPTER 1.

THE PREPARATION FOR THE SCHOOL.

CHAPTER II.

THE ORGANIZATION OF THE SCHOOL.

CHAPTER III.

THE EMPLOYMENTS OF THE SCHOOL.

CHAPTER IV

THE GOVERNMENT OF THE SCHOOL.

CHAPTER V.

THE AUTHORITIES OF THE SCHOOL.

SCHOOL ECONOMY.

By School Economy are meant all those arrangements that tend to make the school a fit place in which to impart instruction, and all those conditions that render teaching effective. That schools may be badly arranged, and that certain conditions may exist which are unfavorable to success in teaching, are unquestionable facts; and hence the teacher should understand School Economy. Without this knowledge, his labors must be ill directed and may be fruitless.

The whole subject will be divided into five chapters, as follows:—

CHAPTER I.—THE PREPARATION FOR THE SCHOOL.
CHAPTER II.—THE ORGANIZATION OF THE SCHOOL.
CHAPTER III.—THE EMPLOYMENTS OF THE SCHOOL.
CHAPTER IV.—THE GOVERNMENT OF THE SCHOOL.
CHAPTER V.—THE AUTHORITIES OF THE SCHOOL

This classification explains itself, and is wellnigh exhaustive.

SCHOOL ECONOMY.

CHAPTER I.

THE PREPARATION FOR THE SCHOOL.

PREPARATION is required for every important undertaking. Preparation must be made for building a house, for constructing a railroad, for taking a journey, for painting pictures, for growing fruit, for rearing animals; and so for the School. The nature of this preparation will depend, in each particular case, upon the end intended to be accomplished, and the means which can be used in its accomplishment. In making preparation for the School, the following particulars must be regarded:

I. School-Sites.
II. School-Grounds.
III. School-Grades.
IV. School-Studies.
V. School-Houses.
VI. School-Furniture.
VII. School-Apparatus.
VIII. School-Records.

I. School-Sites.—Too little attention has been paid to the location of school-houses. Not unfrequently a school-house is located along some dark alley or noisy street, half in a road and half in an adjacent field, at an angle of a cross-road, or upon a narrow strip of land where two roads fork. All have seen it placed upon ground low and marshy; on a common, rocky and exposed; or high up on a bank by the roadside. In such locations,—disturbed by noises; attracted by passing vehicles; suffering from heat, cold, dampness, want of light, or miasmatic exhalations; blunted in taste and, perhaps, corrupted in morals,—pupils cannot pursue the work of education with full profit to themselves or full satisfaction to their teachers.

Several things must be taken into consideration in selecting a site for a school-house. The most important of them are:—

1. Convenience of Access.
2. Suitability of the Grounds and Surroundings.
3. Healthiness of the Neighborhood.
4. Beauty of the Location.

1. Convenience of Access.—Each Common School house is designed to accommodate with school facilities the people who inhabit a certain district of territory, and should therefore be so located as to furnish the best accommodations to the greatest number without doing injustice to any. Theoretically, taking distance alone into consideration, the place for the location of the school-house is that to reach which the least possible distance must be travelled by all the children who attend the school. This will not often be the centre of the district; for

the distribution of the population, the direction of the roads, and the intervention of obstacles, as mountains and streams, will nearly always render it best to choose a different location. All that is insisted upon here is that those whose duty it may be to locate school-houses should do it with reference to their convenience of access, but by no means with reference to this consideration alone. In towns, especially, it is often best to increase the distance of the school-house from the population to be accommodated, for the purpose of securing a more eligible location for it.

2. SUITABILITY OF THE GROUNDS AND SURROUNDINGS.—No school-house should have attached to it less than a half an acre of ground; and a lot larger in extent should be procured whenever possible. The best shape for a school-yard is rectangular, the length extending north and south, and bearing the ratio to the breadth of about three to two. The ground selected for a school-yard should be level or slope gently toward the south; it should be dry, free from obstacles that would interfere with the children's play, and susceptible of a reasonable degree of ornament. The air ought to be allowed to circulate freely about the school-house and the school-grounds, and the sunlight to baptize them with its health-giving beams.

The surroundings of a school are to be considered of almost as much importance in locating it as its grounds. The work of the school cannot be well done amidst noise and confusion. The clatter of a mill or a factory, the sounds which come from a smith or a carpenter shop, the noises of the busy street or the thronged highway,—all are apt to divert the mind from study. Still worse is the near proximity to the school of a store, a railroad station, a butcher shop, or a tavern; as occurrences at such places are sometimes calculated not only to distract the attention of pupils, but to vitiate their taste or corrupt their morals. It is best to locate a school-house a little distance from the street or the public road, and away from other buildings. It may be sheltered on the north side by a wood, but the other sides should present an unobstructed view in all directions.

3. Healthiness of the Neighborhood.—This point needs only to be stated to secure assent; and yet it is not uncommon to find school-houses located amid the dense population of a city, where children are compelled to breathe the impure exhalations arising from streets, stables, sewers, and thousands of lungs; near marshes, stagnant bodies of water, or rivers whose subsiding waters leave vast accumulations of vegetable matter to decay in the autumn sun; or in low, damp situations, where heavy vapors hang about them in the morning long after the glad sunshine has begun to play all over the neighboring hill-sides, or the chill night-dews fall before the day's work is done. Of doubtful benefit is that benevolence which provides for the education of the mind at the sacrifice of the health of the body.

4. Beauty of Location.—Very seldom in the past have those who selected sites for our school-houses allowed themselves to be influenced by beauty of location; and yet it is a very important consideration. A school-house so situated that the children

who frequent it can look out in all directions upon scenes of romantic wildness or quiet beauty will teach many lessons better than they can be learned from books. We are taught unconsciously by the objects that surround us; and towering mountains and peaceful valleys, golden grain and shaded forests, rough wild rocks and pleasant gardens, villages dotting the neighboring plains, and vessels gliding along the distant river,—all have truth for the intellect and beauty for the heart. Scenes like these leave upon the susceptible mind of a child a deep impression. Accustomed to look upon the beautiful in nature, he will learn to appreciate the beautiful in life. Thus instructed, he will be more apt to shun the low and the grovelling, the profane and the vulgar, and to exemplify the sentiment, "How near to what is good is what is fair!"

II. School-Grounds.—It is not less important that a school should have connected with it appropriate grounds than that the school-house itself should be well built or properly furnished. But to such an extent have those whose duty it is to provide these grounds neglected it, that in many cases schools have no grounds at all, and in others they are much too small to subserve the purposes for which they should be designed. Where they do exist, they are often found uncared for, and without good fences, shade-trees, walks, or flowers, and, not unfrequently, covered with heaps of stone and rubbish, overgrown with briers and brushwood, or made unhealthy by stagnant pools of water, and useless for the purposes of play by rocks and stumps and the unevenness of the ground.

Upon this subject it is proposed to consider—

1. The Arrangements of School-Grounds.
2. The Advantages of School-Grounds.

1. The Arrangements of School-Grounds.—The principal arrangements necessary to be made respecting school-grounds will have reference to their *size, shape, plan, apparatus, and care-taking.*

Size.—In cities and towns where ground cannot conveniently be procured, or where the means of a district will not justify the outlay, the school-authorities must be content with small play-grounds well used. A play-ground of a half an acre in extent may be made to subserve many of the purposes of an ungraded school in a rural district, provided that but a small part of it be appropriated to ornament, and that the children be restricted to certain kinds of games, plays, and gymnastic exercises. It is far better, however, wherever suitable ground can be obtained at any thing like a reasonable cost, to procure a whole acre, or even two or three acres.

Academies, Normal Schools, and Colleges, especially such as furnish boarding accommodations to their students, should have, according to their circumstances, from five to fifty acres attached to them and properly laid out in botanic gardens and play and pleasure grounds.

Shape.—The shape of school-grounds containing a half an acre or an acre should be rectangular, as before stated. The length should extend north and south, and the school-house should front toward the south. With larger grounds the shape is not so important; but they should always form a compact body.

Plan.—Supposing that the front of the grounds will border on a street or a highway, it is best, when the grounds are not more than an acre in extent, to place the school-house at about the distance of one-third their length from the front, and on a line extending lengthwise through the middle of the grounds. A neat and strong fence should enclose the grounds. A walk should extend from the front entrance to the house, and walks should also extend to both sides on a line with the front of the house. A close and high board fence should extend from the centre of the house behind to the centre of the fence at the back end of the grounds. This arrangement will divide the grounds into three divisions. The two spaces behind the house should be used for play-grounds, in mixed schools, one for each sex. A shed placed immediately behind the house and extending into both play-grounds would furnish shelter in wet weather. The space in front should be laid out in grass-plots with shrubbery and beds for flowers, and a few rustic seats for the studious or those seeking rest from play might be placed under its shade-trees. The engraving of a school-house, designed for a common, ungraded school, which is inserted as a frontispiece to this work, will convey a better idea of what is meant than a description.

Plans for designing extensive school-grounds must be left to the taste of school authorities, or to be determined by their means of gratifying it. They may embrace only the grading of a place for play, the planting of a few trees, the laying out of a few walks, and the arranging of a few beds of flowers, or they may comprehend all the arts known to the landscape gardener. No place can be named where these arts could be turned to better account. Blessings upon the benefactors who shall connect with our higher institutions of learning, grounds diversified by hill and valley, by grove and copse and cluster, by lawn and nook and glen; who shall make walks and drives wind about them; build here and there arbors, retreats, and summer-houses; cause streams to meander through them, and, now and then, swell into little lakes; place fishes in their ponds, waterfowl upon their lakes, and fawn in their groves; erect fountains where best the leaping of their diamond jets could charm the eye; and set up statues of the good and great whose mute but eloquent voices might speak to the young of learning and of virtue.

Apparatus.—Such apparatus for play as is used in the games of ball, foot-ball, base-ball, cricket, marbles, &c., the pupils will furnish for themselves: they will also procure stones, and sticks, and sand, and clay, and find use for them; but there are other kinds of apparatus for the play-ground which the school-authorities should furnish. Among the most useful of these, for boys, are a ball-alley, a rotary swing, a climbing-stand, a balancing-bar, and a vaulting-horse. Girls will use swings, jumping-ropes, brick-blocks, and bows and arrows. Such apparatus as that now mentioned will answer the purposes of play and exercise in a day-school; but all bcarding-schools should have a room set apart for gymnastics and supplied with the most approved apparatus. Here the pupils should receive regular and systematic training from a competent teacher.

Care-taking.—School-Directors or School-Committees should first put the school-grounds in order; but, after he comes into possession, the teacher ought to be held responsible for their care-taking. It is his duty to keep a clean and tidy school-room, and it is equally his duty to keep the grounds in good condition. It is true that the destructive propensities of children, uncontrolled, often lead them to do mischief,—to throw down fences, to cut and bark trees, to cover doors and furniture with uncouth and obscene figures; but it is emphatically the teacher's duty to prevent these acts, and no better proof of a teacher's want of qualifications need be asked than his inability to do so. This propensity of the young to cut, scratch, deface, and destroy school-property should be corrected. They do not thus misuse the property of their parents; and good management in school will prevent it there. Teachers may create such a spirit among their pupils as not only to prevent them from doing harm to the school-property, but to render them willing and ready to assist in protecting it from the trespasses of others. They can be taught to love neatness and order, to guard affectionately the trees and flowers about the school-grounds, and to take pride in protecting and preserving then

2. THE ADVANTAGES OF SCHOOL-GROUNDS.—The following advantages may be expected to result from school-grounds well arranged and well provided with

apparatus: *the invigoration of the health of the pupils; the removal of particular causes of disorder from the school; the promotion of study; the caltivation of taste; the furnishing of occasions for imparting certain kinds of instruction; and the presentation of opportunities for studying the disposition of pupils.*

The Invigoration of the Health of the Pupils.—Children require free, exciting bodily exercise. They cannot be healthy without it. When confined for a long time, they become restless and unable to study. They need pure, fresh air, which is seldom found except out-of-doors. Nature thus indicates that periods of exercise should alternate with periods of study. The bones must be strengthened, the muscles toughened, the blood made to circulate briskly, and the whole organism of the body made to perform its functions healthfully, in order that a sure basis be had upon which to erect the superstructure of mental education. There must be a healthy bodily organization to insure a healthy mental organization; and, while a school-room is necessary to induce the latter, a well-arranged play-ground is the best means of promoting the former. No gymnastic exercises can be contrived equal in value to jumping-the-rope, rolling hoops, ball, or cricket.

The Removal of particular Causes of Disorder from the School.—The exercises of a school situated upon a street or by the side of a highway must suffer great interruption from noise, and be considerably disturbed by the curiosity pupils evince to see every passing object. At play, in such circumstances, without a play-ground, the pupils are themselves in constant danger from horses and passing vehicles, and sometimes give much annoyance to travellers. In situations removed from such thoroughfares, but in which no school-grounds are attached to the school, pupils are apt to trespass upon the neighboring fields, sometimes to the damage of fences and growing crops; or to play in the house, thereby injuring the furniture, and producing scenes of uproar and confusion.

Play, fun, and frolic, most children will have. It is natural to them; and I have no feeling in common with that pedagogical asceticism which laments this disposition in the young, or chides children for its reasonable indulgence. An active, wide-awake child is less likely to throw his life away to no purpose, than a moping, dull one. School-children should neither sit listlessly about the school-house during intermission and noon-time, nor should they be allowed to run up and down the highway, to the neighboring creek or wood, through the village, over the adjoining fields,—anywhere and everywhere their fickle fancies may prompt. Both are extremes, and both are wrong. Praise given to the hard-working student who does not rise from his desk at play-time, is injudicious praise; and the teacher whose care does not follow his pupils while engaged in play, neglects a very important part of his duty.

To avoid these causes of disorder in the school-house and out of the school-house, a good play-ground well provided with appropriate apparatus is absolutely indispensable. Here, within the hearing of the teacher and under his eye, with no danger to themselves and little opportunity of disturbing others or trespassing upon their rights, pupils could take the liveliest exercise and enjoy the merriest games unmolesting and unmolested. Quarrels would be few where the teacher's eye might witness them, and vulgar or profane language would be seldom heard where the teacher's ear might catch the unpleasant sound. The hour of play over, the pupils would return to the duties of the school-room, fresh, vigorous, and ready for work. The propensity for fun and mischief would have exhausted itself, and most, if not all, would be willing to submit quietly to the necessary restraints of study-hours.

The Promotion of Study.—It cannot be doubted, from what has already been said, that children would attend school more regularly, be more attentive to their studies, learn more and learn it better, if school-houses were pleasantly situated, school-grounds properly arranged, and school-plays properly conducted.

Our ability to study is greatly influenced by surrounding circumstances. No one can sit down in a cold, dark, gloomy, uninviting room and study well; at least persons whose interest has not become completely absorbed in study cannot do so; and this fact has as much significance in reference to school-grounds as to school-houses.

Let children have suitable opportunities for play, for working off their animal energy, and their progress in study will be greatly accelerated. If this be done, they will work more industriously, and be able to endure, without loss of health, much more mental labor.

The Cultivation of the Taste.—We have around us silent teachers. Mountains and valleys, lakes and rivers, green fields and clustering villages, the setting sun, the clouds of heaven, the grand old ocean, —all that is beautiful or sublime in the works of nature and art, elevates the mind and cultivates the taste; while, on the other hand, disproportioned, inharmonious, deformed, or neglected objects excite no train of pleasurable emotions, and familiarity with such tends to lower the standard by which we judge of the beautiful. The youthful mind is peculiarly susceptible to influences of this kind, and it cannot be doubted that the unimproved and uninviting grounds about our school-houses tend to deaden the natural sense of beauty and refinement instead of quickening it. If school-grounds were as we have shown they should be, their silent teachings would ever tend to the culture of the noblest feelings of the human heart; and, instead of that ruthless disposition to destroy, that rough, rude conduct, and those careless habits, which so often characterize the pupils of our schools, all might have their taste elevated, refined, and purified.

The Furnishing of Occasions for imparting certain Kinds of Instruction.—The most prominent use of a play-ground is to enable the pupils to obtain conveniently relaxation and exercise. When systematic gymnastic training is required, the teacher must conduct the exercises. The games and plays of children must be allowed to proceed without unnecessary interference on the part of the teacher; but he can sometimes, if in sympathy with children, make suggestions respecting old plays, or propose new ones, that will much increase the interest taken in them. Children may be taught how to play.

Occasions will present themselves, too, when the teacher can find in the play-ground attentive listeners to the relation of an anecdote or story, or the reading of some interesting book. If a teacher will take a seat under a shade-tree near the school, and offer to tell his pupils their names and something concerning all the flowers, minerals, fossils, shells, or insects they will bring to him, he will need considerable knowledge of Natural History if he is able to keep his bargain. Let it be remembered that the greatest of the ancient philosophers taught in groves and gardens.

The circumstances of the play-ground may be used to impart important moral lessons. On the play-ground the real character of pupils shows itself; and the quick judgment of the true teacher will tell him when he may give a hint that will awaken attention to the right and the wrong, or plant the seed of a moral truth that will grow up in the heart, and produce fruit a hundredfold. Even the presence of the teacher on the play-ground, while it need detract nothing from the fun or frolic, will be beneficial in elevating the general tone of enjoyment. Unkind words will not be spoken, nor selfish deeds be done, when he is by; and good qualities soon grow habitual. Instances, indeed, are not wanting in which, when rebellious natures had stirred up discontent among the pupils, and appearances indicated the subversion of the teacher's authority, he was able, by judicious management on the play-ground, to arrest the rising tumult and win all back to obedience and respect.

The Presentation of Opportunities for studying the Disposition of Pupils.—The success of school-government, and even of teaching, depends very much upon the knowledge the teacher possesses of his pupils' dispositions. It is on the play-ground that pupils first encounter opposing desires and clashing wills, and the teacher can see manifested there, much better than in the school-room, all that play of passion and all those springs of action and diversities of character incident to social life. Each individual is himself on the play-ground; and the teacher, if he freely mingles with his pupils while at play, can scarcely fail to gather information that will aid him in his school-room duties and prove beneficial to the school.

III. School-Grades.—Pupils can be classed according to the studies which it is thought best they should pursue. A system of graded schools provides a separate school or a separate room for each class, or for as many classes with slightly different attainments as can be conveniently accommodated in the same room. Without some system of this kind, the education that could be furnished by a Common School system would be very imperfect.

What is designed to be said on the subject of school-grades will have reference—

1. To the Plans of Graded Schools.
2. To the Objects of Graded Schools.

1. Plans of Graded Schools.—Plans of graded

schools involve considerations respecting, first, *the number of grades*, and, second, *the manner of grading.*

The Number of Grades.—No principle can be found that may be used to determine the number of grades in a system of graded schools. Pupils cannot be classed according to age, and studies admit divisions in a hundred places as well as in ten. The gradation of schools is, therefore, a matter of convenience, and its nature must be determined by circumstances. Custom, however, seems to have fixed three general grades, called, respectively, Primary Schools, Grammar Schools, and High Schools. The rudiments of an education are imparted in the Primary School, the Grammar School carries on the work, and the High School completes it. Where no Grammar Schools or High Schools exist, or where it is inconvenient to patronize them, the Academy and the Seminary take their place; and those who wish to pursue their studies beyond the course contemplated by these classes of institutions resort to the College or the University.

In large cities or towns, Primary Schools are divided into several grades, very frequently into six or eight, and Grammar Schools are likewise divided into several grades, mostly into three or four. It is very evident that, in fixing the number of grades for a particular locality, certain knowledge may be agreed upon as proper to be imparted in the Primary Schools, certain other knowledge as proper to be imparted in the Grammar Schools, and the remaining branches of the course may be reserved to be taught in the High School; but in this division of a course of study, as well as in all subdivisions of it, the arrangement must be arbitrary The grades of the schools might be used to determine the studies, just as well as the studies to determine the grades. Both studies and grades must be adjusted to one another and to the circumstances of the locality.

Some help to those needing it, however, may be rendered by the following statements, which are inferences drawn from the results of the systems of grading schools, adopted in many places. They are intended to apply only to our present social condition.

There ought to be a school for every fifty pupils who are accustomed to attend school in a district. In thinly populated neighborhoods there may be a school for a less number. One teacher is wanted for such a school; and he must classify his pupils as best he can.

Wherever from fifty to eighty pupils can conveniently attend a school, it should have a recitation-room attached to the school-room, and an assistant teacher should be employed. Such a school can be divided into two divisions, a Primary division and a Grammar division, although both divisions would occupy the same room except when reciting.

When the number of pupils attending one school is increased to from eighty to one hundred and twenty, there should be a school-room and two recitation-rooms, a Principal and two assistant teachers. Such an arrangement will be open to the objection that it brings older and younger pupils together and subjects them in some respects to the same discipline; but on the whole it will be found the cheapest and best mode of grading—if grading it can be called—for the stated number of pupils.

In a rural neighborhood or a village where from one hundred and twenty to one hundred and fifty pupils can be conveniently collected into one place, the school-house should have three apartments, two for Primary Schools and one for a Grammar School; or, if preferred, there can be three houses, two for the Primary Schools and one for the Grammar School. The pupils in the Grammar School will be to those in the Primary Schools in about the ratio of one to three. Provision must be made for pupils in Grammar and Primary Schools in about the same ratio until their number reaches six hundred, when —and not safely before—a High School can be established. With High, Grammar, and Primary Schools the ratios of pupils in the different grades respectively, will stand about one, three, and eight; and, consequently, of the six hundred pupils fifty will be found in the High School, one hundred and fifty in the Grammar School or Schools, and four hundred in the Primary Schools. If but one Grammar School be provided, there should be three distinct classes, with three teachers; if three such schools be provided, each school can be occupied by pupils of one grade. The pupils attending the Primary Schools can be divided into eight grades, if so many be desirable, and they can either be accommodated in one large school-building or in separate schools.

From six hundred up to any higher number, the relative number of pupils attending each grade of schools will not be much changed, and school-accommodations can be made accordingly. It ought to be remarked, however, that it has been found best in large cities to raise the grade of a High School somewhat above that now contemplated, thus necessitating a rise in the grades of the schools below it.

The Manner of Grading.—Incidentally, in speaking of the number of grades, something has been said in regard to manner of grading; but it is deemed best to make the subject as clear as possible by presenting it under a distinct head.

The first system of graded schools that will be noticed may be called the Union Graded System. This system consists in bringing all the pupils of the several grades to one building designed for the purpose, and uniting them under one Principal or Superintendent. Of course, separate apartments are appropriated to the Primary, Grammar, and High Schools, and to as many subdivisions of these as may be deemed expedient. A Union School with an attendance of six hundred pupils would require about twelve teachers and a general Superintendent. Eight teachers should be employed in the Primary department, three in the Grammar department, and one, with such help as could be rendered in this department by the Superintendent, would be sufficient for the High School. If the grades of pupils be made to correspond with the number of teachers,—as they should be,—it becomes an interesting question as to whether it is best to assign a separate room to each grade and each teacher and let each teacher hear his pupils in all their studies, or whether it is best to provide rooms large enough to seat the pupils belonging to several grades, have recitation-rooms, a Principal, and the needed number of assistants. My own well-matured conviction is that in a Union School having an attendance of six hundred pupils, which we are taking as the type of this class of schools, the best manner of grading is to provide four apartments,—the first two each large enough to seat two hundred Primary pupils, the second designed to accommodate the one hundred and fifty pupils who would attend the Grammar School, and the third arranged for the pupils of the High School. Each of the first should have connected with it three recitation-rooms; the second, two; and the third, one. One Principal and three assistants should be employed in each of the Primary Schools, one Principal and two assistants in the Grammar School, and one teacher and the general Superintendent could do the work of the High School. I cannot give at length here my reasons for this opinion; but it will be found to secure better system in the general working of the school, better discipline among the pupils, and more effective teaching,—better system and discipline because the Principals would be chosen with reference to their executive abilities and disciplinary qualifications, and more effective teaching because each teacher could be engaged in teaching those branches in which he took most delight or was most successful. The time the pupils spend in passing in good order from one class-room to another, or from study-hall to class-room, need occupy but a few moments, and the movement will relieve them from the weariness of sitting. All the teachers in such a school must, of course, unite their efforts in caring for the moral and spiritual welfare of the pupils under their charge, who, it seems to me, must be greatly benefited by the varied instruction of this kind which they would then receive.

Separate Graded Schools differ from Union Graded Schools in this: in Union Schools, the pupils are all brought to one school-house and graded there; while in separate schools, a school-house is provided for each grade of pupils, and a teacher employed to take charge of them. The school-houses designed to accommodate the Primary pupils may be placed in different parts of the district; but the location of Grammar and High Schools must be more central.

A system of Graded Schools for a city or town may consist partly of Union Schools and partly of Separate Schools. Local circumstances sometimes render it inconvenient for young children to walk the distance necessary to reach a Union School; and in such cases it is wise to provide separate Primary Schools for them.

In regard to the relative advantages of the Union and Separate Graded Systems, it might be remarked that the Separate Graded System places the schools at a less distance from the pupils, avoids sudden dangers as from fright or fire, and lessens the evils of noise, confusion, and evil association, which, unless the school-grounds be very commodious and the school-discipline very exact, will prevail where hundreds of children are brought promiscuously together. On the other hand, it should be stated that Union Schools can be managed more cheaply, they admit better gradation, and can be subjected to a much more complete supervision. In good hands, as a working machine, Union Schools have decided advantage over any other system.

What has been said has reference to schools in cities and towns. Something must be added concerning the manner of grading schools in the country. Of course, grading schools in country districts is only practicable in thickly settled neighborhoods. Here it is practicable; and the schools will never produce their full fruits without it.

If the old school-houses were out of the way, the best manner of grading schools in rural districts would perhaps be to divide a township into districts containing each a school-going population of from one hundred and twenty to two hundred, and then build two or three Primary Schools at convenient places, and locate a Grammar School somewhere near the centre of the district. The younger pupils would thus enjoy school privileges by walking a short distance, and the older pupils could obtain a better education by going a little longer distance. If people really felt the value of a graded school, a near approximation to this result could often be obtained without much change in existing arrangements as to school-houses.

Another mode of securing the advantages of graded schools in rural districts will be named,—not so complete as the preceding, perhaps, but against which much less opposition would be made. This plan consists in bringing together wherever practicable—and it is practicable in every thickly settled rural district—from fifty to eighty pupils of all grades, and providing seats for them in the same school-room, but to which a recitation-room should be attached. The teachers should consist of a Principal and one assistant, and the pupils should be divided into two grades and subdivided into classes. One of the teachers should remain in the school-room all the time, while the other could hear classes, uninterrupted, in the recitation-room. Some classes that could best be heard in the school-room, might be; though this would not very often be necessary. Where from eighty to one hundred and twenty pupils could conveniently assemble at one house, there should be two recitation-rooms and two teachers.

The advantages of such a system are very great. It enables the older children in a family to lend their protection to the younger ones in going to and coming from school. It enables the school-authorities to accommodate the increasing number of school-children without building new school-houses. All that is necessary is to enlarge the old ones, where they are sufficiently good to warrant it. It enables these same authorities to procure the services of the very best teachers as Principals, since they could pay them good salaries. The assistants could in many cases be chosen from among the oldest and best-qualified pupils; they might not be needed all the time, and would not expect large compensation. Under the direction of a competent Principal, they would do their work well. If selected because they desired to become teachers, the system might do much to provide its own teachers. With such a large number of children from whom to gather pupils, the Principal of each of the schools graded upon this plan could find employment for ten months in the year; for should the public schools be open a less length of time, a private school would be well patronized. In this way, teaching would become a permanent business, and a long step would be taken towards constituting it a profession.

2. THE OBJECTS OF GRADED SCHOOLS.—Some of the most prominent objects the friends of education have had in view, in advocating a system of graded schools, are the following: *they economize the labor of instruction; lessen its cost; make teaching more effective; promote good order in school; prompt the ambition of pupils; provide instruction in the higher branches of learning; and remove the necessity of children's leaving home to obtain a good education.*

They economize the Labor of Instruction.—In ungraded schools there is much unnecessary expenditure of time and labor. Several teachers may each have a small class in a branch of learning, whose recitations require about as much time as if all the classes were combined. Less interest, too, is always taken, both by pupils and teachers, in small classes than in those which are larger. Graded schools diminish the number of classes, and thus economize the labor of instruction.

They lessen the Cost of Teaching.—If graded schools decrease the number of classes, they likewise decrease the number of teachers required to conduct them, and in this way lessen the cost of teaching.

They make Teaching more effective.—As has already been said, ten or fifteen pupils will make more rapid progress in a class than two or three. But the chief reason why teaching is more effective in graded than in ungraded schools is because in the former no advantage can be taken of the teacher's special tastes or special talents. When a teacher is compelled to teach ten or a dozen different branches, as must be the case not unfrequently in ungraded schools, he can make but little special preparation for teaching any of them; and if he is more fond of some branches than of others, has a better knowledge of them, or succeeds better in teaching them,—and this will always be the fact,—he has no alternative but to do his best in the unfavorable circumstances in which he finds himself. A well-managed graded school has its teaching-forces so distributed as to do the most effective work.

They promote good Order.—Graded schools admit, from the very nature of their organization, better system and better discipline than would be possible if the same number of pupils were distributed in ungraded schools. The government of a school is not so easy where large and small pupils prepare and recite their lessons in the same apartment, as many sources of disturbance arise which their separation would remove. The easiest school to govern, other things being equal, is one in which all the pupils in the school-room prepare their lessons at the same time and recite them at the same time.

They prompt the Ambition of Pupils.—A pupil who enters a graded school has something in addition to the usual motives to prompt his ambition. He knows that there are higher schools, he sees his companions transferred to them, and he naturally works harder to hasten his own going. If judiciously managed, the constant spur of such a motive may be made to do much good.

They provide Instruction in the higher Branches of Learning.—Respecting the value of what are called the higher branches of an education, there is but one opinion among those who are competent to judge; and that is, that no one can be able to appreciate the true worth of knowledge who neglects the study of them. To avoid distinctions in society, to bring out all the talent a people may possess, as well as to allow the privileges of liberal learning to be enjoyed, wherever possible, by the poor and the rich alike, the course of study in our Common Schools ought to be so extended as to embrace a number of the higher branches of learning.

For one teacher to give instruction in an ungraded school, in more branches than Reading, Writing, Arithmetic, Geography, and Grammar, is wellnigh an impossibility. Either our schools must be graded, or the education of the great majority of our people must stop at this point.

They remove the Necessity of leaving Home to obtain a good Education.—It has been shown that the schools even in most of our rural districts can be graded, and, when graded, that the higher branches of learning can be taught in them; and this removes all necessity of leaving home to obtain a good education. Some writer upon the subject of education says, "All schools are a necessary evil." What he means is that, if education could be obtained in the family, it would be much better than in a school of any kind. Whether this is true or not, it is certainly true that the dangers of school-life—and they are neither few nor trifling—increase in proportion to the distance the child is removed from the family.

When children can be with their parents all the time except the six or eight hours they spend at the District School in company with other children of the neighborhood, they are comparatively safe; but the moral danger becomes very great when young persons are placed at even the best-regulated boarding-schools, where the watchful eyes and constant promptings of loving parents cannot follow to shield them from harm. If parents rightly appreciated this one view of the matter, the earnest educator would not have long to wait for the establishment of graded schools.

IV. School-Studies.—The thoughtful educator finds no more difficult problem than that which is to determine the branches of knowledge which should be embraced in a course of school-studies, and arrange the order in which they should be pursued. The performance of this task will not be attempted in this volume, as the discussion of the subject would involve principles which do not come within its scope. But, in order to render as much help as possible to the teacher, some practical suggestions will be made in regard to studies for *Primary Schools*, *Grammar Schools*, *High Schools and Academies*, and *Colleges*. Details must be left to those who write specially upon this subject.

1. Studies for Primary Schools.—Children enter our Primary Schools at the age of five or six years. They already possess considerable knowledge, and the teacher should begin his instruction where that knowledge ends, and follow as closely as

possible the methods—nature's methods—by which it was acquired.

The most prominent kind of instruction that should be imparted in our Primary Schools is Lessons on Objects. A better name would perhaps be Intuitive Exercises. These lessons are adapted to the mental condition of young children, and intended to gratify their curiosity, discipline their senses and their powers of observation, develop their thinking faculties, and improve their language. The matter of such lessons consists of the most important qualities and phenomena of objects; and, to make the instruction effective, each class should receive two lessons daily. Some well-arranged system should be followed in selecting objects for lessons, and in conducting the recitations. Suitable apparatus is an indispensable auxiliary to success in Object Teaching. Books treating of this subject must be referred to for further information.

Children in Primary Schools ought to be taught the names and the sounds of the letters of the Alphabet; and they ought also to receive careful instruction in Pronouncing, Spelling, Defining, Elementary Reading, and Oral Composition. They may write, as soon as they are able, accounts of things seen or heard of by them. The committing and speaking of pieces is an old exercise, but by no means a useless one. Appropriate narratives, descriptions, and stories may be read to such children with great profit to them.

The studies of Drawing and Writing must claim a large share of attention in the Primary School.

Pupils in Primary Schools will take great delight

in performing elementary Arithmetical Exercises, and may be shown some of the simplest Geometrical truths.

Little songs and hymns should be committed and sung. Both teacher and pupils will be the better for it.

2. Studies for Grammar Schools.—Object Lessons must be continued in the Grammar Schools, the objects chosen for lessons and the manner of imparting the instruction concerning them being adapted to the age and acquirements of the pupils. In this manner, much knowledge of such sciences as Botany, Mineralogy, Geology, Chemistry, Natural Philosophy, and Physiology can be profitably imparted. No instruction that could possibly be given in a Grammar School can exceed this in value.

A list of Grammar School studies must embrace Spelling, Defining, Reading, Composition, and the Elements of Grammar. One year is quite long enough for pupils to spend in the study of Grammar before entering the High School. They can generally learn all of it they can comprehend in that time, and the remaining time usually wasted upon this study can be much better employed in studying the Elements of the Natural Sciences, as before suggested.

Geography may be studied from a text-book, and likewise the History of the United States.

Instruction in Drawing and Writing must continue in all the grades.

Elementary Arithmetic, both Written and Oral, can be completed in the Grammar School. If desirable, considerable progress might be made in the studies of Elementary Geometry and Elementary Algebra. Better these than Higher Arithmetic.

Pupils in Grammar Schools should be taught to sing by note. Vocal Music is very appropriate, both at the opening and the closing of the school.

3. Studies for High Schools.—The principal studies embraced in a High School Course are included in the following classification:—Language, Inductive Sciences, Deductive Sciences, and History; and the teacher will not make any great mistake if he require his pupils to devote about an equal length of time to each class.

In Language, Grammar, Rhetoric, Composition, Elocution, and English Literature must be carefully studied; and if the study of any of the modern or ancient languages be contemplated, and no progress have been previously made in them, it must be now commenced, and pushed forward as far as time and other circumstances will admit.

From the many Inductive Sciences, it may be a somewhat difficult task for the High School authorities to select such as should be embraced in the High School curriculum. The following branches, however, cannot well be omitted:—Geography, Botany, Zoology, Geology, Astronomy, Natural Philosophy, Chemistry, Physiology, and Psychology.

The most prominent place among the Deductive Sciences is generally given to Mathematics. Of Mathematical branches, there should be studied in the High School, Arithmetic, Algebra, Geometry, Trigonometry, and their various applications. The elements of Logic, Ethics, Æsthetics, and Political Science, or Metaphysics generally, may be studied with great profit by those whose minds are sufficiently matured.

History, as studied in a High School, should consist of a Compend of Universal History, together with Detailed Histories of the most noted nations of ancient and modern times. The history of the several sciences and arts should be included in this course.

What has now been said in reference to a course of study for High Schools, it is conceived, will apply, with slight modifications, to the courses of study designed for Academies and Seminaries.

4. Studies for Colleges.—Language, Inductive Science, Deductive Science, and History, constitute the chief studies of Colleges, as of High Schools and Academies. The relative values of these several classes of studies are differently estimated in different institutions; but the application of a true standard would probably reveal the fact that no one class, either on account of the truths it embodies or on account of the discipline it furnishes, can establish any stronger claims upon the pupil's time than the others. Too much time, probably, is now devoted in our colleges to the study of Language, and, it may be, to Mathematics, in proportion to the time devoted to other studies. If students in college can make four recitations daily, I would have them recite once in a branch of study belonging respectively to each of the classes above named. This conclusion is not stated hastily, but only after mature deliberation.

Language, as studied in a College, should embrace English Literature, Composition, and Elocution. The classic languages of Greece and Rome should be thoroughly mastered. If the student has time, he should add to his other acquirements a knowledge of French and German, or other modern languages. Some investigation into the science of language itself may crown the work of this department.

The popular knowledge of the Inductive Sciences which students may have obtained in High Schools and Academies must be made precise and systematic in the College. Students must be taught to look deeper down into nature, and to take broader views of the facts and laws which they witness. It is un necessary to name particular studies, for all seem equally valuable; and fresh truths may still be gathered from the great store-house in which they were placed by God himself.

The Deductive Sciences start out with universal principles which are revealed by the reason, and are completed by the addition of the new truths which are found contained in these principles, by a process of logical evolution. It is in this field that nearly all the great philosophers have labored, and the results of these labors constitute the proudest monuments of the human intellect. In this department, the students in our Colleges should study the Higher Mathematics, Rational Physics, and several branches of Metaphysics, as Rational Psychology, Logic, Ethics, and Æsthetics.

The cou-se of reading in History may be extended in the College to embrace the History of Science, the History of Art, the History of God's dealings with men, the Bible, and the most difficult of all studies, the Philosophy of History.

Professors in a College are supposed to be ac

quainted with all that is known respecting the branches they teach, and to be able to conduct the student in making original investigations. Teaching in the lower schools must consist, in good measure, in making pupils acquainted with text-books; but in College they should be taken beyond text-books and made to gather the fruit of knowledge fresh from the garden of nature.

V. School-Houses.—It is not within the design of this volume to treat at length of the construction and arrangement of school-houses. To practice teaching successfully requires a suitable place and proper means to carry on the work. It is for this reason that any thing is now said in reference to the subject, and most that will be said will be confined to suggestions in regard to Common School houses in rural districts, where such information is so much needed.

The particulars respecting school-houses which require notice are—

1. Size.—The size of a school-house should depend mainly upon the number of pupils it is intended to accommodate. A house designed for an ungraded school to be taught by a single teacher should not contain less than nine hundred square feet Such a house will furnish room for vestibules, closets, platform, &c., and leave sufficient to seat about fifty pupils and to hear their recitations. A house built to accommodate from fifty to eighty pupils, and provide them with a recitation-room, should contain not less than fifteen hundred square feet; and one to accommodate from eighty to one

hundred and twenty pupils, with two recitation-rooms, should have an area of something like two thousand square feet.

2. Form.—The best form for school-houses in rural districts is rectangular, the door entering at the south end, and the north end being without windows. The dimensions of the three kinds of school-houses contemplated in the preceding paragraph may be, respectively, the first thirty-eight feet by twenty-five, the second fifty-two feet by thirty, and the third fifty-six feet by thirty-two. The ceiling in all cases must be from twelve to sixteen feet high, as it will add to the beauty of the room and to the health and comfort of its occupants.

3. Internal Arrangements.—All school-houses should possess rooms for hats, bonnets, shawls, overcoats, umbrellas, dinner-baskets, &c.; recitation-rooms, or convenient spaces for pupils during recitation; a large platform for the teacher, and for use at examinations and exhibitions; places for book-cases and apparatus-closets; a large surface of blank wall for blackboards; and seats for all the pupils, with aisles between them for ingress and egress. The diagram on page 35 will indicate better than any description the manner of making provisions for all these desiderata in an ungraded Common School.

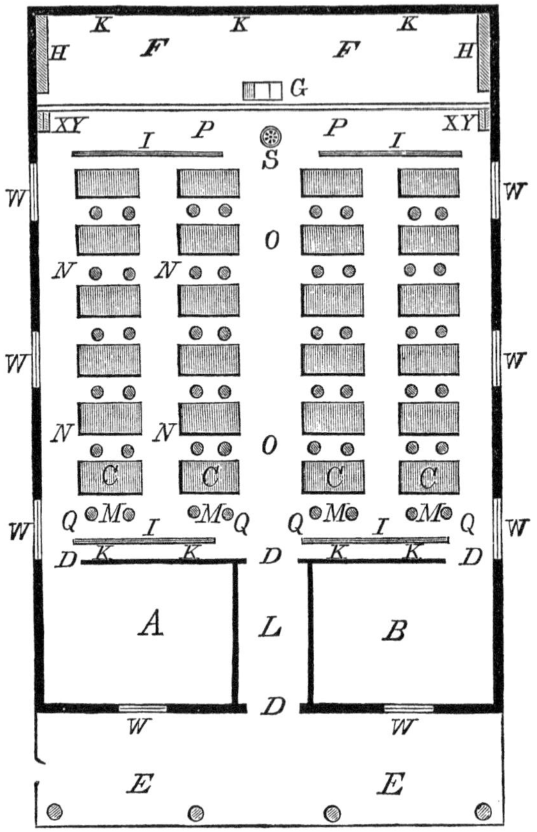

A. Clothes-room for boys, 8 ft. by 9.
B. Clothes-room for girls, 8 ft. by 9.
W W W W. Windows.
D D D D. Doors.
E E. Portico, 6 ft. wide, columns sanded.
F F. Platform, 15 in. high, in two risers.
L. Passage, 6 ft. wide, lighted by a window placed above the door.
S. Heat Register: if a stove is used, it must be placed near the centre of the room.
X Y X Y. Smoke-flue and ventiduct the latter in front.
G Teacher's desk or table.

H H. Cases for books and apparatus.
K K K K. Blackboard-surface.
I I I I. Recitation-benches, those back, when not in use, to be placed on the platform, and those in front against the partitions.
C C C C. Desks, 4 ft. long, 1½ ft. wide, and from 25 to 29 in. high.
M M M M. Seats, from 12 in. to 16 in. high.
N N N N. Aisles, 1½ ft. wide.
O O. Main aisle, 3 ft. wide.
Q Q Q Q. Space back of seats, 3 ft. wide.
P P. Space front of platform, 3 ft. wide.

In connection with the foregoing plan of an ungraded Common School, it may be useful also to present the design of one with a recitation-room attached to the school-room and calculated to accommodate pupils sufficient to employ two teachers.

It is not deemed necessary to explain the several parts of this design, as the letters are used in the same way as in the preceding diagram. The recitation-room is made ten feet wide, and supplied with seats and plenty of blackboard-surface. The book and apparatus cases are placed in the recitation-room, as more convenient. One good furnace will heat both rooms. The school-room has been furnished with seats for eighty pupils: by making it somewhat larger, it would seat one hundred and twenty pupils, in which case the recitation-room could be enlarged and divided, and two assistant teachers should be employed, as elsewhere stated.

Space is economized by having double desks; but single desks are better than double ones in several respects. Each pupil likes to have his own desk; and he will take more care of it than if he possesses it in partnership with another. It promotes order, too, by separating the pupils.

The aisles between the desks ought, if practicable, to be wider than one and a half feet, as this width will scarcely admit of quick passage between them, and entirely precludes certain gymnastic movements which are quite essential to the health of pupils and ought not to be overlooked. The partitions between the school-room and the clothes-rooms should be made movable. The walls of a school-house should be painted stone-color, or a lightish

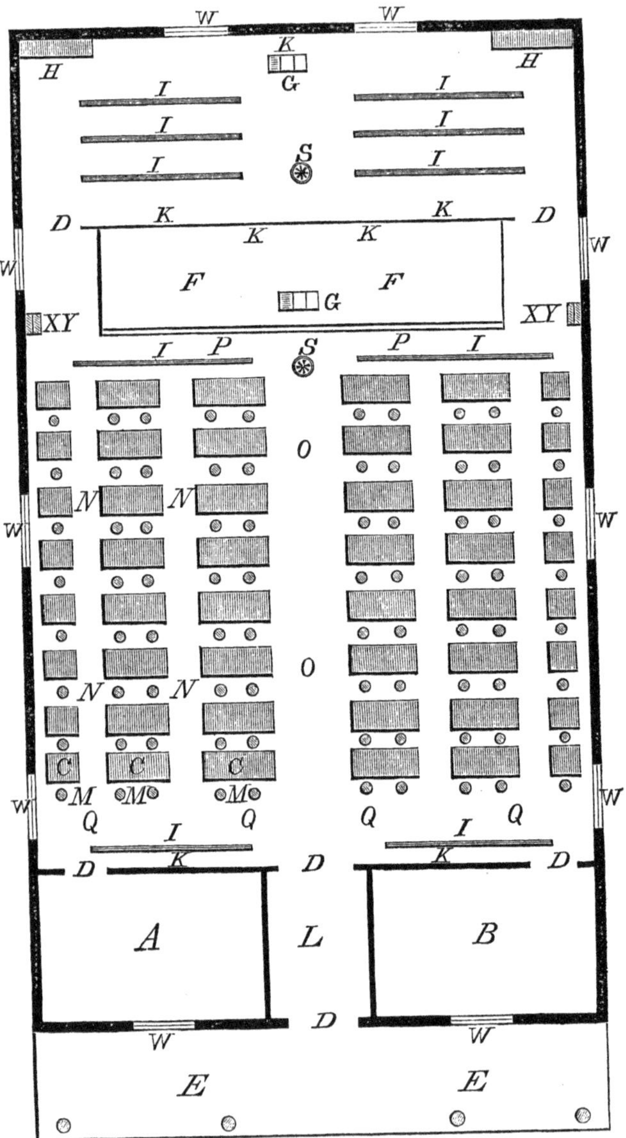
W
W
K
H
G
H
I
I
I
I
S
I
I
D
K
K
K
K
D
W
W
F
G
F
XY
XY
I
P
S
P
I
O
N
N
W
W
O
N
N
C
C
C
M
M
M
W
W
Q
Q
Q
Q
I
I
D
K
D
K
D
A
L
B
D
W
W
E
E

brown; and cherry or walnut is the best color for school-furniture. For plans of larger school-houses than these, as well as for full details in reference to the subject, the inquirer must resort to some work on School Architecture.

4. Recitation-Rooms.—The shape generally most convenient for a recitation-room is rectangular; and one in which the work of the recitation is mostly written out upon blackboards should be about twice as long as wide. Schools requiring several recitation-rooms may appropriate one to the hearing of classes in each study or each class of studies taught in the institution, and adapt the room, its furniture and apparatus, to the end it is intended to subserve. For example, one room might be appropriated to Mathematics, and be supplied with tables, blocks, models, diagrams, mathematical instruments, and books for reference; another, to Geography and History, and be supplied with Tellurians, globes, maps, charts, gazetteers, stereoscopes, pictures, antiquities; another, to Natural Science, whose cases should contain a full supply of apparatus, and whose shelves should be filled with choice specimens from every department of nature; and still another, to Art, around whose walls should hang specimens of writing and drawing, engravings, paintings, and in whose niches might be placed a few pieces of statuary. A hint is all that is here intended; and school-authorities must make the application for themselves. That something of the kind might be done in every Union School, Academy, or College, does not admit of a doubt, and, if done, there is just as little doubt ot its benefits. A recitation-room, arranged with taste in

the spirit of these suggestions, would of itself be a silent but most effectual teacher, and pleasant associations would ever cluster about it.

5. The Cellar.—The uses of a school-house cellar are, to keep the floor dry, to store away fuel, and to furnish a suitable place for locating the stove or furnace. The cellar can also be used, when properly lighted and ventilated, as a place for play in unpleasant weather; and it ought to be constructed with reference to that end. When thus used, the ceiling should not be less than eight feet in height, and extend at least two feet above the surface of the ground. The inside walls should be roughly plastered. An entrance must be provided, at some convenient place, from the school-room to the cellar.

6. Lighting.—Light is necessary to health. Facts show that people who live in well-lighted houses suffer less from disease than those who are surrounded by circumstances which either in whole or in part exclude the light. Plenty of light, too, renders a room more cheerful and inviting.

The best place, probably, of admitting the light is from the roof by a sky-light. In that case it would be steady, equally distributed about the room, and free from shadow. As such an arrangement is not often practicable, the next best mode of admitting light is from rows of windows placed on each side of the school-house. Light coming from behind casts shadows in front, which render the light unequal, and when it comes towards the eyes it is apt to injure them by its glare. All school-house-windows ought to be provided with shutters, but curtains at least are indispensable.

7. Heating.—The common mode in which our school-houses are heated is very objectionable. A stove is generally placed near the centre of the room, and in cold weather those pupils who sit close to it often suffer from the heat, while those who sit at some distance from it as frequently suffer from the cold. The temperature of the several parts of a school-room heated in this manner differs many degrees. The locality of the stove, too, is generally covered with dust and dirt, or cumbered with fuel; and sometimes it becomes the point where the idle gather to put in their time and the mischievous collect to carry on their tricks. The noise made in keeping up fires, and the smoke arising from them, are sources of annoyance.

To avoid these disagreeable effects, the heating apparatus should be located in the cellar. A small part of the cellar would answer for heater and fuel. Only a small heater would be needed to heat a single room, and such can be had at a price little above that of a large stove; or a stove may be used, if surrounded with a tin casing so as to force all the heat through the register into the room above, instead of distributing it about the cellar. If only so much cellar be excavated as to allow space for the location of a heater and for the storing of fuel, entrance may be had to it from the school-room by means of a trap-door placed where it will be least in the way. Care must be taken that the air which feeds the heater be pure and fresh. Heated air thrown into a room at any point will diffuse itself quite equally throughout the room.

If a stove *must* be placed in the room, it should

be surrounded with a tin casing made to extend from the floor to about one foot above the top of the stove. There should be a door in the casing for putting in fuel; and a trunk for the conveyance of fresh air should start outside of the building, run under the floor, and communicate directly with the stove. This arrangement will distribute the heat much better about the room, and avoid those cold currents of air which always, in a room heated by an ordinary stove, sweep along the floor from the bottom of doors and windows, and openings in the floor or walls.

Large school-buildings are generally kept warm by furnaces which heat the air, or an apparatus which generates steam; but no description of these can be given here.

8. VENTILATION.—All the windows of a school-room should be hung with pulleys, in order that they may be easily raised or lowered. If windows and doors are skilfully used, a tolerably good degree of ventilation can be secured. The ventilation will be much more perfect if the arrangement be adopted which is indicated in the designs representing the internal arrangements of a school-house. In this arrangement, the smoke-flue starts from the cellar and runs out at the roof; and, starting at the floor of the school-room, a ventiduct is carried up in front of it, and separated from it by a sheet-iron partition. In this way the smoke in the flue will heat, and of course expand, the air in the ventiduct, and make it rise in a strong current, while the air in the ventiduct will not interfere with the draft in the flue. The smoke-flue should be about twenty-four

inches by nine inches, and the vent-duct the same. The stove or furnace may have two pipes, one running to each smoke-flue. The ventiduct should have two registers, one at the ceiling and the other at the floor, though during the school sessions—unless the room be too warm—the upper one should be closed. Impure air is heavier than other air, and will generally find egress from near the floor.

Nothing can be said in a work like this of the complicated arrangements necessary for ventilating large buildings; and those who want information must seek for it elsewhere.

VI. School-Furniture.—Some suggestions are deemed appropriate in respect to school-furniture. They will be made under the following heads.

1. Desks and Seats.—Pupils in a school-room should sit facing the teacher, and all should have assigned them seats and desks adapted to their height, neatly constructed, and so designed as to place the occupants in comfortable positions. The seats may be from twelve inches to sixteen inches in height, and the desks, if intended for two pupils each, may be from twenty-five inches to twenty-nine inches in height, eighteen inches wide, and four feet long; and if for one, two feet long, the other dimensions remaining the same. A desk and seat will occupy a space upon the floor of nearly or quite three feet in length. If seats could be so contrived as to remain firm when placed horizontally to allow the pupil to lean forward easily to write upon his desk, and then could be made to have an inclination backwards when the pupil desires to read or study,

it would add much to his comfort in sitting, and something, perhaps, to the comeliness of his figure. Both desks and seats should be firmly fastened to the floor. Inkstands should never be set in the desks, because their lids are apt to be left open or broken off, and the desks around them are almost always stained with ink.

The teacher will find a table placed near the centre of the platform more convenient than a desk, especially if there be cases for books and apparatus; and these seem indispensable. The teacher's table should not be stationary.

Backs ought to be provided for the recitation-seats, and these seats should generally be movable. A seat might be placed in front of each of the desks next to the platform, and others, attached to these with hinges, might, when needed, make the connections across the aisles, and, when not needed, rest upon the top of those in front of the desks.

2. Platform.—A platform a few feet square might be sufficiently large for the teacher's table; but there are numerous occasions in every school when the pupils are required to recite before spectators, and at such times classes appear to much better advantage on a platform facing the audience. For this reason, the platform should extend the whole width of the school-room, and be at least six feet wide. Its height ought to be about fifteen inches, with two risers. The proper place in ungraded schools for book and apparatus cases is at the ends of the platform.

3. Blackboard.—The blackboard is an indispensable article of school-furniture; as much so as the plough to the farmer, the plane to the carpenter, or

the scalpel to the surgeon. It can be used to advantage in all recitations in all studies.

A blackboard should be placed immediately behind the platform and extend its whole length, and elsewhere all around the school-room wherever suitable blank wall can be taken advantage of. I never heard a good teacher complain that he had more blackboard-surface than he could use. The teacher will want blackboards for his classes while engaged in reciting, and also for others who are preparing to recite. Young pupils can be profitably employed in drawing or writing on blackboards while the teacher is hearing the lessons of older pupils.

The blackboard may be five feet wide, and extend to within two feet of the floor.

The best kind of blackboards are made of slate. They can be had four or five feet square; but they are too costly for general use. If wood is used, it must be well-seasoned pine or poplar, of fine quality, and the blackboards must be well made and carefully painted.

A cheap and serviceable black-surface for walls may be made by the following recipe:—

4 pecks of white finish, or white coating.
4 pecks of beach or other fine sharp sand.
4 pecks of ground plaster.
4 pounds of lampblack.
4 gallons of alcohol or good whiskey.

This quantity will make a mixture sufficient to cover twenty square yards of surface. A little flour of emery will prevent the mixture from "setting" immediately, thus giving time to put it on the wall with the necessary care. If emery be not used, only a small quantity of the mixture can be put on at a time; and this is perhaps, on the whole, the best plan.

The wall which is intended to be covered with the black-surface should be plastered like the rest of the room, with the exception that the black mixture takes the place of the white coating and is put on in the same manner. After the black-surface is on the wall, it must be carefully dampened and rubbed, in order to fill up all the pores and make the surface hard and smooth. If the old surface be well moistened, a new surface, composed of the same mixture, can be applied. The slate-surface now prepared by manufacturers in Philadelphia, New York, Boston, and other places, is in some respects superior to any blackboard-surface known, except the real slate. The Report of the Board of Education of Chicago for 1862 contains the following recipe for making blackboard-paint: To make one gallon of the paint, take 10 oz. pulverized pumice stone, 6 oz. pulverized rotten-stone, $\frac{3}{4}$ lb. of lamp-black, and mix them with alcohol enough to make a thick paste. Grind the mixture very thoroughly in a paint-mill, and then dissolve about 14 oz. of shellac in the remainder of the gallon of alcohol. Stir the whole together, and the paint is ready for use. This paint, if well applied, will make a good surface.

A frame should be placed around all blackboards, with a trough at the under side to catch the dust. Hooks should be attached to them on which to hang pointers and rubbers. Prepared chalk and talc are used for blackboard-pencils.

4. MISCELLANEOUS ARTICLES OF FURNITURE.—The operations of the school can hardly proceed with the necessary regularity and system without a clock. It is a silent monitor, ever reminding both pupils and teacher that time is passing. The constant lesson it teaches is, "Be ready."

A little sweet-toned bell, to be used in calling out and dismissing classes, and, now and then, to arrest the attention of those who are disturbing the order of the school, must be found among the articles of school-furniture. If the school-house have no belfry, the teacher must have a large hand-bell to call the pupils from the play-ground.

A couple of settees or a few chairs, for visitors, cannot well be dispensed with.

Pointers, rubbers, brooms, mats, scrapers, wash basins, buckets, umbrella-stands, &c. need be no more than named.

VII. School-Apparatus.—It has not always nor everywhere been considered necessary for the school to be furnished with apparatus of any kind. This was a mistake. The teacher can be greatly aided in his work by having at his command appropriate apparatus. The eye seems to be the most open inlet to the mind; and when a child sees a thing, it is more effectually impressed upon his memory than if it had been described to him many times.

Among the articles of apparatus which should be found in all schools are the following:—a set of cards for teaching the Alphabet, Pronunciation, Spelling, and Elementary Reading, with a stand to hang them upon; several sets of Letter Blocks, and a chart of Elementary Sounds; Writing-Charts; cards for Drawing, both large and small, to suit classes or individuals, and a set of objects for Drawing; a Numeral Frame, and sets of Square and Cube Root Blocks; a Globe, a set of Outline Maps, and a Tellurian; charts of History; a case of minerals and curiosities, a large collection of objects for Object Lessons, some pictures and engravings intended for the same purpose; a Thermometer; a Dictionary, a Gazetteer, and a few other well-selected books for reference in the several studies. All these articles of apparatus can be obtained or made without much difficulty or expense. No Common School should be without them.

High Schools, Academies, and Colleges should be well provided with Philosophical apparatus, and be made rich in cabinets, libraries, collections of maps and charts; and even paintings and statuary are not out of place.

School-apparatus, if well cared for, will last a long time; but if roughly handled, it may be destroyed almost as soon as procured. To keep it safe, it must be used carefully and skilfully, and, when not in use, every article should have its place in the proper case or closet, where close doors, well locked, will keep dust, insects, and rude hands away from it.

In our Common Schools the teacher should be held responsible for the safe-keeping of the school-apparatus, as well as for the taking care of the school-grounds, school-house, and school-furniture. The defacement and destruction of school-property by the hands of pupils will not occur under the superintendence of a well-qualified teacher; and one who neglects his duty in this respect should be held to a strict account by his employers. For me, it is a sad sight to see the enclosure of a school-ground broken down, the grounds themselves filled with rubbish, the walls of the school-house, both inside and outside, covered with uncouth figures, the doors and furniture cut almost to pieces by generation after generation of ruthless whittlers, the apparatus lost or out of order; and in seeing such sights I have almost ceased to wonder at the hesitation of School-Directors and School-Committees to improve the school-property. It is for teachers to apply the remedy.

In rural districts, when the school is not in session, the apparatus should be removed to some private dwelling where it will be cared for, and the house itself should be placed in charge of the nearest neighbor who will guard the property from abuse.

VIII. School-Records.—In discussing the subject of School-Records, it will be convenient to speak—

1. Of the Forms of School-Records.
2. Of the Objects of School-Records.

1. The Forms of School-Records.—School-records, to be most useful, must be adapted to different kinds of schools, and to schools under different circumstances; and for this reason I have doubted whether it was best to present any forms of them in this book. The importance of the subject to teachers and school-officers decided the question in the affirmative; and it is hoped the forms pre-

sented will be valuable to some for what they are, and to others for what they suggest. I do not see how the work of registration can be simplified and made complete in any school without using the whole set, or others which answer the same ends. Four forms will be presented,—viz.: A REGISTER OF ADMISSION AND WITHDRAWAL, A REGISTER OF ATTENDANCE AND DEPORTMENT, A CLASS REGISTER, and A SUMMARY REGISTER. Of course, any of the forms can be dispensed with if it is desirable, or a blank book can be readily ruled for the forms "A" and "D." Books for the forms "B" and "C" should be printed, as they require considerable ruling, &c.

The form of Register on page 50 explains itself. It may not always be necessary to make a record of all the items indicated in it, and, if not, any of them can be omitted. Such a Register will be more convenient if accompanied with an Alphabetical Index. The Index can be made by numbering the names in the Register, 1, 2, 3, &c., and attaching the same numbers to the names arranged alphabetically.

The names in the Register on page 51 constitute the roll of the school which should be called immediately after the opening exercises in the morning, and again just before dismissing in the afternoon. All pupils answering to their names at the morning roll-call may be marked /, those answering to their names at the evening roll-call may be marked \, and those present at both roll-calls Λ. Any one who is absent at the calling of the roll in the morning should have a . placed opposite his name, which, if he be present in the evening, and be able to give a satisfactory explanation of his tardiness,

A.—REGISTER OF ADMISSION AND WITHDRAWAL.

NAME OF SCHOOL.

Term Beginning .... *Ending* ....

Names of Pupils.	Age of Pupils.	Residence.	Names of Parents or Guardians.	Occupation of Parents.	Date of Entrance.	Date of Withdrawal.	Reason of Withdrawal.

B.—REGISTER OF ATTENDANCE AND DEPORTMENT.

NAME OF SCHOOL.

Month Beginning .... *Ending* ....

Names.	M		T		W		Th		F		M		T		W		Th		F		M		T		W		Th		F		M		T		W		Th		F		Nos. for the Month.	
	A	D	A	D	A	D	A	D	A	D	A	D	A	D	A	D	A	D	A	D	A	D	A	D	A	D	A	D	A	D	A	D	A	D	A	D	A	D	A	D	A	D

the teacher can change into a figure denoting his partial presence. If no such explanation be given, the teacher must, in addition, express the fact by giving him a low mark in the deportment column. If the pupil be absent altogether, he should receive a 0 in the attendance column, and the space opposite his name in the deportment column be left blank, until it is seen whether he will bring a satisfactory excuse for his absence; when, if so, he should receive the same number as if present, and if not, a 0. The deportment should be marked at the evening roll-call. When several teachers are engaged in the same school, it is their duty to report promptly to the Principal all improper conduct which they may have noticed, in order that it may be noted at the proper time in the Register. Habitual tardiness, repeated truancy, and incorrigible bad conduct, should be punished by dismission from school.

The most convenient scale of marks which I have been able to find is the following:—5, 4, 3, 2, 1, 0, meaning, respectively, *very good*, *good*, *middling*, *rather bad*, *bad*, and *very bad;* or, as applied to attendance and study, the last three degrees should read, *rather poor*, *poor*, and *very poor*. By *very good* attendance, *very good* deportment, and *very good* study, a pupil should receive the number 5 for each, daily; which, for a week, would be 25 for each, and for a month, 100 for each. This is the highest number attainable. As regards attendance, tardiness, whether excused or not, necessitates a deduction from the full number accorded to punctual presence; and no credit can be given, in the attendance column, for absence, no matter from what cause it occurs. As regards deportment, *unexcused* tardiness should be marked as low as 2 or 3, *unexcused* absence can rightfully claim nothing more than a 0, and all other conduct and deportment must be estimated fairly by the teacher and marked accordingly. The sum of the numbers attained by each pupil for the month is designed to be placed in the last column of the Register of Attendance and Deportment, for easy transfer to the Summary Register.

The Class-Register is designed to record the names of the pupils in the several classes of a school, and to mark the degrees of excellence in their recitations. As many Class-Registers will be needed as there are teachers in a school. The same figures are used as in the Register of Attendance and Deportment, and with the same significance. The space opposite the name of a pupil who is absent from any cause is left blank, as the question of the absence itself is to be settled under the head of deportment; and all others are to be carefully marked according to the knowledge of the lesson which they evince. The sum of the numbers received for all the days of a week will give the number for that week, and the sum of the numbers received for four weeks will give the number for a month. The highest number for a month, as in attendance and deportment, is 100.

In the column designated *Relative Standing*, it is intended to mark the members of the class, *first*, *second*, *third*, *fourth*, *fifth*, &c., according to their relative scholarship.

The column headed *Marks of Transfer* is designed

C.—CLASS REGISTER.

Class .... *in* ....

Month Beginning .... *Ending* ....

Names.	M	T	W	Th	F	Nos. for the week.	M	T	W	Th	F	Nos. for the week.	M	T	W	Th	F	Nos. for the week.	M	T	W	Th	F	Nos. for the week.	Nos. for the m'th.	Relative Standing.	Marks of Transfer.

to aid the school-authorities, especially when the schools are graded, in making promotions from a lower class to a higher one, or from one grade to another. If, in the opinion of the teacher of a class, a pupil should remain where he is, the space in this column opposite his name should remain a blank; but if he thinks he should be advanced, he fills it with a +, or if placed in a lower class, with a —.

At the end of every month, the teacher should add together the numbers each pupil has received in his different studies, and divide their sum by the number of studies: the quotient will be his *general number for study*, which should be transferred to the Summary Register. Where several teachers are engaged in the same school, each teacher monthly should arrange the members of his several classes alphabetically, place opposite each name the proper number, so far as attainable from the data in his possession, and hand his report to the Principal, to be modified by the reports of the other teachers and then transferred to the Summary Register.

In this Register the names of the pupils ought to be arranged alphabetically. The Summary Register itself, when carefully filled up, will be a synopsis of all that is done in the school.

The numbers for the term are obtained by adding together the several numbers for the different months contained in it. He who has the highest number for attendance will stand *first* in this respect; and so in regard to deportment and study.

2. The Objects of School-Records.—Some of the objects of school-records might be inferred from

D.—SUMMARY REGISTER.

NAME OF SCHOOL.

Term Beginning .... *Ending* ....

Names.	Nos. for 1st Month.			Nos. for 2d Month.			Nos. for 3d Month.			Nos. for 4th Month.			Nos. for 5th Month.			Nos. for 6th Month.			Nos. for Term.			Relative Standing.		
	A	D	S	A	D	S	A	D	S	A	D	S	A	D	S	A	D	S	A	D	S	A	D	S

the forms already presented; but it will be proper to make a more definite statement of them.

To aid the Teacher in his Work.—The great economist of time and labor is system. A loose organization is never an effective one, in a factory, in an army, or in a school. With such a set of school-records as has just been described, the little trouble it takes to keep them will be ten times more than compensated for by the increased efficiency of the school, and the pleasure that arises from contemplating the results of nicely adjusted machinery. Without them, the teacher's rewards and punishments, praises and rebukes, promotions and degradations, must necessarily be ofttimes inconsiderately made. He will have no substantial foundation upon which to base his administration of the affairs of the school.

To give Information to Parents and School-Officers.—The Registers, if carefully kept, will contain an abstract of the history of the school, and of each pupil in it. It can there be learned when every pupil entered school, how long he continued his attendance, and why he withdrew; how many days he was absent or tardy, how well he conducted himself, what branches he studied, and what progress he made in them; and these and other things recorded in the Registers are just the information parents and school-officers desire most to obtain. Besides, the Registers furnish the means of comparing one school with another, in the same district, and the schools of one year with those of preceding years.

To furnish Educational Statistics.—Our educational statistics are extremely unreliable, and inferences based upon them are, therefore, apt to be fallacious. This arises from imperfect school-records or an imperfect manner of keeping them. Our State authorities whose duty it is to make school-laws and administer them need accurate information concerning the condition of the schools; and to furnish such information is one of the objects of school-records. They ought to furnish particularly, every year, the whole number of children of school-age in each school-district, the whole number that attended each school, the average number that attended each school, the expense per scholar, the number of grades into which the schools are divided and the number of pupils in each grade, and what branches are studied in each school and each grade; and, although all of these statistics cannot be gathered wholly from the school-records, they cannot be obtained without these records.

Questions relating to the higher interests of education, too, can only be determined at last by a resort to the unequivocal truths unfolded by statistics: I mean questions concerning the relations of education to the value of property, to labor, to crime, to government, and to religion. The simple facts recorded by careful teachers may one day solve the great problem of human civilization.

To exert a beneficial Influence upon the Pupils.—I speak from a large experience when I say that school-records judiciously used are among the most potent means open to the teacher of securing regular attendance, correct deportment, and attention to study among the pupils in a school. Many do not regard a rebuke that passes away with the utterance of it, or a punishment that will be soon forgotten, who will be averse to seeing their derelictions of duty placed permanently upon a record. In the system of school-records previously explained, it will be observed that care is taken to sum up the numbers obtained by each pupil for each week, each month, and each term, that every pupil may observe what kind of a history of himself there is being recorded. The teacher will do well sometimes to read the numbers for a month, or the relative standing of the members in a class; or he may send abstracts of each pupil's record in attendance, deportment, scholarship, and average standing, to his parents.

While school-records may exert all the beneficial influence upon the pupils in a school that is claimed in the preceding paragraphs, an injudicious teacher may do his school more harm than good by using them in the way suggested; and even in the hands of one who is most careful, there is danger that the nobler motives to study, such as the love of truth and the conviction of duty, will be subordinated to a desire for honor, or be lost sight of in the struggle for success. If properly used, however, school-records will always prove a valuable auxiliary in the management of a school.

CHAPTER II.

THE ORGANIZATION OF THE SCHOOL.

THE organization of the school is the part of school-economy which treats of the adjustment of the school-machinery, the assignment of positions and duties to pupils, and the adoption of regulations necessary to control the school-operations. A good school-organization enables the teacher to do the greatest amount of work in the least amount of time, and to do it most efficiently; it makes the government of the school more easy and more effectual; and it places pupils in circumstances most favorable to their advancement in learning.

In the discussion that is to follow, chief reference will be had to the organization of Common ungraded schools; but, as occasion offers, hints will be given as to the manner of organizing other kinds of schools.

The subject can be more conveniently treated of in two sections, as follows:—

I. The Temporary Organization of the School.
II. The Permanent Organization of the School.

I. The Temporary Organization of the School.—The most skilful teacher, in taking charge of a new school, will be unable to foresee all the circumstances that may tend to modify the arrangements which ought to be made for its well-working; and this creates a necessity of a temporary organization, to last until experience furnishes data for making it permanent. As the success of such an organization will depend upon the principles involved in its formation, some suggestions respecting them are deemed appropriate.

It is important to make a good beginning in teaching. If the teacher exhibit want of skill the first day in school, it may create a prejudice against him in the minds of his pupils that cannot for a long time be removed. A teacher can hardly be placed in a more awkward position than to have many inquisitive, sharp-eyed children gazing at him, and not know what to do with them. Many children are good judges of character. Their quick instincts soon inform them whether their teachers possess the necessary qualifications for their position. They hasten to school the first day, watch eagerly every word and motion of the new teacher, form an estimate of his character and ability, and hurry home to relate their impressions of him. They are good critics, too; and that teacher will be fortunate with respect to whom, on this first day of school, their criticisms are favorable.

System in any kind of business is necessary to success. A captain could not command a vessel, a superintendent manage a factory, or a general marshal an army, without a systematic plan of operations. The same truth applies to the organization of a school. Teachers have commenced the work of teaching without knowing what to do or how to do it; but, although practice made some skilful, it was always at the expense of the best interests of their pupils, while others met with such poor success, and were so conscious of it, that they took the earliest opportunity to escape from a position which, with more preparation, they might have adorned.

It is generally a good plan for a teacher to visit a neighborhood in which he is unacquainted before taking charge of a school in it. No necessity will exist for visiting all the patrons of the school, as the most essential information can be had from such school-officers as may live in the district, or from those citizens who take the deepest interest in the school.

The information most necessary to the teacher in organizing his school will relate—

First, *to the views of the neighborhood respecting schools.*—The people of different neighborhoods differ in their views of education and the methods of obtaining it, as they do with respect to other things; and, whether these views be enlightened and liberal or otherwise, it is very important that the teacher should be acquainted with them. It is not meant that a teacher should always conform to the wishes of his patrons in adjusting the affairs of his school, for by pursuing a different course he can frequently convince them of their error; but he should always treat these views with becoming deference, and to do so he must know what they are. Young teachers often lose much by their injudicious disregard of public opinion. Reforms in school affairs, as well as in all else, can only become permanently established by being made gradually.

Second, *to the methods of managing the school and imparting instruction pursued by his predecessor.*—Not that these should be closely imitated on the one hand, or severely criticized on the other; but the teacher should acquaint himself with them as thoroughly as his opportunities will permit, for the purpose of making a safe connection between the instruction the pupils have received and that which he intends to impart to them, and to avoid a violent transition from one mode of governing to another. This information can perhaps be better obtained from some intelligent friend of education in the neighborhood than from any other source, though many facts can be gathered from the pupils. A conversation with his predecessor would enable a teacher to learn much, both with respect to the school and its patrons.

The great object of the teacher's first day's work in school is to make a favorable impression upon the pupils by winning their confidence and respect. To this end, the teacher should be at the school-house early the first morning. The house itself should be pleasantly arranged, and the teacher should await the new-comers. Busy hands in cottage, farm-house, and mansion, soon make ready the children of the neighborhood, and, almost without breakfast, they hurry away to school, for the news has spread that they are to have a new teacher. They come! The teacher need have no fear for the first comers; they will give him little trouble. But by ones, twos, and threes the children flock towards the school, and among them it is not difficult to point out some who are rude and rough; others, polished and polite; some, gay and lively; others, shy and reserved; some, bold and mischievous; others, modest and respectful:—in short, the teacher has about him a miniature world. He will act wisely if he meet them as they come, talk with them, ask their opinions respecting the arrangement of the furniture, and inquire of them concerning the previous management of the school. Dr. Franklin said, "It is a good way to make your enemy your friend to ask him to do you a favor." The teacher will find that even bad boys, bent upon mischief, will be made better by consulting them or asking their help. Besides, something may be done in this way to awaken a feeling of school-patriotism. If parents come to the school with their children, they should be welcomed and consulted.

It may be well to state to some of the pupils informally at what time school will open: they will spread the information; and precisely at the hour named, order may be readily secured by ringing a small bell. The pupils will be likely to take the seats they formerly occupied; near friends will seat themselves together; or, if the desks are of different heights, they may arrange themselves somewhat according to size or age. The selection of seats will have been generally made before the opening of the school. The teacher may watch the choosers, and learn the reasons for their choices; but he should not authoritatively interfere. If asked, he may point out suitable seats, but should make no permanent arrangements.

As soon as the pupils have taken their seats, a teacher who understands the nature of his work will commence the organization of the school, knowing what to do and how to do it. No position, however, can be more embarrassing to one who has made no preparation for teaching, who has provided no plan of operations, than to have a houseful of children before him, looking at him, criticizing every movement he makes, and not know how to proceed with his work. What seems most necessary to be done first, is to make some needful general regulations. This course is best, because it will be calculated to prevent the formation of bad habits which subsequent effort may not easily correct, and also habituate the pupils at the start to conform to a system. Loose arrangement in the beginning will eventually prove a fruitful source of trouble.

The regulations thus instituted should be *temporary*, and the pupils should so understand them. Many of them, doubtless, will become permanent,—the more of them the better; but, since some of them may be changed, it is the best policy to consider all of them as in force only for the present. Frequent changes in laws beget a want of confidence in the lawmaker; and school-regulations are not an exception to the general rule. I do not know which plan would be productive of the most evil,—to adopt at first a permanent set of rules for the management of the school, or to allow the pupils to do as they please without any rules at all; but I am certain that both will prove, in a very large majority of cases, unsatisfactory. Of course, this does not apply to schools whose objects are fixed, or whose teachers do not change.

The most important of these regulations will concern—

1. THE SEATING.—It will often be well for the teacher to state that the pupils may occupy the seats they have chosen, or which have been assigned to them, for the present, but that they are not yet theirs permanently, and, if good order requires it, changes will be made. It may be well for him to remark, further, that in some schools pupils desire to sit near together for the purpose of talking or playing, and that, though he hopes such may not be the case with them, he thinks it best to be prepared to protect those who wish to study from disturbance by making arrangements, without seeming to trespass upon the rights of any, to prevent it.

2. THE TIMES OF OPENING AND CLOSING THE SCHOOL.—This information is necessary both to the pupils and their parents. Punctuality can be best secured by being exact in the beginning.

3. THE HOURS OF RECESSES OR INTERMISSIONS.—These will depend upon the circumstances of the school; but *some* hours should be temporarily fixed upon at once. They can be easily changed if it become necessary.

4. LEAVING SEATS AND ASKING QUESTIONS OF THE TEACHER.—The best *temporary* arrangement, probably, that can be made in these respects, is to require every one who wishes to leave his seat or ask a question of his teacher to hold up his hand, and the teacher, noticing it, will grant or withhold liberty to do so, as he deems best.

5. WHISPERING.—Whispering is a very difficult thing to control, either under a temporary or a per-

manent school-organization. The practice I recommend is for the teacher to say to the pupils that the school room must be still in order to study and recite well, that low talking is apt to become loud, and that those who talk much will most likely waste time by it; but for him then to add that, since it happens sometimes that one pupil may have a proper communication to make to another, or a proper question to ask him, the privilege of whispering will be allowed, provided it be done in such a way as to disturb no one. Such a regulation will be satisfactory to pupils, and no opposition will be manifested to the additional provision that, in case whispering become a source of disturbance in the school, it will be prohibited. This plan will enable the teacher when he comes to prohibit whispering entirely—and this will be found in most schools to be the best policy—to throw the responsibility upon the pupils, where it justly belongs, instead of seeming to act in an arbitrary manner. I know no better plan than this; and *some* plan should be adopted the first day.

6. General Deportment.—A detailed system of school-rules enforced the first day will not affect pupils favorably. They may not be well adapted to the circumstances of the school, and thus may seem to imply a want of skill on the part of the teacher, and the pupils, unable to appreciate their necessity, will consider them arbitrary. The most effective rules relating to deportment are those which are forced upon the teacher by the circumstances of the school and in ful. view of the pupils. Such rules can be justified by what has happened, not by what might happen On the first day, therefore, I recommend

the making of but one rule in reference to deportment,—"*Do right.*" This rule embraces all cases, and the appeal for its justice is made directly to conscience.

7. WORK.—It will be well to assign work at once, more for the sake of giving the pupils something to do, than for the sake of what will be done by them. In graded schools, when teachers know what studies are to be pursued, and where the lessons are to be commenced, no delay for the purpose of ascertaining these things will be necessary; but it will frequently happen that a teacher cannot know how to form his classes, what branches are to be studied, nor at what points the several studies should be commenced, without special inquiry and examination. Such inquiries and examinations require some time; and, while the teacher is engaged with them, how are the pupils to be employed? Miscellaneous lessons, which are reviews of what they have previously studied or which furnish good tests of their present knowledge, may be assigned; but perhaps it is just as well to ask all to prepare the next lessons in their several studies to those they previously studied when last at school. All these arrangements need require but a few moments of time; and while the pupils commence their work, knowing what is expected of them, the teacher can take pencil and paper, and pass around among them, taking down their names, ascertaining whether they have complied with the conditions of admission, and, if so, the kind of books they have, the branches they have pursued in the past, and those they desire to engage in at the present. This done, a short

time will suffice to make a *temporary* arrangement of classes, and to commence recitations. The evening of his first day in school the teacher can most profitably spend in registering the names of his pupils, and adapting his regulations to the circumstances of his school as ascertained from the experience of the day.

The pupils must recite the first day more in groups than in classes; and the recitations must be general in their character, and conducted in reference to the end of obtaining exact information in regard to the attainments the pupils have made in the several branches they have previously studied. Several days must sometimes be spent in these experimental recitations or examinations, before the teacher can bring order out of the confusion, by forming classes and commencing the new instruction at the point where the knowledge of his pupils ends.

In managing the school and conducting the recitations under his temporary organization, the teacher will need to call into requisition all his tact and talent. Many can keep machinery in operation which they could not contrive; and young teachers will find it more difficult to organize a school than to manage it when organized. Several days, and in some cases a week, may be allowed to elapse before the teacher should venture to give his pupils permanent seats, make permanent regulations for the school, or arrange a permanent programme of study and recitation. Some approach, however, may be made daily to this desirable end.

II. The Permanent Organization of the School.—No organization of a school, however well considered, can be permanent in the common acceptation of the word. A teacher can never foresee all the elements which should enter into the calculation in the arrangement of his plans. The word *permanent*, then, as used here, must not be understood to mean unalterably fixed, but only that degree of permanency possible under the circumstances.

As no professional skill can devise plans that will be adapted to all kinds and grades of schools, what is intended to be said will have reference to the leading principles which must be observed in permanently organizing a school; and each teacher is expected to possess the ingenuity necessary to apply them so as to meet the peculiar requirements of the state of things by which he is surrounded.

In organizing a school permanently, the teacher must make—

1. General Provisions in Regard to Study.
2. General Provisions in Regard to Order.

1. Provisions relating to Study.—Provisions relating to study must be made with reference to the following circumstances:—

1st. *The Branches to be taught in the School.*

2d. *The Branches to be studied by each Pupil.*

3d. *The Text-Books to be used.*

4th. *The Formation of the Pupils into Classes.*

5th. *The Distribution of the Classes among the Teachers.*

6th. *The Arrangement of Times for Study and Recitation*

1st. *The Branches to be taught in the School.*—In a preceding section, some remarks were made with respect to a general course of study for schools; here it is proposed to make some suggestions concerning the selection of branches of learning to be taught in a particular school. In making such a selection, the teacher must regard the object of the school, its grade, the requirements of school-officers, and his own time and ability.

If the object of the school be a special one, its course of study must be arranged with reference to a special end. Some schools aim to prepare pupils for higher schools, and others have in view preparation for a particular kind of business: all such must so direct the studies of their pupils as to secure most effectually their special object. If a general education is contemplated, such an arrangement of studies must be made as will be best calculated to attain it. A general education has four objects: to obtain truth, to promote discipline, to elevate ideals, and to impart skill. Truth is desirable for its own sake; and education strengthens the body and the mind, expands our aspirations, and renders men more fit to perform the work of life. All of these objects must be considered in arranging a course of study; and, when well understood, there is no antagonism in the efforts necessary to be made for their attainment. A teacher may be making his pupils active business-men and good citizens at the same time that he is enriching their minds with stores of the noblest truth, holding up for their contemplation the purest ideals of perfection, and enlarging their powers by free, strength-giving exercise. With these objects in view, the teacher must select such studies, subject to other conditions, as will be best calculated to promote them. What it is thought these should be under the most favorable circumstances, has already been stated; what they *must* be under particular circumstances, can only be left to the teacher's judgment.

In an ungraded school, the course of study is completed within itself; but in a system of graded schools, each school or grade has its particular studies, the general course of study extending through all the grades of the system. The studies of a particular school in such a system, depending upon its grade, can only be determined in connection with the studies of the other schools of the system of which it is a part.

Sometimes school-officers, Directors or Controllers, assume the duty of arranging courses of study for the schools under their charge; but, if so, they must do it subject to the general principles already indicated for the guidance of the teacher. Such arrangements are binding upon teachers who remain in the employ of those who make them

It is not to be expected that a teacher can find time, or that he will possess the ability, to teach every thing; and this may have something to do in fixing upon the studies for a school. It is the teacher's duty to spend his school-time most profitably for the whole school. If he has a large school and devotes much time to a few pupils who are engaged in the study of some special branch of learning, he may do injustice to other members of the school. It is not meant by this that he ought not to devote more time to pupils in the higher classes than to those in the lower classes, for he may do this without encroaching upon the rights of any, since the members of the lower classes will soon enter the higher ones; but it *is* meant that the teacher's time during school-hours is not his own, and each pupil is entitled to a proper share of attention; and no studies should be introduced into a school that will necessitate a violation of this principle. It seems scarcely worth while to add that a teacher ought not to undertake to teach to others what he does not know himself. By hard study a teacher may prepare lessons in advance of a class; but the experiment is a dangerous one.

2d. *The Branches to be studied by each Pupil.*—Two modes of fixing the number and kind of studies to be pursued by each pupil in a school are practised in institutions of learning. By the first, a general course and a general order of studies are prearranged, each pupil is examined upon entering, and such studies are assigned him as it is deemed best he should acquaint himself with in the beginning, and such an order is followed in his course as his progress may justify. By the second, the course and order of studies are determined by the teacher's judgment formed from the circumstances that surround him, the interests of the school, the wishes of parents, and the tastes or talents of pupils. These modes differ in this: in the former, the controlling consideration is the nature of the branches to be taught, and the general ends of study; while in the latter, more influence is allowed to particular circumstances. When pupils enjoy the liberty of either attending a school or not, the school-authorities have an undoubted right to adopt a course of study and compel all members of the school to pursue it; and this plan is more systematic, and probably, on the whole, in institutions designed to impart a general education, is productive of more good than any other. No complete gradation of schools or arrangement of classes would be possible without it. Many schools have been crippled in their working by an effort to conform to individual wants. Still, the particular interests of a school, the wishes of parents, and the tastes or talents of pupils, cannot be wholly overlooked; and the question becomes an important one as to the influence which ought to be allowed to them.

It can easily be conceived that a school with a fixed course of study may find that its interest demands at times a departure from it. It may be done to take advantage of some unforeseen circumstance or to accomplish some special end, to accommodate the course of study to the length of time pupils can attend school, or to the nature or amount of their home-work; but in so doing the teacher must be careful that the school as a whole suffers no detriment.

Parents have a deep interest in their children, and some deference should be paid to their wishes respecting the branches of study which they are made to pursue. A school should remove children as little as possible from the influences of home, and, as school-authorities derive all their powers primarily from parents, their wishes should never be disregarded unless the general good demands it. No parent, however, can reasonably expect that his child should receive more than a just proportion of the teacher's attention, or that the general interest of the school should be sacrificed to secure for him some special favor. If a parent insist that his child should study some branch of learning for which he is found not to be prepared, his demand ought to be kindly but firmly refused; but if he is prepared, and the general good of the school suffer no detriment from it, the parent's wish should be complied with, though the teacher may think some other branch more suitable.

Tastes in regard to particular studies are often the effect of habit. Most pupils may be brought to like any branch of learning; and there are branches upon the study of which it is worth while for the teacher to insist, even against his pupil's antipathies. But pupils study more devotedly, make better progress, are more contented, when engaged in learning those branches for which they have a taste. Talents are not alike in kind or quality as exhibited by the human family. All persons cannot succeed in all things equally well; and it is right that each should have a chance to succeed in that in which he may succeed the best. The teacher may, therefore, when the general good of the school permits it, allow individual pupils to exercise their peculiar tastes in the selection of studies, or to use their peculiar talents in the acquirement of some special science or art. Not that he can heed every individual whim with regard to study; but he may watch the development of real tastes and real talents for particular lines of pursuit, and give them such encouragement as circumstances permit. In the economy of mind, something is lost to the world by a fixed routine of study.

In arranging studies for individuals, care must be taken to fix upon a proper number. It is easy to induce pupils to undertake too much, and it engenders bad habits to allow them to undertake too little. They should engage in the study of just as many branches as they can study well, and no more. Pupils now generally engage in too many studies at a time. It not unfrequently happens that pupils have on hand ten or fifteen branches in which they are required to recite daily lessons. This practice defeats the end of study, and should be everywhere abandoned.

It does not seem best to confine a pupil to one kind of studies. A proper variety imparts more general culture, and gives more zest to study. The mind, too, becomes less easily fatigued when it can change from one study to another than if it is engaged all the time in the same kind of work, as weights can be carried farthest by changing hands.

Not only is it important to assign proper studies to each pupil, but to select for him the right place to commence his work. In finding this, the teacher should carefully inquire as to what knowledge the pupil already possesses concerning the subject, and begin his instruction where that knowledge ends. No one can ever thoroughly master a subject who does not first study its elements, and afterwards ascend to its more difficult principles.

3d. *The Text-Books to be used.*—Text-books are used in all kinds of schools, and some arrangement must be made respecting them before classification can take place or recitations commence. Some suggestions will be made with respect to the use of text-books, directions for selecting them, and the importance of their being uniform in the same school.

Text-books cannot well be dispensed with. They aid both the teacher and pupil. It is freely admitted, however, that a school might be taught without the use of text-books. Teachers in ancient times taught almost altogether by conversations and lectures; but this mode of teaching was, before the invention of the art of printing, in great part a matter of necessity. At the present day, in our higher institutions of learning, lectures are delivered to the several classes; but in such institutions students are expected to understand the subject-matter of the text-books and to be prepared for original investigations. It is admitted, likewise, that knowledge communicated from the lips of a living teacher has a freshness and a vitality that no dead text-book can give it. But, while all this is true, it is still maintained that good text-books may be used with great advantage to a school. They present the object-matter of a branch of knowledge in a proper form for study. If no text-books are used, the teacher must communicate orally all the facts and principles of a subject, and afterwards the pupils must write them out, study and recite them; and in doing this some discipline may be gained, but much time is lost. The worst result I have known arise from it is, the misconceptions to which pupils are liable from the necessary rapidity of oral expression. An exception must be made in favor of young pupils: with them oral instruction is much more effective than the more formal mode with text-books. Still, even in their case text-books cannot be wholly dispensed with. If the object-matter of a study be furnished in a text-book, pupils can carefully prepare it, and the time of the recitation can be occupied in reciting what they know, and in hearing what additional matter the teacher may have to present. A well-written text-book has the subject of which it treats arranged in a proper order; and this is a very important consideration in teaching. Some teachers who dispense with a text-book merely present a mass of fragments, a rude conglomeration of facts and principles. It is better to have a bad system in teaching than no system at all,—better, even, to have the questions put and answered in the language of the text-book, bad as that is, than to have the memory clogged with disconnected fragments of knowledge without language to make it known or power to use it for the accomplishment of any important practical end. Text-books, however, must be used, not abused. A teacher should know all that is contained in the text-book, and more. While he may exact a close study of it, requiring his pupils to commit its definitions and rules, he should merely make it serve the purpose of a *text* to his own instruction, and be able at any time to lay it down and proceed with the recitation without it. In this manner the object-matter of a study can be concisely and systematically presented, the pupil may have before him, for careful investigation, correct definitions, well-expressed rules, exact arguments, apt illustrations, and appropriate examples, and the teacher can have a *text* for such further comment as he may deem necessary. These advantages are as effectually lost without the use of a text-book as by a slavish dependence upon one.

Some directions may aid in the selection of text-books. A text-book should exhaust the subject of which it treats, or present a complete outline of it from the point of view from which it is considered. Not that any one book can contain all that is known concerning a branch of knowledge; but, without attempting this, a text-book may present all its leading facts and principles arranged into a system. A book of science may be a statement of facts, an enumeration of experiments, a series of speculations, an exposition of theories; but a text-book is unlike such a work, and contains a systematic arrangement of the known definitions, axioms, facts, and truths of a science, with such a number of examples as may be deemed necessary to impress them upon the mind of the learner. No man can write a good text-book upon a subject until he has looked all through it and about it and has a clear knowledge of the whole. A text-book is rather the history of a science than an exposition of a science. Writers of text-books should leave much for the teacher to add and for the pupil to find out. They should present an exhaustive series of *texts*, and leave the details to be mainly supplied by teachers and books of reference. Our text-books have converted a large number of teachers into mere machines; and it is time it was understood that they are not intended to relieve teachers from the trouble of thinking. When a branch of study is treated of in a series of books, what is here said applies to the whole series, and not to any one of the books of which the series is composed.

Text-books ought to present a logical arrangement of the several divisions of the subject upon which they treat. This truth has already been stated, but its importance demands a stronger presentation of it. Some of our popular text-books are very much at fault in their arrangement. Their authors seem to have thrown the different parts together disjointed and disconnected, and filled up the interstices with such loose details as first presented themselves. A proper arrangement would furnish a reason for the place of each division, chapter, section, and paragraph. A text-book, in fact, ought to be a rigid piece of practical logic.

Text-books should be interesting in matter. The authors of text-books should incorporate into them the most important principles, the most suggestive facts, the most striking phenomena, that belong to the subject written upon. They should have in mind before them the class of pupils for whom they are writing, and write as they would talk to them. With the whole material of the subject before them, they should select only that which is most valuable and most interesting. No temptation to appear learned, to dwell upon favorite theories, to use fine language, should divert them from the purpose of presenting the most important truths in the most agreeable manner. Nor is it necessary, to make a text-book interesting, that every thing in it should be explained or simplified. A healthy mind always feels the deepest interest in that which it has worked hardest to obtain. Idle students may be found in great numbers; but an author of a text-book should not presuppose them, lest he encourage habits which he should strive to prevent.

Text-books should be appropriate in style. Avoiding the extremes of the dry style on the one hand, and the florid style on the other, text-books that are not simply formal—as works on Mathematics or Grammar—should be written in a style plain and simple. An apt figure introduced now and then may reveal some hidden beauty, or a single glance of the imagination may open up to the astonished student the glories of the ideal world; but a text-book full of fancy-flights, however it might intoxicate its readers, could scarcely serve to instruct them. Students may read, in connection with the study of text-books, works beautified with all the refinements of thought and language, may follow the imagination of some Milton or Goethe, some Hugh Miller or Louis Agassiz, in its sublimest flights, and be the better for it; but the works of such writers are seldom well suited for text-books. We want clearness, precision, and strength in a text-book, and all ornament should be a subordinate consideration. Firm foundations and substantial walls are wanted for a building, before carving, gilding, or fresco-work can adorn it, or painting or statuary find a place within its halls.

Text-books should be adapted to the capacity of the class for which they are intended. In many schools the text-books are too difficult for the pupils who use them. Parents are many times ambitious to have their children study branches of learning with high-sounding names and use books with high-sounding titles, and teachers sometimes, at least, do little to check this dangerous ambition. No plan could be better calculated than this to destroy all interest in study. It imprisons thought; and the blank, impenetrable darkness, into which the pupil is compelled always to look, soon creates despair in seeking light. A child may learn whatever he can learn; but it is worse than folly to attempt to teach him what he cannot understand. Hence text-books should be written and used adapted to his capacity. One of the most serious errors in text-books is the placing of the higher and more difficult parts of branches of learning in such close proximity to the elementary parts. Quite young pupils can learn the elements of Grammar or Arithmetic; but when advanced beyond them they soon begin to lose interest in study, and consequently make little progress. The fault is in the text-book, or the teacher who follows it, and not in the children. They cannot be expected to take much interest in what they are unable to understand. An immense amount of time is squandered every year in this fruitless labor, and tens of thousands of promising children are made to contract thereby habits of idleness, if not of vice. Text-books for Primary Schools should contain the elements of several branches of learning, instead of both the elements and higher parts of one branch, and text-books for advanced pupils might then omit the elements altogether.

A series of text-books ought to be adopted in every school, and the use of all other kinds should be prohibited. In favor of such a uniformity of text-books it needs not that a long argument be presented. If not absolutely necessary to classification, it aids very greatly that work; it makes teaching more effective, and avoids that confusion of definitions and rules which must arise in a school where the books of several authors upon the same subject are in use. The cost of text-books is a small loss, compared with the gain of having them uniform.

4th. *The Formation of the Pupils into Classes.*—Two principles are recognized in the formation of classes in our American schools. The first requires all the members of a class to study the same branches; the second permits pupils to recite different studies in different classes. The classification of a school according to the first principle can be made much more complete than when done according to the second, and the stimulus to exertion is much greater in a fixed class than it can be when pupils recite one subject in one class and another subject in another. A teacher who adopts the second principle, however, can better accommodate his classes to the unequal attainments of his pupils, and, probably, better satisfy the wishes of pupils and parents. On the whole, I prefer a classification based upon the first principle—a *close* classification—to one based upon the second, a *loose* classification; and if pupils are better versed in some studies, and less advanced in others, they can equalize their attainments by devoting more attention to the latter, and, if circumstances render it necessary, some special classes can be formed to meet the views of parents or the tastes of pupils. I recommend in our Common Schools, therefore, a close classification, with such departures from it as overruling circumstances may make expedient.

Data for the formation of classes must be obtained by a formal examination or by experimental recitations, as previously described. With accurate data, the work of classification will present little difficulty in a school where the number of classes is fixed, and where such pupils only are admitted as can enter the classes; but in schools where the classes must be formed to suit the multifarious attainments of the pupils, this work requires careful management. It seems appropriate to speak of the advantages of classification, the impediments in the way of classification, and the manner of forming classes.

Classification economizes time. The teacher can do much more work when he need only listen to the recitations of whole classes, instead of the recitations of individuals; when he need not repeat to each pupil explanations or illustrations of the lesson or additions to it. The time thus saved by the teacher can be used greatly to the profit of the pupils.

Classification enables the teacher to make special preparation for hearing the recitations of his classes. If a teacher has pupils engaged in many different studies and in all parts of the same study, it is obviously impossible for him to make the necessary special preparation for his work; and his teaching is, consequently, less effective than it would otherwise be.

Classification stimulates pupils to more diligent

study. The common experience of teachers reveals the fact that pupils will study more diligently to make preparation for a class-recitation than for a recitation by themselves. The presence of numbers in the class-room, and the competition of classmates, will sometimes prompt even dull minds to activity. There is such a thing, too, as a class *esprit du corps*, the advantage of which is lost when each pupil recites by himself or in a small class.

Classification tends to increase the teacher's interest in the instruction he imparts. Animation on the part of a teacher is essential to good teaching. A dull teacher will make a dull class. A clergyman would hardly take a very warm interest in preaching if he had but a single listener. The delivery of the best oration would be spoiled without an audience. The same principle is applicable to teaching. A teacher is roused up to earnest effort when a large class awaits his instruction.

Classification enables pupils to help one another. The members of a class help one another by their silent presence, but still more by proper criticism. If the teacher is compelled to correct all mistakes, the recitation is apt to grow monotonous; while class-criticism renders it lively, and is advantageous both for the critics and the criticized.

Certain impediments lie in the way of securing a complete classification in schools; and these must now be considered.

Diversity of text-books is such an impediment. When the pupils in a school, of equal attainments, have been furnished with the same kind of books, their formation into classes is comparatively easy.

If there is a want of uniformity in the text-books of a school, the teacher should apply for a remedy to the proper school-officers; or, failing here, he may apply to parents, either directly or through their children. If this application is made in a proper manner, in most cases it will result favorably to the teacher's wishes. Should it not, the case is still not a hopeless one, for the teacher can form his classes just as if the books were uniform, and modify his teaching to suit the circumstances. Nearly the same subjects are treated of in all text-books; and the teacher can assign some topic for a lesson, and the pupils can each use his own book in preparing for the recitation. A recitation can take place with respect to a rule in Arithmetic, a part of speech in Grammar, a country in Geography, a division in Natural Science, a period in History, even if the subject-matter be learned from different books. It is acknowledged that such a mode of reciting would add very much to the teacher's labor, confuse the pupils, and clog the recitation; but it is thought to be a less evil than an excessive multiplication of classes; and sometimes even good may result from it.

Irregular attendance of pupils is such an impediment. Public school-authorities everywhere complain that pupils attend school irregularly. Private schools are patronized by classes of people who, as a general thing, more highly appreciate education, whose circumstances enable them better to dispense with the services of their children at home, or whom, perhaps, a pecuniary motive prompts, and hence equally loud complaints are not made by them. Irregularity of attendance, wherever it occurs, inter feres greatly with the classification of a school; but, at the worst, the teacher can classify such pupils as do attend regularly, and proceed to instruct them. He can permit irregular pupils to enter the classes, and perhaps they may be made to feel the want of a knowledge of the lessons recited during their absence, and can thus be induced to be more punctual in their attendance. If pupils attend so irregularly that they can derive no profit from the instruction given to the classes of which they ought to be members, the teacher may devote to them the few minutes which would be their share of time in an equal division of it among the pupils. They can justly claim no more. But, while this would probably be the best mode of procedure under the most unfavorable circumstances, the teacher may many times do something to correct the evil. There are numerous instances in which irregular attendance has been almost wholly corrected under the judicious management of a skilful teacher. Irregular attendance is either the fault of the teacher, the parent, or the pupil. If it is the fault of the teacher, he should correct it by teaching and managing better,—by making the school attractive, presenting strong motives to punctuality, interesting the pupils in their studies, and inducing them to love school and teacher. To tell how to do this is the great purpose of this book. That it may be done, is attested by multitudes of facts. If the irregular attendance is the fault of the parent, the teacher ought to seek an opportunity of pointing out to him its disadvantage to the pupil as an individual and to the school as a whole. One visit of the teacher to the parent or of the parent to the school has frequently brought about a right understanding of the matter, and secured the application of the proper corrective. The pupils may be the most blameworthy parties. The parent may send them to school, the teacher may be ready to receive and instruct them, but they find attractions by the way, and become truants. If parents and teachers co-operate, truancy cannot be of frequent occurrence. An arrangement may be readily made by which the parent can inform the teacher whenever his children have been detained at home, and by which the teacher can inform the parent whenever they do not attend school. As many parents will object to writing excuses for the absences of their children, the teacher may supply himself with a few hundred excuse-cards, upon which is simply printed, "Excuse the bearer." These may be distributed to the patrons of the school, and one of them should be returned to the teacher by each pupil who has been necessarily absent. At the end of a term, all the cards should be returned to the teacher, preparatory to the arrangements for a new term.

Laws have been made in some foreign countries, and in some localities in this country, punishing truancy, and punishing parents for not sending their children to school. In favor of such laws, it is argued that if the state has a right to educate the children of the state and deem this work to be to its interest, it would follow that no parent can deny his child this education without violating his duty as a citizen, and no child can habitually absent himself without endangering the state's interests and thus making himself liable to punishment. On the other hand, it is maintained that the legitimate function of the state in reference to schools is ended when it generalizes into laws the wishes of majorities of citizens and aids good citizens in the enforcement of these laws, and that it transcends its right when it undertakes to force unwilling parents to send their children to school, or to punish children for their non-attendance. In all a state can do respecting the establishment of systems of education, it must have in view the end of public order; and, while the state may be convinced that education tends to promote public order, it can in no rightful way punish until some overt act of crime or disorder has been committed; and it is evident that the mere refusal of a parent to send a child to school, or for a child to refuse to attend school, is not such an act. The state may adopt systems of education, may hold out inducements to secure regular attendance; but, if any do not attend, the state must wait, before inflicting punishment for non-attendance, until its bad consequences manifest themselves by open acts of wrong. Laws designed to compel the attendance of children at school are contrary to the spirit of our American institutions; and, if not, such laws are extremely impolitic, owing to the difficulties that must arise in enforcing them. Teachers, therefore, should look to other means as a remedy for irregular attendance; and if no help come thence, they must philosophically do the best they can, consoling themselves with the reflection that their successors may be privileged to teach among a wiser generation of people.

Having pointed out the advantages of school-classification, and having shown how impediments which lie in the way of such a classification can be removed, supposing that the teacher has in his possession the necessary data concerning his pupils' attainments, something must now be said in reference to the manner in which classes may be formed. No two pupils can be found in a school who are exactly alike in scholarship; and if the teacher forms his classes by putting only those in one class whose attainments are precisely alike, he will have each of his classes composed of a single pupil. The best he can do is to carefully survey his material, calculate the amount of school-time, decide upon the number of classes he can hear recite, and then classify his pupils by putting those in one class who are most nearly alike in scholarship and ability. If pupils fall behind their class during a term, or gain a position in advance of it, it is the teacher's duty to make the proper transfers; and it might be added that a faithful discharge of this duty greatly promotes the good of a school. Large schools can be classed much better than small ones, because there are in them more pupils of nearly the same qualification. In assigning lessons to classes whose members differ in ability, the teacher must adapt the lesson to the pupils who represent the average capacity of the class; because in this way only can he avoid discouraging the poorest scholars in the class by assigning lessons that are much too hard, or creating habits of idleness on the part of the best by giving work which costs them little effort. If the lessons are assigned in this way, the teacher can so manage the recitation that the honest, hard-working pupils may accomplish something every day and be stimulated by success to further exertion, the smart, active pupils find something in the lesson worthy of study and quite equal to their ability, and the idle of both classes incur, by frequent failures, the just consequences of their misspent time. By judicious management, the members of a class who are quite unequal in ability can be gradually brought to work more evenly in practice.

The size of classes must depend upon the age of pupils, the kind of study in which they are engaged, the form of the recitation the skill of the teacher, and the amount of work the teacher has to do. Young pupils recite better in small classes than in larger ones. Their attention can be better retained, and frequent questions will excite greater interest in the lesson. It is possible for a skilful teacher to amuse a class of fifty young pupils and to mingle some instruction with the amusement; but his teaching would be much more effective with a class one-fifth as large. Advanced pupils may with less loss than beginners be formed into large classes; but, even with such, the class should not be so large that the teacher cannot ask at least one leading question of each of its members during a recitation. Some members of a class may be required to recite a greater part of the lesson one day than others; but if many are repeatedly overlooked, and allowed to pass away often from the recitation without being noticed or called upon, there will soon be some who will calculate the chances of escaping the responsibility of answering any questions at all, and will prepare themselves accordingly. This result is not uncommon even in College classes. It is more convenient to have large classes in some studies than in others. Classes in Spelling, Writing, Drawing, Vocal Music, &c., may be larger than those in Arithmetic, Grammar, &c.; because in the former class of studies all the pupils can recite simultaneously. If a class meet a teacher to hear a lecture from him, to receive instruction which he is to impart himself without asking any or many questions of the pupils, it may be much larger than if the purpose of meeting be a drill, an examination, or a close and careful inspection of what each pupil has learned and the manner in which he has learned it and can reproduce it. In other words, the form of recitation may modify the size of a class. A skilful teacher can manage a large class without the same disadvantages resulting to it as if managed by one who has had little experience. This is self-evident. With a large school, and a great variety of studies in which to hear recitations, a teacher may be compelled, as the choice of evils, to form larger classes than he would deem politic under more favorable circumstances.

5th. *The Distribution of the Classes among the Teachers.*—What is said in reference to the distribution of the classes of a school among its teachers can only be applicable to schools in which more than one teacher is employed; but in such schools it is a matter deserving consideration.

The several teachers in a school ought to be employed with reference to the qualifications which fit them to perform the work desired to be done. No teacher can impart instruction in all branches equally well; and school-work should be divided into several departments, and each department be assigned to the teacher who can perform its duties to the best advantage. A wise economy of the teaching-force of a school would direct that each teacher should teach those branches which he can teach best, and undertake to teach no more of them than he can teach well. Teachers sometimes attempt to listen to recitations in twelve or fifteen different branches in a day. In such cases they must try to teach some branches for which they are badly qualified, they can make but little preparation for the recitations, and they must be unable either to satisfy themselves or do justice to their pupils. If due regard be paid to these principles, large schools may be organized with an efficiency impossible of attainment in any other way. By this arrangement, too, each teacher may be made responsible for a department of study, and, as he feels a special interest in it, he will naturally strive to make it successful. It needs scarcely be added that the work of the school should be equally distributed among the teachers, and if one branch of instruction does not furnish a sufficient amount of work for a teacher, his department may be made to include several kindred branches. It must be taken into consideration, however, that some branches are more difficult to teach, and, consequently, require more preparation on the part of the teacher, than others.

If the principle, that it is best to assign to each teacher those branches which he is best qualified to teach, be observed, each class may have a different teacher in each different study. This is no small advantage to a pupil. If he recite always to the same teacher, he may become familiar with certain lines of thought, but he will most likely be confined to them. He might be trained by a more unvaried discipline, but it is a discipline in one direction. He becomes imbued with his teacher's peculiar opinions, acquires his manners, and is apt to create a little world in which his teacher is the reigning sovereign and himself the most conspicuous citizen of the realm. It is much better for all pupils to have different teachers, with different tastes, talents, and opinions; but it is very important that this should be the case with advanced pupils. In speaking of graded schools, such arrangements of school-buildings were provided for as would admit the carrying out in practice of the principles now stated; and I am well satisfied that a school so organized will work much more efficiently than one in which the pupils of each grade recite all their lessons to a single teacher.

6th. *The Arrangement of Times for Study and Recitation.*—Classes should receive general directions as to the time of preparing their lessons. It is the misfortune of many, that when they have several things to do, and have adopted no particular order of doing them, in their doubt as to which they ought to begin first, they neglect the whole. System, rigid system, is as valuable in its results, when conformed to in preparing lessons, as it is in other things. These general directions may have reference, first, to the advantage that will arise from having times for study, and, afterwards, it may be proper to suggest that certain studies might be best prepared during school-hours and certain others out of school-hours. A more particular arrangement of the order to be observed in preparing the several studies in which a pupil may be engaged, ought to be left mainly to the pupil himself. It is perhaps impolitic generally to insist upon the members of a whole class attending to the same studies at the same time, though this may be done with young pupils and with classes whose members possess equal attainments, with good results; but, when pupils have made out their own programmes of study-time, it will be well for the teacher to make himself acquainted with them, because, in calling pupils' attention to their work, a command directing them to the performance of a particular duty is much more effective than one directing them to the performance of a general duty. Whenever a teacher deems it expedient to assign the same time to all the members of a class for the preparation of a lesson, it may with propriety be stated in the school programme.

In institutions where boarding and lodging are furnished to pupils, regular times must be appointed for retiring, for rising, for devotional exercises, and for recreation, as well as for preparing lessons and reciting them.

The following outline of a Student's Programme may aid in systematizing the student's work. It will only be filled up so far as to illustrate the manner of doing it. Each student should fill up one for himself, and hang it near his desk or study-table. Once adopted, he should suffer no ordinary circumstance to prevent him from working in exact accordance with it. In a short time habit will render a compliance with its requirements more easy, and the good results will soon more than compensate for the trifling inconvenience which may at first be experienced from the fixed line of duties that it enjoins.

STUDENTS' PROGRAMME.

(NAME OF SCHOOL.) (DATE.)

TIME.	GENERAL DAILY DUTIES.	SPECIAL DUTIES.
5 A.M.	Rise.	Sabbath. — Read Scriptures from 8 to 9 A.M.; attend Church at 10; and Bible-Class at 2 P.M. Saturday Evening. —Attend Meeting of Society at 7 P.M.
5.20 A.M.	Study Grammar.	
6 A.M.	Take a walk.	
6.30 A.M.	Breakfast.	
7 A.M.	Study Latin.	
8 A.M.	Attend Opening Exercises of the School.	
8.30 A.M.	Recite Arithmetic.	
9.30 A.M.	Recite Botany.	

The time and length of each recitation must be fixed. Without this the work of the school would go on very irregularly, and with little satisfaction to the teacher and little profit to the pupils. The principal data for determining the time and length of recitations are the length of the school-day, the number and kind of recitations to be heard daily, and, when several teachers are employed in the same school, the number of teachers and the amount of work to be performed by them, and the rooms in which the recitations are heard. These differ in different schools; and the only comprehensive principle that can be stated concerning the matter is, that the time and length of recitations in all schools should be such as to insure justice to all classes and all individuals, and to secure the greatest possible efficiency in the school. A few particular suggestions, however, may be of service to young teachers.

With advanced pupils, one recitation daily in each regular branch studied will be sufficient. Recitations may take place on alternate days, or less frequently; but it will be found everywhere that, while pupils can study more branches at a time in this way, their interest in study will not be so great, nor will their work be so thoroughly done. The best plan is to assign a daily lesson in each branch studied, and make it of such a length that it can be well prepared, and have a daily recitation in it. This is not intended to discourage teachers from having special exercises on miscellaneous subjects at any time they may deem them advantageous to the interests of the school.

With young pupils in ungraded or Primary schools, the recitations should be frequent and short. Children of six or eight years of age have difficulty in attending closely to a recitation for a long time, and yet they will be pleased with the variety of exercises brought about by frequent recitations. Besides, they cannot be expected to study much apart from the recitation.

Theory would demand the hearing daily of all the lessons that the pupils in a school can prepare, and the setting apart of a sufficient time to attend to all the requirements of the recitation. Theory would also demand the recitations to take place at hours when the pupils are best prepared to recite, or at which the teacher can best impart his instruction or they can best profit by it. Practice must conform to the theory as nearly as circumstances will admit.

In ungraded schools, the younger pupils might recite first after the opening of the school, both in the morning and the afternoon. They are supposed to be ready at any time, inasmuch as they have little preparation to make.

Older pupils may recite, first, those lessons which it was found most convenient to prepare out of school.

The most severe studies should not be recited near the close of the school day. Recitations in Reading, Writing, Spelling, or Vocal Music, would be best calculated for the last hour of the day. Writing and Drawing Lessons should not immediately follow active physical exercise.

In all schools there are certain general exercises that cannot well be dispensed with. Of this character are moral lessons, lectures upon subjects not regularly studied, or special instruction in certain branches which an economy of time will demand should be given to the whole school.

Frequent reviews of the subjects studied will tend to deepen the impression upon the minds of pupils, promote a clearer understanding of what is studied, and do much to connect the fragmentary daily lessons into a connected whole. For these reasons they are valuable, and a place must be provided for them in making general arrangements in regard to study.

A programme of the operations of a school will be presented on a subsequent page; and all that is intended here is to inform the teacher as fully as possible in regard to the principles which concern its construction, so far as that is related to times and lengths of recitations. It needs only to be remarked, further, that Superintendents or Principals of schools with a number of teachers working under their direction, should frequently visit all the classes while reciting, should require at least weekly reports from all the teachers as to their condition; and when they find that some change in their Programme will make their schools work more efficiently, and only then, they should change it.

2. Provisions relating to Order.—Provisions relating to order must embrace the following particulars:—

1st. *The Conditions upon which Pupils may be admitted into the School.*

2d. *The School-Limits.*

3d. *The Length of the School-Day.*

4th. *The Time and Length of Intermissions.*

5th. *The Opening and Closing Exercises of the School.*

6th. *The Calling out and Dismissing of Classes.*

7th. *The Granting of Special Privileges.*
- A. *Leaving Seats.*
- B. *Speaking to one another.*
- C. *Asking Questions of the Teacher.*
- D. *Making Complaints to the Teacher.*
- E. *Receiving Help from the Teacher.*

8th. *The Transaction of General Business.*

9th. *The Administration of Discipline.*

1st. *The Conditions upon which Pupils may be admitted into the School.*—These conditions generally have respect to locality, age, and scholarship. In the case of our Common Schools, the State laws, and the authorities properly authorized by them, impose the conditions. Each town or township is divided into convenient school-districts, which are about equal in population, and the children of such districts are required to attend their proper school. This arrangement causes all the schools to be nearly equal in size, and, when fully carried out, effectually prevents the evil of having some schools too large, while others are too small. The age at which pupils may attend school depends wholly upon circumstances. Schools have been so conducted as to be proper places for children three or four years old, although our school-laws do not often admit them before the age of five or six; and, if a person has been deprived of the opportunity of learning previously, it is praiseworthy for him to make the effort at twenty-one, or beyond that age. It is not unusual to see in the Night Schools of our cities, men who have reached the age of fifty years. The qualifications necessary to admit a pupil into a particular school depend upon the grade of school and the course of study adopted in the system of schools of which it is a part.

In schools managed by individuals or corporations, the locality from which pupils must come, the age, and the degree of scholarship required for entering, are determined by private considerations. The ends for which schools are established are so various, and the circumstances that surround them so unlike, that even with those that are called by the same name there is little uniformity in any thing.

2d. *The School-Limits.*—By school-limits are meant the grounds connected with the school-house, upon which the pupils have a right to play, and to the extent of which they have a right to go without obtaining the special consent of the teacher. Teachers of schools with play-grounds attached to them sufficiently large, need have little trouble in fixing the school-limits, as the boundaries of the grounds themselves should limit the distance the pupils may go away from the school-house during intermissions. More difficulty, however, will be experienced in keeping pupils within proper bounds when the place for play must be the highway, a neighboring wood, a wide-extended common, or when the privilege of play in some adjoining field is granted by its owner. In such cases the distance from the school-house the pupils may be allowed to go may be made to depend upon the teacher's means of communicating with them, and the time that might be lost in collecting them from play.

In no case should pupils be suffered to trespass on the neighboring property without the owner's consent. It looks badly for the teacher, and promises unfavorably for his pupils, when the trees near a school are stripped of their bark or their foliage, when fences are thrown down or destroyed, or when growing crops are injured, or fruit stolen. A distinct understanding should be had between teacher and pupils as to the school-limits and trespasses upon surrounding property.

3d *The Length of the School-Day.*—It is quite easy to adopt extreme views in regard to the proper length of the school-day. The sight of feeble children, who are confined seven or eight hours a day in school, who recite one or two lessons every hour, which have to be prepared out of school-hours, who have no time to play, and soon lose all taste for it, is enough to warrant the conclusion that less study and more exercise would be beneficial. A few sights of this kind, accompanied with rumors that death or insanity has somewhere occurred from too hard study, are sufficient to excite public attention and to set the newspapers to talking about the matter. The cry is, "The Innocents are murdered!" and excitable school-authorities hasten to forbid study out of school-hours, restrict the number of studies in the schools, and reduce to three hours the length of the school-day. This is one extreme.

A teacher takes charge of a school in a neighborhood in which the people work hard but do not think much. He finds his pupils strong, but dull. They can lift, and run, and labor, but can scarcely be induced to study. He calls into requisition all the motives that can arouse their mental energies. The ordinary school-days are too short for his work. He meets his pupils in the morning, in the evening, during noontime, on Saturdays, and visits them at their homes; and, with all this exertion, they do not make very rapid progress. Under these circumstances, it is not to be wondered at that the conclusion is reached, that ten hours are not too long a period for the length of a school-day. This is the other extreme.

It is true that some pupils study too much and are confined too closely; and it is equally true that others study too little, and work until their brain seems hardened into muscle. It is clear, therefore, that the induction of a general rule from one class of circumstances would lead to error. The age of pupils, their occupation, the locality in which they live, the constancy of their attendance at school, their state of health, their temperament, must all be considered in determining the length of the school-day.

In a Primary or Infant School, the children ought not to be confined in the school-room more than a half or three-quarters of an hour at a time. The length of the school-day may be five or six hours, but periods of study should alternate very frequently with periods of play. In an ungraded school in which there are young pupils, they must be allowed to spend much of their time upon the play-ground. They can be taught to go out and come in at stated periods without troubling any one or interrupting in any way the rest of the school. I think this arrangement is better than that which permits young pupils to attend a school in the morning and older ones in the afternoon, or opens a summer school for one class and a winter school for the other.

A farmer's son, who works hard for eight months in the year, and who walks a mile to school after having spent an hour or two in cutting wood or foddering cattle, and returns home again at the close of the school-day to engage in similar tasks, will not suffer from close confinement in school for a length of time that might endanger the health of a delicate city girl, who rides to school, never works, seldom breathes fresh air, and whose diet is often highly stimulating. The length of the school-day in the country may generally be longer than in cities; and two sessions a day are better everywhere than one. Those who attend school constantly require more exercise daily while at school than others who attend school but a few months in the year.

Parents must take proper care of their children who are delicate. School is not the place to nurse sick people. They require special attention, which no teacher who does his duty to his whole school can render. Precocious children, or those whose temperament leads them to study too closely, must be watched and warned. If no injustice be done to others, some special privileges may be allowed them, which may be calculated to restore to their mental nature its equilibrium.

Weighing all the circumstances as best I can, I give it as my opinion that in country schools a session of three or three and a half hours in the forenoon, and one of the same length in the afternoon, for five days in the week, with proper intermissions and proper attention to exceptional cases, will not injure any one or prove too long for the work to be done. In city schools, two hours and a half or three hours for each of the two daily sessions will be quite long enough.

In all these estimates it is understood that proper attention is paid to ventilation and to certain simple hygienic rules in regard to sitting and standing

The singing of a song at intervals will quicken the life of the school-room, and tend to promote health. Short gymnastic exercises, too, may be given, either with some simple apparatus, as dumb-bells, wands, or rings, or without it.

Hard and prolonged study is not injurious to health, if proper exercise is regularly taken and proper attention is paid to diet. On the contrary, it is only in this way that good scholars can be made. Those who expect to become good scholars by attending school three hours a day and preparing no lessons out of school-hours will, most likely, be disappointed. Ripe culture and rich scholarship are attained only by long and hard work. If evils have arisen from too much study,—and no doubt such is the fact,—it is more owing to the weak, sickly bodies children bring with them to school, and to the unnatural mode of life which so many lead, than to any injury the work of the school is calculated in itself to produce. The evils have a seat nearer the heart of society, and the school merely manifests them. Let children have a strong natural constitution, be trained to work, eat proper food, dress in a healthy manner, sleep well, breathe pure air, shun all luxuries, and, my word for it, neither six nor ten hours a day of hard study will do them injury. But if they are permitted, from the age of five upwards, to attend parties at night, sip wine, smoke cigars, indulge in confections, make love to babies like themselves, eat what they please, sleep when they please, and go where they please, all expense for true educational purposes might as well be saved; for under such management the shattered constitution cannot endure study for three hours a day, even if the race itself does not become extinct or helpless.

4th. *The Time and Length of Intermissions.*—No intermissions are needed in schools where the pupils are required to be present only at recitation-time. They can take exercise during the intervals between the recitations. In other schools the number of intermissions will depend upon the age of the pupils and the length of the school-day. Primary Schools ought to have an intermission at least every hour. Children in such schools may very profitably spend one-half of their time on the play-ground. Schools composed of pupils over fourteen years of age should have an intermission of an hour or an hour and a half at noon, and one of fifteen or twenty minutes in the middle of both the forenoon and the afternoon sessions. The intermission at noon is designed for a dining-hour and for relaxation, and the others may be used for the purposes of play, gymnastic exercises, or conversation.

5th. *The Opening and Closing of the School.*—It will promote general good order, as well as be beneficial in itself, to have a proper mode of opening and closing schools. To commence a day's work in school abruptly, or to close it in confusion, is neither in accordance with good taste or good judgment.

An appropriate way of opening a school is as follows. A few minutes—always a fixed time—after the pupils have been called to assemble, may be allowed them to get seated; and then the roll may be called. If all are not present, the exercises should proceed without them, during which no one should be permitted to enter the school-room. When all are quietly seated, the teacher may read a hymn, and invite the pupils to join him in singing it. He may then read a selected chapter from the Bible, or have the pupils all engage in reading a Bible-lesson. When agreeable to the patrons of the school, a few brief comments upon the text may convey valuable information, as well as direct the spirit of inquiry towards the investigation of religious subjects. A short, simple prayer may follow, the pupils bending forward their heads in token of humility, and the teacher, returning for himself and for them thanks to the Good Giver for all blessings received, and petitioning Him for blessings coveted. If the form of oral prayer should be objectionable, especially with pupils old enough to appreciate it, silent prayer may be adopted. In this mode of prayer, both teacher and pupils bow their heads and for a few minutes hold silent communion with their Maker. The ceremony is very impressive. Each one is taught to turn his own heart to God, and thus devotional feeling is cultivated in a way with which the strictest sectarian can find no objection.

The Bible should be used as a text-book on religion in all schools. It is considered as the word of God by all denominations. There are serious objections to its use as a text-book in Reading; but the reading of it at a special time by teacher or pupils, as previously indicated, both creates respect for the Book and love for the truth it inculcates.

The afternoon session may be opened with a cheerful song. If deemed expedient, the roll may be called, as at the opening of the morning session.

To save the time required to call the roll twice every day, an arrangement may be made by which pupils can report their own attendance. For this purpose let a board of suitable size be procured, and prepared as described in the following diagram:—

THE REPORTER.

NAMES.	ATTENDANCE.			
	FORENOON.		AFTERNOON.	
A A	Present.	Tardy.	Present.	Tardy.
( )	• B	• B	• B	• B
( )	•	•	•	•
( )	•	•	•	•
( )	•	•	•	•
( )	•	•	•	•
( )	•	•	•	•
( )	•	•	•	•
( )	•	•	•	•
( )	•	•	•	•
( )	•	•	•	•

The board may be painted black, the cross lines white. Small pins or pegs should be made to fit the holes B B B B, and painted green. Boxes to hold them should be placed at the bottom of the board. The words used at the heads of the columns may be written on paper and pasted upon the board. The names of the pupils, plainly written, are intended to be kept in their places by the little morocco slips A A. Thus ready for use, this article of apparatus, which we have called a Reporter, is hung against the wall at some convenient place, and each pupil, at the opening of the school, morning and afternoon, goes to it, takes a pin from the box, and puts it in the designated hole opposite his name. If tardy, he places the pin in the Tardy column; and, if absent, the holes opposite his name remain vacant. A little care on the part of the teacher will cause the whole to be done quietly, quickly, and accurately, and the result will be to secure more regularity of attendance. Where the school is a mixed one, there ought to be two boards:—one for the girls, and one for the boys. After school, the teacher may transfer the report to his Register, and place the pins again in the box for use next morning.

A school may be nicely closed in the following manner. The school-work and school-business for the day are supposed to be completed. The pupils are ready to depart. All are quiet. The teacher starts an appropriate hymn or song, and all sing it together. I have marked the effect of this parting music hundreds of times, and hundreds of times have my own burdens been made lighter and my own heart been gladdened by it.

At the tap of a little bell, one section of pupils rise; at another, they pass out, and a second rise; at a third, the second section pass out, and the third rise; and so on until all are gone. The whole arrangement is very simple, and is carried out with little noise or confusion.

6th. *The Calling out and Dismissing of Classes.*—It is the practice of some teachers to announce the recitation of a certain class, and allow its members to take their places with little regard to order, and at the end of the recitation permit them to return to their seats in the same confused manner. Such a practice is apt to create much disturbance in the school-room, and sometimes shakes the desks and diverts the attention of those not members of the class called out.

Other teachers call out and dismiss their classes by mentioning the name or number of each member of the class desired; but this plan, while it avoids the disorder occasioned by the preceding one, generally requires too much time.

The method of calling out and dismissing classes with a little bell is probably the best that can be adopted. A single tap of the bell may be used to call the attention of the class, a second may indicate that its members shall rise at their seats, and a third that they shall take their places upon the recitation-seats or repair to the recitation-room. If a class is large or there is any danger of confusion, it may be divided into sections, or all those occupying one seat or one row of seats can come and go together.

7th. *The Granting of Special Privileges.*—Under the head of Special Privileges are classed leaving seats, speaking to one another, asking questions of the teacher, making complaints to the teacher, and receiving help from the teacher. All these things are sometimes necessary to be done; and, if no time be provided when they may be done lawfully, some of them will be done unlawfully and thus interrupt the regular exercises of the school.

In small schools with considerate pupils, these privileges need not be special, but pupils may be permitted to enjoy them whenever they see fit to do so, and the school will be but slightly disturbed thereby. Pupils may not desire to leave their seats or to speak to one another; or, if they do, they may carry out their desire in such a manner as to disturb no one. They may have no questions to ask of the teacher, no complaints to make to him; or, if they have, they may seize those opportunities at which he is at liberty to attend to them. But more frequently it will be found, if no special arrangement be made concerning such things, trifling as they may seem, that the teacher will be continually interrupted by requests to do several things at once, and disorder will arise in the school.

The best arrangement I have been able to discover by which to dispose of the granting of these special privileges, is to provide suitable times at which general liberty may be given to enjoy them. At these times the regulations of a school in session need not be suspended, but merely relaxed so far as may be necessary to accomplish the end in view. No loud talking or noise can be permitted; but a few minutes—not more than five—may be granted during which pupils are allowed to leave their seats, talk together, ask questions of the teacher, or receive help from him. If the first intermission be fixed about the middle of the forenoon session, one of these periods of *suspended business* may come about the middle of the time between the opening of the school and the first intermission, another, between the first intermission and the intermission at noon-time; and the afternoon session may be divided in the same way. If this arrangement be adopted, the school-day will be divided into eight periods of recitation, three of intermission, and four of suspension of the regular work.

Some additional suggestions are deemed essential to enable the young teacher to operate his school upon the plan now proposed.

The granting of these special privileges should be refused, unless under extraordinary circumstances, at all times except during the periods set apart for it. Neither should the granting of them at these periods be a matter of course: the pupil must always indicate his want by holding up his hand, and the teacher must judge whether it is proper to grant it.

Pupils should not be suffered to leave their seats when it is possible for the teacher to wait upon them at their seats. It is better, generally, for the teacher to go to them than for them to come to him.

The most difficult thing to regulate among pupils according to the plan now proposed, or, indeed, according to any other, is their speaking to one another, or whispering. The difficulty will be greater if the school-room is not well seated. If the pupils are crowded together on long benches, they will be much more liable to talk than if placed on single seats some distance apart. Loud talking in a school-room during school-hours interrupts the school-work. Low talking is apt to become loud, and, if not, it will most probably lead to a waste of time. It is sometimes necessary, however, for pupils to speak to one another; and the plan just explained seems to afford ample privileges to the pupils and yet protect the interests of the school. If the teacher has reason to think that his pupils do not waste time in talking, or if they do not trespass upon the rights of others in so doing, he need make no regulation concerning the matter. He may even allow whispering at all times if he can succeed in securing less interruption to the school and less trouble to himself by regulating it than by totally prohibiting it except at certain stated times. But it is presumed that neither of these contingencies will often happen, and that the wisest plan is to make the provision already indicated. I know it is said that, if the teacher allow whispering whenever it is necessary, he will not be bound to notice every supposed violation of the rule; but if he prohibit it wholly, he must inflict some punishment for every violation noticed, and among talkative children this punishment has to be inflicted so often that the task becomes a very unpleasant one for the teacher and produces little good effect upon the pupil. This difficulty is acknowledged, and is best met by inflicting upon offenders those mild punishments which are the simple consequences of their conduct, as the forfeiture of seats, or seats upon a bench provided for the purpose, where they can talk to no one. The difficulty will grow less as good habits are formed. On the other hand, the objection loses much of its force when it is seen that ill consequences of greater magnitude will arise from attempting to regulate whispering, for the teacher is not often able to tell for himself when his rules are violated. He must depend mainly upon the pupil's own confession, and thus may hold out a temptation to falsehood in the first place, and, in the second, risks the danger of punishing only those who are honest, while those who are willing to speak falsely may readily escape. It is not supposed that all whispering can be prevented by any plan; but that which is here suggested, if carefully followed, will, it is hoped, prove to be generally a satisfactory mode of disposing of this troublesome subject.

Pupils should not be encouraged to make complaints against one another; but still there will be occasions when such complaints ought to be made, and when great injustice would be done were the teacher not to hear them. Pupils, too, have other grievances than those which come from wrongs done to them by their school-fellows. They may be unwell, their books may be lost or torn, the apparatus they are required to use may be out of repair, their seats may be uncomfortable from heat, or cold, or want of light, and for the removal of these and other like causes of complaint, the pupils ought to be allowed at some time to apply to the teacher.

This is not the place to discuss the amount of help a teacher should render his pupils in preparing their lessons. It will be admitted upon all hands that he may render some help; and, if he occupy all the time during which, four times a day, the regular business of the school is suspended, in doing it, he can hardly exceed in this respect the safe limits of sound policy.

8th. *The Transaction of General Business.*—More or less general business must be transacted in all schools. Notices must be given, appointments must be made, regulations must be introduced and explained, classes must be arranged, and various items of miscellaneous business must be attended to, and the question is whether the teacher will have a stated time for doing such work, or whether he will do it whenever it occurs to him, or whenever circumstances suggest it. To have a stated time for doing it is much the best plan, because in that way no class need be disturbed, no pupil need be interrupted in his studies, and both teacher and pupils will be more at liberty to attend to the matter in hand.

The most appropriate time for transacting general business is immediately preceding the closing of the school. The day's work is then done, all the business of the day can then be settled up, the necessary arrangements for the morrow can then be made, and the teacher can rest with no unfinished business on his mind to distract his attention or to absorb his time.

The teacher will find it convenient to note during the day such items of business as he desires to bring before the school, and at the appointed time he can attend to the whole at once.

9th. *The Administration of Discipline.*—Elsewhere, under the head of School-Government, will be discussed the subject of School-Offences and their punishment. Here it must be taken for granted that there will be offences and that there must be punishments; and the question to be determined is when the administration of discipline shall take place.

Individuals offending against the rules of the school may be corrected either privately or publicly. Private correction is very much the best in a vast majority of cases; but very rarely, and with peculiar offences, the correction must be made before the whole school.

If the correction is to be made publicly and the offence be a trifling one, it may be done during the time appropriated for general business; but if the offence be a very grave one, a more suitable time could not be selected than immediately after the completion of the whole day's work. In anticipation of the time that will be taken up in administering the contemplated discipline, the afternoon exercises may be somewhat shortened. The reason this hour should be fixed upon is because it is unlikely that after the infliction of punishment or the arousing of strong feeling either teacher or pupils will be fit for their usual duties. Some teachers dispense with one of the intermissions and occupy the time in the administration of the needed discipline; but the fact that a privilege is thus taken away from the pupils, may create prejudice against the teacher or his mode of punishment.

It is very seldom that a teacher should interrupt his work to correct an offence. An uplifted finger, a shake of the head, a tap of the bell, the quiet removal of a pupil to a place where he has less opportunity to do mischief, may indicate to the offender that the teacher notices him; but the discussion of the nature of the offence, and the application of the punishment for it, should be delayed until an appropriate time is found for attending to the matter. There may occur an open outbreak in the school, as when two pupils quarrel, or some public opposition to the teacher, as when a pupil refuses to obey him; but even in such cases, while the disturbance must be immediately quieted, and obedience at once enforced, the final settlement of the difficulty should be postponed until all parties have had time for reflection, when it can be made with much more satisfactory results.

When discipline is administered privately, it may be done whenever the teacher has leisure, or whenever there is least danger of being interrupted. It may be done at one of the intermissions, before or after school, in the pupil's room, or at his home in the presence of his parents, or in the office of the teacher.

It seems proper to conclude this chapter with the presentation of a form for a School-Programme. This form is more simple and more complete than any other with which I am acquainted, and readily admits modification to suit circumstances.

After what has been said in the preceding pages, this Programme will not require much further explanation. A few observations, however, must still be made. When there are but one room and one teacher, of course the last two columns will be unnecessary. They are intended to exhibit the form of a Programme for a graded school in which several teachers are employed. The selecting of the classes which should recite during each Recitation-Period, and the fixing of the length of each recitation, are left to the teacher, who must be governed by the circumstances of his school. Several classes may be heard by the teacher during each Period; or, if there are more teachers than one, by each of them. If teachers hear different classes on different days, it can readily be so stated in the Programme. Special arrangements must be made for such general exercises as reviews, lectures, &c.

PROGRAMME.

TIME.	EXERCISE.	ROOM.	TEACHER.
	Opening Exercise.		
	First Recitation-Period.		
	Regular Business Suspended.		
	Second Recitation-Period.		
	Forenoon Intermission.		
	Third Recitation-Period.		
	Regular Business Suspended.		
	Fourth Recitation-Period.		
	Noon Intermission.		
	Fifth Recitation-Period.		
	Regular Business Suspended.		
	Sixth Recitation-Period.		
	Afternoon Intermission.		
	Seventh Recitation-Period.		
	Regular Business Suspended.		
	Eighth Recitation-Period.		
	General Business.		
	Closing Exercises.		

CHAPTER III.

THE EMPLOYMENTS OF THE SCHOOL

In order to secure an economical expenditure of strength and effort, it is necessary for the teacher to understand what constitute the legitimate employments of his pupils while in school, and in what consists the nature of these employments. To the presentation of this important information this chapter will be devoted.

The employments of the school may readily be arranged into three classes, and the subject-matter before us will therefore be treated of in three sections, as follows:—

I. Study.
II. Recitation.
III. Exercise.

I. Study.—Study is the most important employment of the school. Without it there can be but little progress in learning. The objects of study and the means of securing them must therefore be carefully investigated by the teacher. The following arrangement of topics will give method to the discussion:—

1 The Objects of Study.
2. The Incentives to Study.
3. The Modes of Study.
4. The Characteristics of the Student.

1. The Objects of Study.—The ultimate object of all education is the attainment of the highest possible worth; or, as Kant expressed it, "to develop in each individual all the perfection of which he is susceptible." When God created man in His own image, and gave him powers and capabilities but little lower than the angels, He intended that he should live worthy of his high estate; and the great central end of all education is the attainment of that manhood which God designed for man, and which was the ideal prototype after which He created him.

More particularly, the following may be named as the ends of study:—

1st. *Knowledge.*
2d. *Discipline.*
3d. *Aspiration.*
4th. *Efficiency.*

The Accumulation of Knowledge is an End of Study.—Knowledge may be desired for discipline or for the purposes of life; but it should be desired also for its own sake. Each individual is conscious of a desire to know; and the mere fact of possessing knowledge, considered independently of any use to which it may be put, furnishes the highest pleasure to the possessor. Nature has everywhere truth for the intellect and beauty for the heart. The Naturalist finds them in rocks, and plants, and insects, and animals; the Linguist finds them in the wondrous powers and wondrous forms of human speech; the Mathematician finds them in the mystic properties of numbers and of forms; the Metaphysician finds them in those higher laws, pure as they came from the God-mind, which condition all things; the Historian finds them in watching the great drama which men are playing upon the world's stage; and all are made nobler and better in their contemplation. A true lover of knowledge seeks it for itself, seeks it because God made his soul crave it, seeks it to embalm it in his heart forever. The love of truth, whether found in nature or in the Bible, is a holy love; and happy the teacher who can implant it in the minds of his pupils.

Discipline is an End of Study.—The human body in infancy is weak, it needs to be invigorated and toughened; the human intellect is feeble, it needs to be developed and strengthened; the human passions are wild and rash, they need to be restrained and guided; the human will is fitful and perverse, it needs to be trained to docility and educated to husband and direct its power. This invigorating and toughening of the body, developing and strengthening of the intellect, restraining and guiding the passions, training and educating the will, is discipline; and it is one of the highest aims of study to secure it.

The circumstances that surround the race seem wisely designed to promote the ends both of physical and mental discipline. The earth yields her fruits only after hard culture; and her untamed forests, her barren wastes, her high mountains, her rapid rivers, her stormy seas, and her rocky shores, present such obstacles to the progress of human civilization, that the hand of man is trained to cunning and his head schooled to reflection in the effort to overcome them. What powerful influences prompt the agriculturist to sow and reap; the manufacturer to fashion the raw materials of nature into forms useful and beautiful; the mechanic to invent things new and strange, and to make them; the merchant to send his ships forth upon the pathless ocean on the mission of commerce!—and all these influences are educational, toughening muscle and awakening mind.

Besides, impelled by curiosity, man looks up to the heavens, down into the earth, within himself, and everywhere he finds his eye dazzled with the grandeur of creation, his head puzzled with the riddles he is asked to read, and his heart warmed with the wisdom and goodness which are displayed in all things,—the little as well as the great. The mother places before her infant child a glittering toy, and her mother's heart is gladdened when he takes his first step towards it. This first step a child takes in learning to walk, exemplifies nature's method of discipline. God has adapted the creation to man,—the objective and the subjective correlate,—outer attractions answer to inner impulses,—that the end of discipline might be attained.

It is for teachers to aid nature's efforts. Human nature must be made as nearly perfect as possible. "Be ye perfect, even as your Father in heaven is perfect," says Christ; and all created things respond, "Be perfect." Education is desirable to fit us for the ordinary business of life; but its aim is higher when it imparts a broad, generous culture to all our powers. We want first to be strong men, and afterwards good citizens.

Aspiration is an End of Study.—Nothing tends more to insure the young against the temptations of a low sensualism, to lead them away from an indulgence in debasing pleasures, than an elevated ideal of the purpose of life and of the worth of the human soul. The young should be taught to aim high, to desire to accomplish something noble, to appreciate truly the dignity of the position and the nature of man. The formation of an ideal conception of human perfection, and an earnest longing to realize that conception in life, is what I mean by aspiration; and surely study is worth much even if it only enable us to triumph over the difficulties of a long journey through this wilderness world, and see the Promised Land from afar off.

A person who does not realize the value of a thing will not make the most earnest efforts to obtain it; neither will a coveted prize, if considered beyond his reach, call forth his best exertions. Aspiration must pioneer all noble effort; and study lifts men up to higher, broader views of life, and duty, and God. The scholar may indulge in hopes and anticipations wholly unknown to the ignorant. The tentacula of his mind reach far out and up. His feet may rest upon the earth like those of other men; but his head is up among the clouds, with an ever-widening prospect around him. His ideals lend a charm to life in this world, and light up his bright pathway to another. It is an object of study, therefore, to elevate these ideals, and to stir up in the soul higher hopes and nobler aspirations.

Efficiency is an End of Study.—We study to obtain knowledge, to discipline our powers, to elevate our aspirations; but we can accomplish little for our fellow-men unless we can thereby make ourselves more efficient in the performance of duty. Knowledge latent in the mind can benefit only the possessor; strong muscles unused will do no work; beautiful ideals unpictured will attract no worshippers. Study, then, should aim to make all the forces of our nature available for the interests of society. The talent of acquired lore, of muscular or mental discipline, of divine imagination, must not be hidden in a napkin and buried in the earth. The man of science has no right to conceal the truth he knows; no Hercules can allow himself rest while labors remain to be performed; no artist can refuse to express in stone or on canvas the ideal image born in his own breast; and the world is entitled to all the poetry and music inspired by genius, and to all the revelations from God to man which the holy prophets have ever uttered. Each man, in his sphere, is bound to do what he can. It requires the economical expenditure of all the world's forces to do the world's work. All must hitch themselves to the great car and give their pull, or put their shoulder to the great wheel and give their push.

It is one of the objects of study to make us more efficient,—efficient in all we undertake to do. Knowledge gained should be distributed, the force acquired by discipline should be judiciously expended, and the ideal pictures of the imagination should be displayed, that all may profit by them. Knowledge should not only be distributed, but used. It may be made to aid in all kinds of business, to prevent the impositions practiced upon the ignorant by the unprincipled, to correct the fears and the follies of the superstitious, to assist in the work of morality and religion, to ennoble the pleasures of mankind: these and other such uses has knowledge, and the scholar must so use it, or he fails to appreciate the gift, and wrongs the Giver.

While it is maintained that efficiency is one of the objects of study, it will be noticed that by this is not meant mere efficiency in buying, selling, and managing affairs; but any efficiency is meant which performs labor, either with head or hand, adds new facts or principles to science, or presents purer ideals for the admiration of mankind,—any efficiency, indeed, which tends to make society better, wiser, or more happy.

It must be added that the object of study is sometimes an improper one. If an education is sought for the gratification of pride, or with the predominant desire of gaining popularity, reputation, power, or position, it both degrades the seeker and the thing sought.

2. THE INCENTIVES TO STUDY.—Taking it for granted that pupils are surrounded with circumstances favorable to study, such as a convenient time, a proper place, and a suitable opportunity,—taking it for granted, too, that the teacher fully understands what are the objects of study,—an in-

quiry is now in place as to the incentives that are best calculated to induce pupils to perform their school-work. We do not exert ourselves without a motive; and just in proportion to the strength of the motive will be the force of the executive effort. A miller might as well expect his mill to run without water or steam, or a sailor his ship to move without wind or current, as a teacher to look for his pupils to accomplish any worthy thing in study without being actuated by motives. The teacher who induces his pupils to work diligently must understand human nature,—must be able to analyze the motives that impel mankind to exertion, and call into requisition those which are proper to be employed in the work of education; and to do this skilfully, no small degree of well-applied effort is necessary.

Before proceeding to name the different incentives to study which have been made use of in school, and to criticize them, it is deemed well to state the most important principles by which it is intended to test them.

Incentives to study ought to be continuous in their influences. They ought not merely to spur pupils on to the attainment of an object and then lose their potency.

Incentives to study ought to arise from the nature of the subject, and the circumstances connected with learning it. They should be natural, not artificial; real, not fictitious.

Incentives to study are best when they are founded upon the positive qualities of each pupil, and are not the result of a comparison of one pupil with another.

It is unwise to encourage a disposition in pupils which may lead them to rejoice in the ill success of their classmates.

All rewards when presented as incentives to study should be given with reference to effort, and not with reference to natural ability.

All rewards when given as incentives to study should be calculated to promote the greatest good of the largest number.

The great end of all study is human perfection; and none but noble motives can lead to the attainment of so noble an end.

In the discussion of Incentives to Study, we will consider—

1st. *Incentives of doubtful Propriety.*
2d. *Proper Incentives.*

1st. *Incentives of doubtful Propriety.*—The principal incentives to study about the use of which a differrence of opinion exists are—*Prizes; Merit-Marks; Emulation; Fear of Punishment; Shame;* and *Ridicule.*

Prizes.—Under the general head of Prizes it is intended to include all those material things which are presented in institutions of learning to such students as are supposed to have made more progress in their studies, or are thought to be more deserving, than their fellow-students. In some schools, medals are used for this purpose; in others, scholarships, books, pictures, money, and privileges of different kinds. Upon the question as to whether prizes should be used as incentives to study in schools, a warm controversy has been carried on among teachers and others interested in education; and it is presumed to be best to state here the chief arguments on both sides, as a basis for the conclusion which will be announced.

The arguments in favor of prizes are—

That long-continued experiment has shown that prizes are useful.—Giving prizes to successful students is a custom which has prevailed in schools and colleges for centuries, and in all parts of the civilized world. It prevails now in a vast number of institutions of learning of different kinds and grades. The argument is that a custom so long-continued and so wide-spread must have some advantages, or it would have been long since abandoned. Franklin approved of prizes; and the Franklin Medals are still given in the public schools of Boston. Sir William Hamilton recently advocated the introduction of a system of prizes into the University of Edinburgh, in the expectation that it would revive therein the languishing interest in certain departments of learning.

That the expectation of gaining a prize increases the interest in study.—It is admitted by all that the student who works merely to gain a prize is not actuated by the highest motive; but a prize is something tangible,—something that his friends and the public can see; and he is accordingly stimulated to exertion. Besides, the teacher can make it understood that the prize is representative in its character,—that it represents correct deportment, hard study, or his own or the giver's approbation of it. There are natural differences in mental capacity. Some pupils surpass others in study, just as some gain the prizes of life while others lose them. Teachers and class-mates will select the most deserving scholars, and bestow upon them in some form their congratulations. The bestowment of a prize is, in such cases, merely a public attestation of their good opinion, and it will be preserved as a happy memorial of their approbation. No one will maintain that a pupil may not strive to obtain the good opinion of teacher, fellow-students, or the public; and can there be any serious objection to the expression of that approbation in the form of a prize? To secure this good will and this public testimonial of it, pupils will study diligently, and with more interest than they would be likely otherwise to evince. Offered prizes have a very marked influence upon the studies of the younger classes of pupils, since they are incapable of appreciating the highest motives.

That the prospect of obtaining a prize promotes profitable competition.—The pupils composing a class compete for a prize. Their relative merits must be judged, and the prize be awarded to the most worthy. In order to attain the highest position in the class, there must be effort made; and, as this effort gives strength, the competition, it is maintained, is profitable. The management of a class under such circumstances may be a delicate matter; great danger may exist that feelings of envy or jealousy will be engendered in the contest; but it cannot be doubted that a teacher who can so manage his class as to avoid this danger, and make the competition fair and honorable and comprehensive enough to embrace the whole class, may secure a rapid ad vancement in study. The actuating incentive may be the prize; but, in the struggle to obtain it, knowledge is acquired and strength developed; and these are among the most important objects of education.

The following arguments may be advanced against the use of prizes in schools:—

That the pursuit of the prize causes pupils to overlook higher motives to study.—That there are higher motives which may be used as incentives to study than the desire to obtain a medal or a sum of money, everybody admits. Does the pursuit of a prize cause pupils to overlook them? It must be confessed that such an effect is frequently produced. A prize is something that can be seen; it can be held up before the gaze of an admiring public; and it is well calculated, therefore, to obscure the more substantial good which it is supposed to represent. A pupil who is striving for a prize talks about it in the daytime and dreams of it at night. He forgets all about the worth of knowledge and the duty of self-perfection, sees nothing but the prize, and hears nothing but the plaudits that will greet its happy recipient.

This transfer of incentives to study from higher to lower, from real and permanent to fictitious and transitory, has a tendency to degrade the student. Nothing adds so much dignity of character to the seeker after knowledge as the consciousness that his object is a noble one. Full of this thought, all his actions are high-toned and manly; and as he triumphs over difficulties, and obtains the rich fruit of his toil, he feels that high pleasure which comes from knowing that he has fought a brave battle and won a proud victory without doing harm to any one.

It quite often happens, too, that the pupils who win prizes, having accomplished what they had striven for, cease their efforts and abandon hard study. Stimulated by the hope of gaining the prize they may have worked diligently; but, that stimulus removed, their interest in study decreases, and they soon become indifferent to it. This is an unfortunate condition in which to leave pupils. It promises little for the future; and it seems better to rely most upon those natural rewards which repay the labor of the student, and which, though constantly used, are always increasing in value.

Careful teaching may induce pupils to think of prizes as the tangible representatives of the real rewards which they hope to gain; and, if so, they can be used with little danger. Few teachers, however, can hope to possess such skill, and, if they do possess it, they will scarcely need the help of prizes to induce their pupils to study.

That the benefits to be derived from the giving of prizes are confined to a few.—If each pupil in a class could receive some testimonial fairly proportioned to his effort and success in study and his deportment as a student, there could be little objection to such a system. It would conform to nature's plan in principle, and, being more tangible, might exert a beneficial influence, especially with pupils in Primary schools. But the system of giving prizes as generally practised is something wholly different. The prizes for which a class or school competes are not often very numerous,—sometimes three or four, but more frequently, perhaps, a single one. They are bestowed, not with regard to *positive* attainments, but with regard to *relative* position. There may be a very slight difference between two competitors; both may be almost equally deserving; and yet one may obtain the prize, while the other is rewarded perhaps by pity for his ill success. By the wonderful principle of compensation, the apparent loser may be the real gainer; but this does not save the distinction made from the accusation of being arbitrary and invidious.

Suppose a class competing for a prize, and observe the result. At first the attention of the whole class may be directed to the prize, and a few good recitations may be the consequence; but very soon some will come to the conclusion that the prize cannot be obtained by them, then others will arrive at the same conclusion, and afterwards still more, until the contest is narrowed down to a very few who strive on to the end. The effect is that those who lose the hope of obtaining the prize can with great difficulty be induced to study at all, and seem to think that, having abandoned the race themselves, their only duty is to watch the runners until they reach the goal and the winner receive the prize. Besides, those who continue the contest are generally such pupils as need no stimulus to exertion. They are more likely to over-work themselves than to work too little. The treatment they need in such circumstances is rather sedative than stimulating. Thus the competition excited by the offer of a prize is apt to injure both the quick and the dull, the industrious and the lazy, one class being induced to work too much and the other being left with little inducement to work at all.

That there is great difficulty in awarding prizes justly —If a prize be awarded unjustly, it will do harm to all concerned,—to him who receives it, to him to whom it rightfully belonged, and to the school-authorities who committed the error. The danger of doing some injustice in awarding prizes is very great. Data furnished by recitations and examinations are subject to many errors; and when the amount of effort made, the facilities of study enjoyed, and the difficulties encountered by the pupils, are taken into the account, there are so many unknown quantities involved in the problem that the shrewdest moral algebraist could scarcely solve it. Those who make the best recitations or appear to the most advantage at examinations are not always the finest scholars or the most deserving students. Some pupils have superior natural ability, which enables them to do with ease what others can accomplish only by hard work; some receive private help, have access to libraries, enjoy ample time for study, and are allowed a pleasant place to study in, while others must help themselves, and study at hours stolen from sleep. The prize should be given to the most worthy. Teachers may be able to make the right selection, but all must admit the liability and the danger of mistakes. True, all praise and censure involve the same liability to mistakes. A teacher may commend the bad and censure the good; but, while this should teach him to be careful as to whom he praises and with whom he finds fault, yet in so doing he generally commits no public wrong, and he can oftentimes repair the private one he has inadvertently done.

That unkind and jealous feelings are apt to arise among those who contend for a prize.—It is not uncommon, when the contest for a prize becomes close and confined to a few, that the other members of the class drop study, divide into parties, and attach themselves to the fortunes of one of the competitors. In such unfortunate circumstances, there are apt to be exhibited the feelings usual at wrestling-matches and horse-races,—there are apt to be those who rejoice equally at the success of their hero and the failure of his adversary; and if the participants themselves do not sympathize with such feelings, they have more control over their passions than most students possess.

That a prize is a fictitious and arbitrary reward for diligence in study or propriety in conduct.—In nature's system all honest effort is properly rewarded. Nature is a prompt paymaster, and she rewards men liberally for every good thought they think and for every good deed they do. As the sower prepares his field, scatters his seed, and expects his crop, so all good thoughts and good words bring forth a natural fruitage of reward.

The system of giving prizes operates upon a principle quite different from this natural system of rewards. The prize is not bestowed for positive merit, but because the merit of the recipient is supposed to be of a higher order than that of others who may have been his competitors. The prize-system virtually supersedes the system of nature, and then suffers a large number of deserving pupils to remain without any recognition of their worth in the standard of value adopted. But, at best, a prize is not a natural reward for hard study or good conduct, and when not used directly as the representative of that reward, its value must be wholly fictitious. The bestowment of it is controlled by no natural law, as such laws require each one to be rewarded according to his merits, and it is therefore an arbitrary reward.

Having now stated the principal arguments for and against the giving of prizes in school, it is proper to conclude the matter with an expression of my own opinion. It is briefly this: that in the hands of most teachers, and as generally practised, systems of offering prizes in schools do much more harm than good. If, however, pupils can be made to understand that prizes are merely the tangible representation of the real reward, and to value them accordingly; if the prizes can be made so numerous that the merits of all can be thus rewarded, and the requisite care be taken that the value of each prize be in proportion to the positive merit of the one who receives it, nearly all the objections to their use would be removed, and they might become an auxiliary in the work of inciting pupils to study. The principle of giving prizes as rewards is not wrong, but it has been wrongly applied. With judicious application its use is safe.

Merit-Marks.—Teachers of Common Schools frequently arrange their classes so that the position of a pupil in the class determines his merit, or at least marks his relative scholarship. The practice of changing places in a class according to an assumed standard of merit, is not subject to many of the objections which can be made against the giving of prizes. Each pupil in the class can be made to occupy the position to which his actual merit at the recitation entitles him; he competes not only with the best scholars in the class, but with those of similar ability to himself, and his place in class is a standard by which his friends and himself can compare his proficiency and progress with others. For young pupils, especially, "place-taking" may be employed with good effect.

In nearly all well-managed schools, a record is kept by which the scholarship and deportment of each pupil are exhibited. The marks used for this purpose are called Merit or Demerit Marks, and they are used as an incentive to study. So far as relates to study, these marks should be recorded during the recitation or immediately after it, and are intended to indicate the degree of proficiency in each lesson. At the end of a week, a month, or a year, these marks may be summed up and read to the pupils themselves, forwarded to their friends, or published to the world. Classes graduating at many of our higher institutions of learning are honored by positions determined by marks made up from those received during their courses of study.

Are such Merit-Marks productive of good? Against their use it may be urged that the keeping of them requires considerable time. This is true, unless the teacher attends to it during the recitation or immediately after it; then the deserts of each member of the class are fresh in his mind, and he has nothing to do but to write opposite each name, in his class-book, the figure denoting them.

Against their use, it may also be urged that nothing but the merit of the recitations can be marked, and that no account can be taken of differences in natural talents, and opportunities for preparation. Merit-Marks for study ought not to pretend to indicate any thing else than proficiency in reciting the lessons. The teacher should make this understood by his pupils. He should also be careful in giving Merit-Marks for deportment to give credit to those who improve their opportunities of study to the best advantage, as well as for propriety in their general conduct. If this be done, no one can reasonably complain of unjust treatment.

Against their use, a more serious objection may be urged, that the attention of pupils is apt to be diverted by them from the high objects for which study should be pursued to the low one of obtaining good marks. To this objection it may be replied, that the great majority of students in all kinds of schools have not formed any high ideals of human perfection, and cannot, therefore, be actuated by motives prompting to their attainment. Teachers must first appeal to such motives as can be made effective, and, afterwards, gradually substitute nobler ones. Merit-Marks, too, like all kinds of reward, should be considered as the symbols of something higher and better. They are, indeed, among the safest of representative rewards, as all pupils may be marked according to their merit, and the record, made daily, is a safeguard against serious mistakes.

In favor of Merit-Marks it may be said that they aid in giving system to the working of a school;

they are a convenient medium of conveying a truthful account of progress in study made by pupils, and their conduct, to their friends; in schools where several teachers are engaged, they furnish to the Principal much needed information; they are almost indispensable in making transfers from one class, or one school, to another; and they can be made, when judiciously used, a safe and powerful incentive to study and good conduct.

That system, however, by which marks for merit are allowed to cancel marks for demerit, I do not approve. There is no warrant for the principle upon which it is based in the moral government of the world. God forgives offences, but he never effaces the recollection of them from the memory of the wrong-doer. Works of supererogation are an impossibility. It is best to let the daily marks received by pupils stand, and make their sum total constitute the record for a week, a month, or a term.

Emulation.—We have no right to seek after that which is unworthy of pursuit. To do otherwise would be to spend time and effort in a bad cause, and to weaken the moral sense. On this point, however, there need be no question here, as all the objects of study are noble objects and well worthy our desires.

Emulation is an effort to equal or surpass another in the pursuit of an object. There may be emulation in school in the struggle to gain a prize, a position, or to obtain good Merit-Marks; but the kind of emulation now referred to, *is simply a desire on the part of some pupils to equal or surpass others in the pursuit of knowledge.* The question now to be determined is as to whether a teacher should present this kind of emulation to his pupils as an incentive to study. Respecting this question, like that respecting prizes, considerable difference of opinion exists among educators; and, hence, it deserves careful consideration at our hands.

It will be acknowledged by all, that the obtaining of a prize, a position, or a high mark of merit ought not to be the end of study. The same is mainly true of those trials of mental strength which spring from emulation; and yet such trials may have something noble and manly about them. A base mind may be made to work for money or for place, but there have been natures so generous as to discard such ignoble motives, and yet be ever willing to test their strength with "foemen worthy of their steel." A prize, in particular, when valued for itself, is an artificial reward; while the complacency which arises from the consciousness of strength and excellence in comparison with others, is a natural reward. In competing for a prize, the contest must be between persons whose relations are intimate, and therefore will be apt to produce ill feelings; while a pupil may emulate the excellences of a member of his class, those of a person who attends another school, those of the good and great whose virtues adorned the age in which they lived, or even those of a personage purely ideal. An offered prize is within the reach of only a small number; but the teacher can always find some one with whom to match even his dullest pupils. Some authority must decide, after a contest for it, to whom a prize belongs, and there is great danger of deciding unjustly; but when emulation simply is the actuating motive, the pupils can mostly decide for themselves. A prize won loses all power as an incentive to study; but a pupil can never long want worthy rivals.

From what has just been said, it appears that emulation is a much safer motive to be used as an incentive to study than the desire to gain a prize; and yet there are some objections to its use, which must be considered.

It is said that *pupils are apt to overlook the true end of study in the heat of rivalship.* I do not object to a trial of strength or skill, either physical or mental, for itself. I believe that such trials, when wel. managed, have much in them that is good in its results. But the true end of study is not to equal or surpass another; and whenever it is lost sight of in a contest for victory, the consequences must necessarily be unfortunate, both intellectually and morally. That the true end of study is sometimes overlooked, when one pupil becomes the rival of another, cannot be doubted; but there is just as little doubt that a judicious teacher can prevent such a mistake. It is the abuse of a good thing; and what good thing may not be abused? Two boys sent upon an errand need not forget to do it because they run a race on the way.

It is said that *emulation tends to produce bad feelings between the contending parties.* This result, it is alleged, may not appear at first, but it grows as a contest becomes more close. That a generous spirit may be made selfish from this cause, that even jealousy and hatred may be engendered, I think, cannot be doubted; and if such is the legitimate result of the employment of emulation as an incentive to study, resort should be had to some less dangerous motive.

A teacher, however, can make use of emulation without incurring such ill consequences. He can terminate a rivalship whenever he deems it best, and he can always avoid such as are close and personal. Standards of comparison may be chosen from without the school as well as from within it.

And, besides, I do not believe that the legitimate effect of a trial of mental or physical strength is to produce bad feelings. It may do this with low and narrow minds; but with the brave and generous, if properly conducted, it never does. The most skilful players in games of ball or cricket, the fastest skaters, and the truest marksmen, are nearly always the best of friends. Their trials of skill teach them to respect one another. Such, too, might be the effect of the rivalship of the school-room. True, now and then unsuspected selfishness will come to the surface; but, in morals as in medicine, the open manifestation of a disease presents the best opportunities for administering the appropriate remedies.

It is said that *the effect of the use of emulation in school is to make ambitious men.*—Ambition may be either good or bad. That unscrupulous ambition which seeks place and power regardless of all other interests, which has drenched the world with blood and filled it with misery and woe, is to be deprecated everywhere. Rather than that schools should become the nurseries of such ambition, let the schools themselves be closed. But no sentiment can be nobler than that ambition which prompts men to do great deeds for themselves and for the race, which has pioneered civilization, marched at the head of reforms, and given the world its science and its art. Ambition is good when directed to good ends, and bad when directed to bad ends. Does emulation encouraged in school necessarily lead to the indulgence of an unworthy ambition?

The use of emulation in school is calculated to make ambitious men; and without such men the whole intellectual and moral world would stand still. Whether the working out of their energies tends to do good or ill to the human family depends upon the manner in which those energies are directed. It is a matter of great responsibility to awaken the ambition of the young, and to count upon giving proper direction to it. It may be like sowing the wind and reaping the whirlwind; but the teacher has no alternative. He aims to make men, and *men* must have ambition. Indeed, he meets with the same difficulty in regard to all the power he evokes and to all the skill he imparts. Education either unchains a devil or frees a man; but the chance of an escape from the bondage of ignorance warrants all risks. These risks, however, should be rendered as slight as possible by the constant vigilance of teachers and parents.

Several special arguments in favor of an appeal to emulation as an incentive to study will be named.

Emulation is a feeling incident to our nature, and therefore has its use.—It is natural to compare ourselves with others. To this is owing the powerful influence of example. Without it the lives of the good and the great would teach us no moral.

The results of a spirit of emulation appear in all nations, and at all times. Nations have competed with one another in commerce, manufactures, science, art, and arms. Individuals have measured strength in pastimes, in trade, in the forum, in peaceful science, and in bloody combat. Children emulate one another in early infancy; and many of the plays of childhood and the games of school-boy days derive all their interest from the efforts of some to equal or excel others. Society is kept alive by competition. We find it in all the avenues of business, in the family, in the State, and in the Church. A power so universally active cannot be doomed to silence in the school-room. The teacher will find it as a part of human nature, and he cannot deny it a use unless he question the wisdom of Him who made man as he is. Not that one man was designed to enjoy a triumph over another's misfortunes; not that some should rise by ruining others; but all were intended to journey through life mutually protected, encouraged, and strengthened. "Iron sharpeneth iron; so a man sharpeneth the countenance of his friend."

The desire of emulation is a part of our nature. It was designed as an incentive to that which is good. The teacher can thus use it.

Emulation can be made a powerful means of securing advancement in learning.—If it be admitted that one person may measure his strength against another's, while both are in the pursuit of some object, that two pupils while studying their lessons may see which of them can perform the work most speedily, then, free from any moral objection, the teacher will have placed in his hands a powerful means of securing progress in study. He can stir up by it not only individuals, but classes and the whole school. Few will be found so indifferent or dull that they cannot be made to feel its influence. My own success as a school-officer was largely attributable to the effort made to induce the teacher and pupils of one school to equal those of another and to hold up to the people of some districts the bright example of others. A teacher may use emulation where higher motives would prove unavailing. Many who would not appreciate the worth of learning can be moved by the desire of doing better than those with whom they may be matched.

Emulation can be used to give culture to character.— If well guarded, emulation among pupils will make them more manly, more generous, and more brave. It will teach them to form more just estimates of their own powers and the powers of others. It often furnishes a cure for selfishness, and gives strength to the will. It can be used to give culture to that radical disposition of the spirit which is termed character.

I know that the general estimate of the value of emulation as an incentive to study differs from that just stated; but, before an objector decide that mine is erroneous, I would like to have him join a well regulated cricket or base-ball club composed of students, play with them for six months, and closely observe the moral effect. There may be games in Mathematics, in the Sciences, in Language; and, according to my observation, all may be made highly beneficial even in a moral sense. Emulation, however, like sharp tools, requires skilful handling. It may do much good or great harm.

Fear of Punishment.—The fear of punishment is not anywhere the highest incentive to the performance of duty; but everywhere there seems to be a necessity for its use. The Creator in His moral government holds out the strongest inducements to well-doing; but, when His laws are broken, He strives to bring the offenders back to obedience by punishments, mild or severe, according to the nature of the offence. The authorities of a State find it politic to inflict fines, imprisonment, and death, upon criminals. True, an individual who obeys the laws of God or the laws of a State merely because he fears the punishment that will be inflicted upon the disobedient, is not acting in a manner worthy of a man or a citizen; but each one must do his duty,—if not from love, then by force.

These principles apply to the use of the fear of punishment as an incentive to study. Pains should not be spared, nor should patience be exhausted, in the effort to induce pupils to study from higher and better motives; but such motives cannot always be made at once effective, and in the mean time lessons must be learned. The idle must first be made to work from some motive, and afterwards their motives can be elevated. Pearls are not appreciated by swine now any better than they were when Christ preached in Judea, more than eighteen hundred years ago For these reasons, I think, the fear of punishment may sometimes be used as an incentive to study.

Lessons learned, however, because punishment is feared, are much less valuable to the learner than if he learned them from a better motive, as they do not in such cases promote healthy mental growth; but they are better than no lessons, and the teacher may choose the least of two necessary evils. The mistake which is apt to be made by the teacher is to continue the use of the fear of punishment as an incentive to study long after he should have displaced it by bringing into requisition higher motives. Moral culture is a growth as well as intellectual; and if the teacher must begin his work with motives addressed to the animal nature, he can only safely end it when the actuating principles are worthy a being created in the image of God.

The punishments inflicted for badly-prepared lessons, it may be well to add, should not be arbitrary in their character. Corporeal punishments of any kind should never be used for this purpose. The punishment should follow the offence as effect follows cause, and be naturally connected with it. It is best that the pupil should fear the punishment as the result of his own folly, and not as the arbitrary infliction of the teacher. For example, badly-prepared lessons might be relearned at recess or noontime. If this were a general rule, the pupils, fearing the loss of the privilege of play, would study more diligently, until, perhaps, they might acquire the habit or the taste for study, when the influence of fear would be no longer needed to secure diligence. Besides, the loss of the teacher's approbation, the forfeiture of the good opinion of the class, the lessening of their own self-respect, the mortification which arises from a failure to perform what others accomplish, the rebukes of conscience for neglect of duty, are natural punishments which are wisely adapted to correct the careless habits of study into which pupils may have fallen.

Shame.—Shame is that feeling which arises from a consciousness of having done something wrong or degrading. Remorse is the reproach of conscience for wrong-doing; shame is the sense of personal degradation. All right-meaning persons experience shame when they have yielded to temptation or failed to perform some duty. Little well-founded hope can be entertained of one who is "dead to shame." There are higher motives by which to prompt idle pupils to the performance of duty than the sense of shame; but the uprising of this feeling is one of the ways in which our nature reacts against a course of conduct that is unworthy of us.

A pupil may feel ashamed when he has suffered his time to pass unimproved, when his lessons have been badly prepared; and he may be induced thereby to abandon idle habits and engage in a manly performance of his duty. Operating in this way, the sense of shame is a proper incentive to study. The teacher may deepen a delinquent pupil's feeling of shame by reminding him of his duty, and by making him sensible of his abuse of privileges; but the feeling should be suffered to arise of itself. An attempt to degrade a pupil in the presence of others—to make him feel little and unworthy—is many times to do him more harm than good. It is quite easy for a blundering operator to blunt a pupil's sense of shame instead of quickening it.

But few circumstances will justify a teacher in making a public exposure of a pupil's delinquencies; and none can ever justify his holding him up to public shame. The faults of pupils are seldom so grave in their nature as to call for the use of means for correcting them that may induce the erring ones to shun the teacher's counsel and his presence and seek the society of the vicious. The loss of self-respect in boys and girls, as well as in men and women, renders their reform hopeless. This loss is suffered by those whose faults are unduly exposed, or whose sense of shame is trifled with.

Ridicule.—Life has its ludicrous as well as its weak side. Men sometimes deserve to be laughed at as well as to be pitied. Democritus and Heraclitus were both right. Ridicule may be used with good effect in rebuking the vices and follies of mankind

Doubtless, the mistakes of ignorant pupils are often very ridiculous. Shall the teacher ridicule them, or permit others to do so, for the purpose of inducing the necessary effort to avoid such mistakes? It is impossible at such times always to avoid a laugh; but I have never seen any good arise from the teacher's attempt to excite one. As with respect to the sense of shame; for a teacher to expose a pupil to public ridicule—to point the finger of scorn at him himself, or to suffer others to do it—is, in a vast majority of cases, to injure him rather than to correct his faults. Still, in private, and, much more seldom, before the school, the lazy and the careless may be made more sensible of their duties by hearing the faults into which they have fallen, or the follies in which they have engaged, exposed to ridicule; and circumstances may even justify the application of its lash to the bare back of some reckless spendthrift of money, time, talent, or privileges. As, however, there are so many higher incentives to study than ridicule, my advice to teachers is that they be sparing in its use, for it ofttimes wounds instead of heals.

2d. *Proper Incentives to Study.*—Chief among the incentives to study which are always deemed proper, are the following:—

The Approbation of the Teacher.
The Approbation of the Parents and Friends of the Pupil.
The Approbation of Society.
The Attainment of an honorable Position in the School
The Pleasure of overcoming Difficulties.
The Gratification of Curiosity.
The Desire of Knowledge.
The Hope of Success in Life.
The Enjoyment of purer ideal Creations.
The Duty of Self-Perfection.
The Satisfaction of doing Right.
The Prospect of Heavenly Reward.

Some of these incentives may include others; but I have thought that the force of the whole is better expressed arranged as they stand. A few remarks will be made with respect to each.

The Approbation of the Teacher.—A teacher who does not enjoy the respect and love of his pupils can never teach them well. He may till the soil of the mind skilfully, but the seed he scatters will have no healthy germination.

The approbation of a teacher who enjoys the respect and love of his pupils is a strong incentive to them to study. Such pupils will often study day and night—sacrifice comfort and health—to please a teacher. What teacher has not seen every feature of his pupils' countenances marked with pleasure—has not known that every fibre of their being vibrated with delight—when kind words of approval cheered their triumph over some difficulty?

What we do is rendered comparatively easy if we are sure that it will be appreciated. A farmer walked through his field where some laborers were mowing. "This is fine mowing," said he,—"the best I have ever seen." The laborers smiled, looked at one another, and worked away with a will that seemed to say, "We can do it better still." This is human nature; and the teacher will find human nature in the school-room.

If a teacher desire to have his pupils do much work and do it well, he must observe what they have done, and let them see that he appreciates merit. A teacher who is never pleased with any thing, who never gives an approving smile or utters an encouraging word, need not expect to have diligent pupils. Some teachers suffer themselves to fall into the habit of finding fault with every thing that does not please them, and of seeming scarcely satisfied with any thing; but the inevitable fruit of such a course of conduct is unwilling pupils and little work. *A teacher should commend where he can, and find fault only when he must.* Honest effort should be encouraged. Kind words, smiles, nods of approval, attentions shown, and privileges granted, should reward the student for work well done. A teacher who enjoys the confidence and good will of his pupils, and who knows how to bestow commendation and when to withhold it, is in the possession of a power which may be made a strong incentive to study.

It is not meant, of course, that indiscriminate praise should be given. The teacher must choose a right time, a fit place, and a proper manner for performing this delicate duty. No pupil should be praised who does not deserve it; nor should a teacher praise every deserving act, as if his approbation was the only reward for it. There is perhaps as much danger in praising pupils too much as in praising them too little; but, in practice, every teacher must be guided by his own judgment.

The Approbation of the Parents and Friends of the Pupils.—When home and social influences are of the right kind, the approbation of the parents and friends of the pupils is a very strong incentive to study, and the teacher may safely appeal to it. Even when parents are indifferent about their own mental and moral improvement, they will nearly always sanction any judicious measures a teacher may adopt for the mental and moral improvement of their children. It is many times unsafe for a teacher to refer to a parent's example; but it is hardly ever injudicious for him to strengthen his cause by citing a parent's opinion. There are very few parents who do not desire their children to learn when they send them to school, and very few children who do not have some regard for their parents' wishes; and these facts may be taken advantage of in enforcing the duty of study. Pupils may be urged to prepare for an expected visit of parents and friends, or for an examination before them. They will desire their teachers and schoolmates to speak well of them before these parents and friends, and they will themselves be glad to carry home the news of their progress, and thus exchange good lessons for encouraging words and approving smiles. Happy the circumstances of that school where the teacher and the relatives and friends of the pupils are equally intelligent, and where all co-operate in the work of instruction!

The Approbation of Society.—Students have not always received the approbation of society. In past times, some learned men were thought by their cotemporaries to have dealings with the Evil One, and others were compelled to suffer imprisonment and death, because they cast their pearls of knowledge before swine, who trampled them under their feet and turned to rend their best benefactors.

But at the present time, in every intelligent community, the scholar is respected. His advice is sought, and his scholarship is a passport to social honors. Indeed, the scholar now ennobles the place of his birth, the house in which he lived becomes almost sacred, and pilgrims from distant lands go sadly to gaze upon his grave.

The hard-working pupils in our Common Schools are not unhonored in their neighborhoods. The people are proud of them. They mark them out for future honors.

This approbation of society—this reputation for scholarship—may be lawfully sought by students; and let no one blame them if sometimes, among higher incentives to study, they permit dreams of such honors to cheer their rugged pathway.

The Attainment of an honorable Position in the School.—All schools have their positions of honor. These may be exhibited by a place in a class, by marks on a roll of merit, or by the silent suffrages of schoolmates; and their attainment is to the ambitious a powerful incentive to study. It is almost worth a fortune to a man to enjoy the reputation of having been the best scholar in a good school; and to graduate with the first honor in a class at college is considered one of the greatest triumphs of life. Nor are such motives unworthy ones.

It is true that but few can expect to occupy the highest positions in a school; but all good students can reach honorable positions, and these, under the judicious management of a skilful teacher, a large majority will strive to attain.

The attainment of an honorable position as an incentive to study is particularly strong in schools where both sexes are educated together. The members of one sex always have more regard for the opinions of persons of the opposite sex than of those belonging to their own.

The Pleasure of overcoming Difficulties.—There is real pleasure arising from the doing of hard things. Boys will lift, and jump, and run, and climb, when no one sees them, and for no other purpose save that of testing their strength. They will work out puzzles, solve problems, and engage in other feats of mental gymnastics, merely for the enjoyment which comes from difficulties encountered and overcome. A vast amount of hard mental and physical effort is expended every day with no end in view but that of doing difficult things. It is one of the ways nature uses to secure that toughening of muscle and that discipline of mind which the world needs to manage its affairs.

The biography of Dr. Kane furnishes a good example in illustration of the principle just stated. Connected with the house of Dr. Kane's father there was a chimney of considerable height above the roof. The difficulty of ascending it on the outside often formed the subject of the thoughts of young Kane as he gazed up at it. It was a temptation he could not resist, and he resolved to scale the chimney. In order to avoid the opposition of father and mother, the hour of midnight, when all were asleep, was chosen. With his brother, whose sympathy in his undertaking he enjoyed, to assist, he mounted the roof, and, after repeated trials, succeeded in throwing a stone, with a rope attached, into the open top of the chimney. The rope being made fast below, and his brother holding on to the other end, the fearless boy began the ascent. Hand over hand he mounts upwards, reaches the top, and, by great exertion, succeeds in seating himself upon it; and the future hero who is destined to explore the frozen regions of the polar sea and brave all its dangers thus triumphs over a difficulty that seemed to challenge his youthful powers. The descent was quickly performed, the rope was hidden away, and the daring boy retired to sleep satisfied.

Science in all its departments presents hard problems and difficult questions. Let the teacher bring them to the attention of his pupils in such a way as to *tempt* them to test their strength. Let him teach them to make long, hearty efforts,—to pull, and tug, and twist, until the work is done. Brave students like to do hard things; and, as they find hard things in science, they are often induced to study in order that they may enjoy the pleasure of overcoming difficulties.

The Gratification of Curiosity.—"*Admiratio est semen sapientiæ,*" says Bacon; and Hamilton has a simila. sentiment, "Wonder is the mother of Knowledge.' It cannot be doubted that the impulse that prompts the young in their search for information is curiosity. Long before they can appreciate the worth of knowledge or desire to seek it for its own sake, their curiosity has led them to notice facts and phenomena and to find out their relations and significance. Nor is this feeling confined to children. Men evince it in their travels into the unexplored regions of the earth, and in their study of the mysteries which are found in all departments of nature.

Knowledge can be so imparted in school as to gratify the curiosity of the pupils. Something new and novel may be taught them every day. They can be constantly delighted with a revelation of the wonders of the air, the earth, and the heavens. Study thus conducted would be like traveling in an unknown land, where every hour brings into view scenes new, and strange, and interesting. It is to be feared, however, that our dull methods of teaching often tend to repress the curiosity of the young instead of seeking to gratify it. Children many times find that book-learning is not the same as what they so readily learned in field, wood, and stream,—as what nature taught them,—and so become disgusted with study.

A teacher should always have in view the gratification of the curiosity of his pupils. Study to the younger pupils should be like turning over the leaves of a picture-book, like opening drawer after drawer of curiosities, like exhibiting ever-changing shop-windows, like looking at successive cases of objects in a museum, like witnessing the shifting scenes of a drama or a panorama. To the older, the objects of study may change less frequently, color and form may excite less interest; but there should be a continual unfolding of new order, new beauty, new laws, and more wonderful facts, to give attraction to it.

The Desire of Knowledge.—The desire of knowledge is one of the noblest incentives to study. In using it, no caution is necessary. A pupil who craves knowledge for its own sake will find a prize in every truth learned. He will not need the spur of position or emulation to prompt him to exertion, and fear of punishment, shame and ridicule, are for influencing other natures than his. Even the approbation of teachers, friends, and society is enjoyed by him more as the reward of his efforts than as the end for which his learning was sought.

The desire of knowledge is not created by artificial means, but is innate. God made the world and stored it with things to be known, and implanted in the bosom of man, for whom the world was designed, the desire to know them. Engaged in trade and traffic, many come to set no store upon that knowledge which cannot be valued in dollars and cents; but it would be well for such persons to remember that things of greatest value cannot be bought and sold, and that God would not create what is unworthy of our study.

Simply to possess knowledge gives pleasure. The mental appetite is thus satisfied. A true philosopher is a lover of wisdom,—not for its practical uses, but for its intrinsic worth. The richest fruits of science are the results of the desire of knowledge.

Teachers will find this desire of knowledge among their pupils,—in some, weak, in others, stronger; but in the majority, it can be made a powerful incentive to study. At first their curiosity must be gratified, as previously shown; but, finally, they should be made *lovers of truth*. This done, earth has few employments that can furnish the same degree of pure happiness as study.

The Hope of Success in Life.—Men who are rightly educated succeed best in business. Education is useful even in the common affairs of life. Learning—not merely a smattering of Arithmetic, Grammar, and Book-Keeping, but *liberal* learning—is an advantage to mechanics, farmers, and merchants, as well as to lawyers, doctors, and clergymen. If making money were the chief end of life, the educated man would enjoy many chances not open to the ignorant. A teacher will do well to show his pupils the relation of the branches they study to the practical affairs of society.

There is such a thing as true honor. What is called honor may be mere tinsel; but there is real respect due to work, and all men may lawfully strive to deserve it. An educated man, other things being equal, can accomplish more for society, is more deserving of respect, and more likely to be honored, than one who has been denied the privileges of an education.

Reputation is not always a bauble. A good name is a treasure not to be lightly esteemed. It is better than riches. Ignorant men have few opportunities to acquire a reputation. Their sphere in life is circumscribed. They move on a low plane. Not all so-called educated men have a desirable reputation; but the names of the great benefactors of mankind in the past and in the present are those of educated men.

Men are unworthy of place and power when they hold them unworthily; but society has positions which are more responsible and which require greater ability in the occupants than others. They are found both in Church and State, and in the affairs of general society. It is not unworthy any man to aspire to fill such positions. They will be filled by somebody. "The office should seek the man;" but no man will be sought unless he is supposed to be qualified, and qualified he can hardly be without an education, either obtained by self-exertion or by the aid of teachers.

Thus it appears that success in life, whether it consists in doing work for society, or in gaining honor, reputation, place, or power, depends very much upon education; and this may be made an incentive to study. Educated men must make the laws of a State, and govern it; must study science, and apply its principles; must write books, invent machinery, command armies, lead reformations, head expeditions, and marshal the general affairs of society. The ignorant occupy the rear in the onward march of human progress, and educated men lead the van. These facts are so open to observation that they can easily be made to exert their due influence in inciting pupils to study. Indeed, with some pupils such influences have rather to be weakened than strengthened; for harm may be done by inculcating the opinion among them that all are one day to become Governors or Presidents, Bacons or Humboldts.

The Enjoyment of purer ideal Creations.—God is truth, and He has embodied this attribute of His nature in His creation. All science consists of truths discovered by men, and arranged into systems. Everywhere other truths await their interpreter. The sum of all the truths known, and all the truths possible, constitutes *truth*, and above all is the ideal standard by which truth is measured,—THE TRUE.

God is beauty, and He has made His creation after patterns of the beautiful in His own mind. How richly is beauty painted on the leaves of trees, on the petals of flowers, on the plumage of birds, in the ever-varying tints of water, and upon the blue sky! How magnificently it is impressed upon nature's sculptured forms, from the tiny blade of grass up to the grand dome of Heaven! How sweetly it is sung in rippling waters, in sighing winds, in the warbling of birds, and in the infant's prattle! Painter, Sculptor, Poet, catch glimpses of this beauty, and would fain express it on canvas, chisel it in stone, or hymn it forth in Poetry or Music. Higher than all this beauty is the ideal conception that comprehends all possible beauty,—THE BEAUTIFUL.

God is good, and all created things proclaim aloud that goodness. It is written upon the dry land, it is echoed forth in the voices of the waters, it is whispered by the winds, it shines from the heavens, the tall forests and the ripening grain nod their assent to it, and man finds it revealed in his own spirit. "And God saw every thing he had made: and behold it was very good." Beyond all that is good is that noblest ideal creation of the human mind,—THE GOOD.

These pure ideal conceptions, The True, The Beautiful, and The Good, cannot be found in a mind darkened by ignorance. To fully realize the pleasure which may be derived from contemplating them, culture is necessary; and there can be few nobler incentives to study.

The powers in which our purest ideals originate are susceptible of improvement. There are those who having eyes see not, and having minds know not, the truth, beauty, and goodness that exist all about them. Ignorance shuts up the senses, and deadens the soul to their influence. Let the young mind once taste of the pure pleasure which ravishes the soul while dwelling in this ideal world, let the young heart once love The True, The Beautiful, and The

Good, and all that exemplifies them, and the labor of study will become light.

> "Scatter diligently in susceptible minds
> The germs of the good and the beautiful!
> They will develop there to trees, bud, bloom,
> And bear the golden fruits of Paradise."

The Duty of Self-Perfection.—The highest type of a man is one who is educated physically, intellectually, and morally,—whose whole nature has received due culture. He who possesses all good traits of character in the highest perfection, and has no bad ones, is a model man. After such a man, ideal or real, we may pattern.

The great purpose of this life is self-perfection. Our duty in this respect is written in unmistakable characters upon our own constitutions. The Bible injunction is, "Be ye perfect." And for this end we have constantly before us an example in the beautiful life of Christ.

Pupils should be made to feel the duty of self-perfection. They should be taught the high purpose of life, the dignity of the human character, the worth of the soul; and they will learn to appreciate the value of growth in knowledge and virtue, and to make the necessary efforts to attain it for them selves.

The Satisfaction of doing Right.—To become more excellent is to exercise the highest prerogative of our nature; and none can doubt that man rises in the scale of being in proportion as he increases his knowledge of God and the works of His hand. The man of science knows that he is making a proper use of his talents when he studies plants and animals, the constitution of air and water, the structure of the earth, the places of the stars, and the mysteries of his own body and mind. For such purposes his powers of intellect were given, and he feels that God will smile upon such a use of them.

It is right to study, because many things surround us that are worthy of it; because "Wisdom is more precious than rubies;" because the acquisition of knowledge ennobles and elevates the mind; because our mental faculties can only be strengthened by exercising them, and we would be false to ourselves, to our fellow-men, and to God, who intrusted their care to us, if we neglect their culture; and because knowledge is profitable in the affairs of life and profitable in fitting us for the enjoyments of Heaven.

No effort is too great on the teacher's part to make his pupils feel that theirs is not a work that can be neglected, but that, on the contrary, it is their sacred duty to become educated. There is wanted sadly more religion in education, and, perhaps, more of the philosophy of education applied in religious teaching. Both education and religion are developing processes, both find something innate in the human soul which can be cultured, and both by different means attempt to impart that culture. It is man's duty to be religious, it is his duty to educate himself; and to be rightly engaged in the pursuit of either, brings with it a complacent spirit and a satisfied conscience.

The Prospect of Heavenly Reward.—If all knowledge perished with the grave, if no hope could be entertained that strength of mind gained here will be strength gained permanently, one of the principal incentives to study would be taken away. This is not the proper place to present the reasons upon which rest our hopes of retaining our mental strength and much of our knowledge in that state of immortality upon which we enter after death; but it may be said that if there were no other reason we would require all that strength and that knowledge simply to understand the justice of our reward or punishment; for "Here we see through a glass darkly, but there face to face."

But, whether the proposition that we retain the knowledge acquired here in the world beyond the grave is capable of demonstration or otherwise, we believe it; and could that faith be stricken from the human heart, it would palsy all educational effort, and eclipse the brightest hopes of the Christian student.

3. The Modes of Study.—Something must be said in this connection upon modes of study; but the design of the present book precludes a full discussion of the subject.

We may study to find out something new, and we may study to acquaint ourselves with what is already known. The product attained by the first kind of study may be called *original knowledge;* and that by the second, *scholastic knowledge;* and, as the processes of attaining these two kinds of knowledge are somewhat different, we may consider—

1st. *Modes of Study in the Attainment of Original Knowledge.*

2d. *Modes of Study in the Attainment of Scholastic Knowledge.*

1st. *Modes of Study in the Attainment of Original Knowledge.*—Original knowledge is of two kinds,—*empirical* and *pure*. It is empirical when derived from experience, and pure when it results from intuitions of the reason. Some rules will be given to guide the student in his search for each kind of knowledge.

With regard to the attainment of empirical knowledge, the following rules are proposed to the student:—

He should set before himself a definite object.—Nothing in nature is devoid of interest; but if one undertake to study every thing he comes in contact with, he can never make much progress, and the knowledge he does obtain can never be arranged into a compact system. A student who would make successful original investigations must select a definite object of pursuit and pursue it indefatigably.

He must carefully observe facts.—This is the great rule to which is owing the rapid growth of modern science. All safe theories must rest upon the basis of ascertained facts; and these facts must be observed carefully, patiently, and with an unbiassed judgment. No other key will unlock the secret treasures of nature.

His observations must be correctly recorded.—An observed fact may not be used for a scientific purpose until years after the observation was made, or by the one who made it; and hence the necessity for a correct record. Much has been lost to science by a neglect of this rule, and many a man has found the labor of years thrown away by failing to make a record of his observations sufficiently exact.

Each fact must be closely examined and critically discriminated from other facts.—Without an observance of this rule, the essential and inherent properties of things cannot be ascertained, nor can the first step be taken towards making a systematic arrangement of them.

All facts must be accurately classified.—Classification is the handmaid of Science in all her departments. Facts isolated and scattered have comparatively little scientific value; but accurate classification helps the memory to retain a knowledge of them, and leads the way to the induction of the laws by which they are bound together.

Generalizations must be faithfully made.—Generalization is the crowning work of empirical science. It should never be done in haste, nor until sufficient data are at command to warrant it. Inconsiderate generalizations have been the bane of science. Hidden errors are prone to mislead at every step, and constant vigilance is required to guard against them.

Anticipations of nature's truths should be cautiously indulged in.—By the anticipations of nature's truths is meant the forming of theories before ascertaining the facts for which they are designed to account,—speculation. A philosopher who has carefully studied the economy of nature, who has patiently made his way up from facts to principles, whose mind has caught glimpses of God's plan in His creation, may, from his stand-point, directly discern a truth or a law from its accordance with the general plan; but one of the great lessons of history is to teach caution in this respect.

With regard to the attainment of pure knowledge, a few rules will also be stated, as follows:—

Learn to distinguish necessary and universal truths from those which are contingent.—When deeply investigated, it will be found that even the Inductive Sciences rest upon a basis—below their basis of facts—of necessary and universal truths. If this be doubted, it is certain that such truths underlie all the Mathematical and Metaphysical Sciences. As a first step, then, in the attainment of pure knowledge, the truths of which it is composed, or from which it is deduced, must be distinguished from other truths. The question, What is an axiom? precedes that as to whether a particular proposition is an axiom, and, indeed, must be answered before any sure progress can be made in the attainment of original knowledge with respect to the pure sciences.

Find the necessary and universal truths upon which is founded the particular subject under consideration.—A definite object is as necessary to success in the acquisition of pure as of empirical knowledge. Having chosen a subject for investigation, the axioms must be found out of which the particular truths sought for can be evolved. For example, the science of Æsthetics is founded upon the idea of the beautiful; and if any one desires to add to what is known on this subject, he must commence by acquainting himself with all the axioms which relate to the beautiful.

Demonstrate the particular truths which are contained in axioms.—This is the principal field in which those labor who seek pure knowledge. Having found the axioms which relate to such ideas as those of time, space, truth, beauty, and right, they proceed to evolve from them, or find by their means, the particular truths of which the noblest of human sciences are made up.

2d. *Modes of Study in the Attainment of Scholastic Knowledge.*—The object-matter of scholastic knowledge, as the student finds it, is contained in text-books and oral discourses. Here, known facts and principles relating to particular sciences are separated from the connections in which they were originally found, and presented in a form convenient for study. The method of studying what is already known may or may not be the same as that by which original investigations are made. A text-book on an empirical science, instead of proceeding from facts to principles, may commence with principles and then prove or illustrate them by a statement of facts, and a text-book on a pure science may take certain truths for granted and treat only of their applications; both of which methods are impossible in the study of what is unknown.

Assuming the possession of properly arranged text-books, a few directions for the study of them will be given to the student.

Begin at the proper place.—A student studies a text-book for the purpose of adding the knowledge it may contain to that which he already possesses. To do this effectually, he must begin at that place in the book at which his own knowledge ends. As a general rule, it is best to commence at the beginning, and then any thing unknown can be investigated, and all that is known can be rapidly passed over.

Take up one thing at a time.—Several studies of different kinds may be profitably pursued at the same time; but in the preparation of a particular lesson it is best to take up one thing at a time. The whole lesson may be at first read over to ascertain its general scope; but afterwards all the powers of the mind should be concentrated upon each part in succession. I am satisfied that many students fail from want of attention to this point. Hurried, desultory study never yet made a scholar.

Pursue a logical order.—Even children exhibit a taste for *related* facts. *Connected* narratives are most pleasing to the young mind. And all sciences have a logical order. If such an order be followed in study, progress will be more rapid, the subject will be better understood, and the knowledge acquired will be longer retained. The rule is a very important one.

Comprehend every thing thoroughly.—What is half understood is worth little, either for discipline or for use. A student should be content with nothing less than the complete mastery in all its parts of every subject he undertakes to study. Thoroughness in study requires close attention to be paid, not only to the thought, but to the language in which it is expressed. Great caution should be observed in coming to fixed conclusions upon controverted points. Prejudices should be guarded against, while the severest tests of truth should be applied.

Fix what is learned in the mind.—What is well understood is not apt to be forgotten; still, means should be taken to prevent the loss of the fruit of hard study. Knowledge is fixed in the mind by repetition and reviews, by connecting its parts together by natural associations, and by making frequent applications of it.

Acquire the power of giving fit expression to what is learned.—Light hid under a bushel is of little benefit; and, if otherwise, we are never quite sure we know a thing ourselves until we can explain it to another.

4. THE CHARACTERISTICS OF THE STUDENT.—Study has its objects to be attained, its incentives to prompt to their attainment, and its modes of attaining them; but the student must possess certain personal characteristics, or the worth of these objects will not be properly appreciated, the force of these incentives will not awaken the requisite energy to attain them, these modes of procedure will not be the most judicious.

Some of the most important of these characteristics are the following:—

1st. *Health.*
2d. *Natural Ability.*
3d. *Love of Learning.*
4th. *An elevated Ideal.*
5th. *Self-Reliance.*
6th. *Perseverance.*
7th. *The Power of Concentration*
8th. *Enthusiasm.*
9th. *Patience.*
10th. *Humility.*

Health.—Such is the intimate connection between body and mind, that the healthy condition of the former is necessary to the healthy activity of the latter. A sound mind can hardly exist in an unsound body. Health, therefore, is necessary to the student; and he should be temperate in diet and free from bad habits; he should enjoy the amount of sleep nature requires, breathe pure air, and take ample exercise. An erroneous Mysticism taught that the good of the soul is consulted by the mortification of the body; the Epicureans, equally mistaken, held that the highest good consists in sensual pleasures; but a better-founded philosophy inculcates the doctrine that the body and soul belong to one being and are mutually dependent, and that the highest good of either can be attained only through the healthy condition of the other.

Bodily health and bodily comfort are necessary to the successful student, and he should be carefully guarded from all influences that are calculated to interfere with them.

Natural Ability.—There may be persons whom no effort could make scholars; but their numbers are not so great as is generally estimated. The public have not yet fully realized what may be accomplished educationally by a determined purpose and skilfully applied labor; but, when they do, it will be found that light may be made to find its way into understandings whose darkness has seemed irremediable. Our institutions for feeble-minded children have shown that even idiots are capable of receiving much instruction.

But, while all minds admit some degree of education, it is not to be expected that those who have received one talent can so improve it as to be able to place themselves on an intellectual equality with those who have improved their ten talents. At least fair natural ability is necessary to one who can reasonably hope to attain eminence as a scholar.

Love of Learning.—Natural talents will not alone suffice to make a scholar. These must be well used; and no other impulse is strong enough to prompt that use but a love of learning. Isocrates had written in golden letters over the entrance to his school this sentence: "If thou love learning, thou shalt attain to much learning." Without it, no earnest, persistent, mind-invigorating efforts will be made to obtain knowledge. Without it, we may build up in the mind a kind of educational superstructure; but it is only a piece of mechanism, not a healthy growth. Without it, indeed, what knowledge may be acquired lies cold in the understanding, and furnishes no nourishment to the soul.

An elevated Ideal.—The ideal of an artist must be elevated in order to paint forms of beauty upon canvas or chisel them from marble; so a student's ideal of the worth of knowledge and the dignity of cultured human character must be elevated before he can do any thing effectually to attain that ideal in himself. People become like the gods they worship. If our ideals be pure, we will be pure. Our thoughts lead captive our wills. With a low ideal of the purpose of life, a young man will read bad books and seek bad society, and even tinge the purest truth with the dark colors of his unchaste imagination. With such an ideal, no man ever accomplished any thing noble. No such man ever left behind him a history that finds admirers among the good. Let all effort be made, then, to have students aim high, and pioneer their course through life with a lofty ideal of its true end. Set before their imaginations a model scholar, and it will be a constant incentive to them to imitate his virtues.

Self-reliance.—A scholar was never made by depending upon others. Self-work is the necessary condition of self-advancement. Every time a pupil receives assistance which by his own exertions he could have dispensed with, he loses an opportunity of strengthening himself: he does worse, for he will thus learn to depend upon others. One person might as well expect another to appease his hunger by eating for him, as to enable him to think by doing his thinking. The tendency of our teaching at this time is to explain, illustrate, and simplify too much; and thus we fail to inure our pupils to that sturdy self-reliance which loves to test its strength by striving to do hard things.

Teachers give too much help to their pupils; but probably more harm is done by the help some pupils give to others. It is not uncommon to meet with schools in which one-half of the pupils do nearly all the thinking for the other half; and this is an evil that requires great vigilance on the part of the teacher to remedy. Keys to works on Mathematics, and text-books in which the questions are all answered, are a nuisance in a school-room.

Perseverance.—A student must not only rely upon himself to do his own work, but he must persevere in the doing of it. No great undertaking can be accomplished without perseverance; but all great undertakings can be accomplished with it. All history illustrates this truth.

It is not an easy task to become learned. No scholar was ever made except by long-continued and earnest effort. Some may be endowed with natural talents superior to others, but still the maxim is true, "No excellence without labor."

The Power of Concentration.—A general perseverance in study even is not sufficient to make scholars. The student must have the power of mental concentration. It is not uncommon to find men who study for themselves, and study diligently, and yet who never attain a high position as scholars, for the reason that they study every thing a little and nothing much. The rays of the sun scattered all about the surface of an object will produce no marked effect; but bring them to a focus, and they may fuse or burn it. It is so in study. A student to be successful must have command of his powers. He must be able to concentrate them upon the subject before him, and suffer nothing to divert his attention.

Too much value cannot be attached to system in study:—system in husbanding the mind's forces for the work; system in preparing the subject-matter to be studied; system in arranging the circumstances under which the task is to be performed; system in bringing to bear upon it the power of a concentrated mental energy.

Enthusiasm.—The word student is derived from a Latin root signifying *zeal, earnestness.*

All great men are in their way enthusiasts.

Without it there would not be full devotion to a work. Columbus, Luther, Washington, would have accomplished little without enthusiasm.

Enthusiasm is warmth of interest in an undertaking, and earnest desire to accomplish some object; and a student who is fired by enthusiasm finds his task easy and pleasant. He does not study because he must. His recitations are not cold and formal. Time never seems to hang heavy upon his hands. Melancholy never broods over him, nor does discontent disturb his meditations. He loves his work, and willingly devotes his time and strength to its performance. Unexpected pleasures meet him at every step. Paths that others have found toilsome, he pursues with delight. Everywhere he finds beautiful scenery, flowers to pluck, and birds to cheer him with their music.

Patience.—How few have schooled themselves to be patient when difficulties are encountered! How few do their best, and are then content with the fruit vouchsafed by Heaven! How few have learned "to labor and to wait"!

Self-reliance sometimes brings burdens that dependent shoulders will not bear; perseverance pledges the whole soul to the performance of a task whose difficulties will scarcely yield to the most persistent efforts; enthusiasm sends all the forces of our nature out to the accomplishment of a work which cannot be performed, and the heart is saddened: these are all occasions for the exercise of patience. The student will need it every day. A want of success may disappoint, it must not discourage, him.

Humility.—Scholars have been accused of pride. Learning is supposed by some to foster conceit and haughtiness. With respect to the truly learned, these opinions are always false. A proud and haughty spirit would never have patience to do the work of a student. He would try to reach the goal of learning by some grand leap, and disdain the slow and toilsome way by which alone it can be approached. It follows that the true effect of learning is humility. "With the lowly is wisdom."

Nature never defers to her investigators. She never waits upon men and proffers her truths. They must knock humbly at her door before she will open it and reveal her secrets. She turns away her face from those who deem themselves already wise.

No one can be a student without comparing the little that is known with the immensity of that which is unknown. We are surrounded with mysteries. By the light of science we can travel a few steps in all directions; but beyond this all is profound darkness; and, seeing it, we realize our own littleness, and the greatness of the Infinite: like Newton, we become as children picking up pebbles along the shore of an unexplored ocean.

II. Recitation.—The recitation is the most delicate part of the school-machinery. All else is but a preparation for it. A failure here is a failure everywhere. The gift of governing well is an enviable one, but good order in a school is an end secondary to that of securing good recitations. No teacher can make good scholars who does not manage the recitation skilfully. It is in this he will need his greatest tact; for he has much to lose or much to gain. If he fail, he will have taught his pupils to hate school and study, will have paralyzed their efforts to learn, and will have created habits that must continue to cripple their energies through life. If he succeed, he will have the proud satisfaction of seeing the budding faculties of the human soul bloom under the culture of his hands; and happy hearts, made wiser and better, will thank him for his kindness and care.

What it is desirable to say concerning the recitation may be embraced under the following heads:—

1. The Objects of the Recitation.
2. The Requisites of the Recitation.
3. The Methods of conducting the Recitation
4. The Preparation for the Recitation.

1. The Objects of the Recitation.—Little is ever accomplished by persons who have no definite aim. One meets with poor success in attempting to catch objects in the dark. Hence it is well to determine at once the chief objects of the recitation.

1st. *It is an object of the recitation to enable the teacher to estimate the daily progress of his pupils.*—If a lesson be assigned to a class of pupils, many of them will work hard to prepare it, and it is just that they should have credit for it from teacher and class-mates; some, it may be, will idle away their time, and it is entirely proper that a public failure and consequent shame should follow. The prospect of the coming responsibilities of the recitation will tend to induce pupils to make the necessary preparation to meet them. At the recitation the teacher can estimate the daily progress of his pupils; and a knowledge of this fact on the part of the pupils makes that daily progress more rapid.

Besides, the recitation enables the teacher to inspect his own and his pupils' work, to measure the intellectual growth of his pupils, to correct the errors into which they may have fallen, and to present judiciously matter for future lessons. The master-workman frequently examines every part of an edifice which he is engaged in erecting. The horticulturist watches daily the plants in his garden, lest some thievish weed may rob them of nourishment or some hungry worm destroy their promised fruitage. It is thus the teacher meets his class and cares for it.

2d. *It is an object of the recitation to enable the pupils to tell what they know.*—All admit that it is an important thing to speak well,—to possess the power of making what we know available in words. It is even doubtful whether we can be said fully to know a thing, until we can embody our thoughts of it in the form of words. Students in reciting frequently rise, confident of their ability to answer a question, but find, when they come to state their knowledge of it, that they cannot set forth their dim ideas in the clear light of words, and then realize that the language of a lesson must be studied, as well as the matter.

The constant training of the recitation is necessary to make clear, precise, strong speakers,—speakers that exhaust a subject and reason logically about it. Next to good thinkers, we want good talkers;

and the recitation furnishes one of the best opportunities of making them,—opportunities that teachers who are awake to the best interests of their classes will not overlook. It is not enough for a pupil to blunder out the answer to a question among many things that have no bearing upon the subject, and some that have no bearing on any subject; it is not enough for the teacher to perceive, through the fog of words, that the pupil has the right idea; but the thought should be stated in appropriate language.

He who studies by himself may become a good scholar, but his progress will be less rapid, his knowledge less general and thorough, and much less available, than that of one who enjoys the advantages of attending well-conducted recitations. One of the principal reasons is that studying without a teacher does not furnish a pupil with an opportunity of telling what he learns.

3d. *It is an object of the recitation to enable the pupils to acquire well-founded self-confidence.*—Many persons may be found who are too timid to give an opinion in public. They may feel that they know as well as others, but they do not like to say. Reciting before a teacher in a class will tend to overcome this excessive timidity.

There are persons, too, in every community who speak without thinking, who rashly venture an opinion on every subject, whether they have investigated it or not. The close criticism of teacher and classmates surely is needed to protect the public from the infliction of mere babbling, and to induce in the young a *well-founded* self-confidence.

4th. *It is an object of the recitation to enable the pu-*

pils to fix in their minds what they learn.—The principle is an obvious one, that the more a subject is thought about, the better it will be understood and the longer it will be remembered. The recitation induces additional thought. It keeps the subject longer before the mind.

But this is not the only advantage of the same kind gained by the recitation. All persons have experienced the fact that their newly acquired knowledge seems more clear and is more deeply impressed upon the mind after a conversation with a friend respecting it. Public speakers understand a subject after having spoken upon it, better than before. The effect of the recitation is similar.

5th. *It is an object of the recitation to enable the teacher to explain and illustrate the lesson, and add new matter to it.*—A teacher ought to know all that the text-book used says upon the subject of a lesson, and ought to be able to ascertain whether the pupils know it; but the recitation furnishes him an opportunity to do more than this. He must be able to explain and illustrate the lesson, and add new matter to it. He must make his pupils feel that he knows more than is contained in the text-book. He should answer questions, elucidate hard points, multiply facts, describe additional phenomena, give the opinions of other authors, and suggest new arguments and new trains of thought. Text-books should purposely leave much unsaid, for knowledge fresh from the lips of a teacher has great attractions for the young, and leaves lasting impressions upon them.

6th. *It is an object of the recitation to enable the teacher to keep before the minds of his pupils proper incentives to study.*—Nowhere else does the teacher come so close to his pupils as in the recitation. Nowhere else is there such an intimate sympathy between him and them. Their minds are then open to receive instruction, their hearts ready to be impressed. Here, if anywhere, a love of learning can be created, and the mind's whole energies summoned to the noble work of obtaining an education.

There are certain moral qualities necessary to success in study. These the recitation furnishes a fit opportunity of strengthening. Industry, perseverance, self-reliance, are virtues with respect to which the teacher in the class-room should manifest a just appreciation. The character can then be cultured.

7th. *It is an object of the recitation to enable the teacher to impart moral instruction.*—When moral instruction is attempted to be formally given, the heart may steel itself against it. Such instruction can be given incidentally with more effect, and the recitation furnishes the opportunity. A teacher alive to the importance of this work will meet occasions, during the progress of every lesson, when he can call attention to a moral truth or give strength to a moral habit. He can scatter, now and then, a good seed which will take root in the fruitful soil that the circumstances of the class have made fallow. A good thought or a noble purpose may even find sustenance in a hard heart, as a seed lodged on a rock may germinate within its rocky crevices and obtain sufficient nourishment to grow. But to impart moral instruction properly requires the most delicate management. No instrument of art is so complex as the human mind,—none so nicely attuned as the human heart: what skill then, is required to place man in harmony with his fellow-men and at peace with God!

2. The Requisites of the Recitation.—The objects of the recitation cannot be attained unless certain conditions are supplied. Such of these as are not more appropriately named elsewhere, are—

1st. *A proper Place.*—The place of the recitation ought to be a room sufficiently large for the purpose, suitable as to temperature, well lighted, well ventilated, and tastefully furnished. If these conditions are wanting, the recitation will lack something in interest and something in good results. Students dislike to be driven to a little, gloomy, untidy room, and hurry away from it as soon as permitted. Let recitation-rooms be made inviting, and each seat and each article of furniture in them will awaken pleasant associations; there will come to be a *genius loci* which invokes to study and seems to applaud the triumphs of the student.

With a little care, a teacher can make even an indifferent room a pleasant one; and the gratifying change which can thus be produced is well worth the effort.

What has been said above has reference to schools having rooms specially appropriated for recitations; and, where possible, this is much the best arrangement. A large majority of the Common Schools in rural districts, however, are taught by a single teacher, and, of course, the recitations must take place in the study-room. In this case, there should be sufficient space allowed to enable the class engaged in reciting, to seat themselves comfortably and engage freely in their work; and this space ought to be so located as to prevent, as far as possible, the recitation from interrupting those engaged in study or from being interrupted by them, and to give the teacher the best opportunity of overlooking the school while he conducts the exercises of a class. The best place for the recitation-seats, probably, is immediately in front of the teacher's platform, as shown in the diagrams given in a preceding chapter, though, for some reasons, it might be well to have such seats placed at the end of the school-room opposite this platform.

2d. *Suitable Apparatus.*—The teacher needs tools. He can work to much better advantage when he has blackboards, maps, globes, charts, pictures, specimens of objects, and other kinds of apparatus, than he can without them. Impressions made through the sense of sight are the most easily understood and the most lasting. It is true that a teacher may teach without apparatus; but so may land be cultivated without ploughs, and the habitations of men be erected without saws and planes.

Recitation-rooms may be arranged with reference to the kind of studies which are taught in them. Mathematical recitation-rooms might be provided with mathematical apparatus; rooms for the classics, with maps and charts of ancient countries and antiquities; rooms for natural science, with philosophical apparatus and cabinets of specimens; and so of those for other departments of study. Rooms thus arranged would teach much themselves.

3d. *Quiet.*—People do things best who do one thing at a time. A teacher cannot well afford to risk a loss of interest in a recitation in consequence of having to attend to other duties while conducting it. It is not very uncommon to see teachers interrupted every moment, while hearing a recitation, with requests to mend pens, to answer questions, to redress grievances, or by the necessity of preserving order. In such circumstances, no teacher can do himself or his class justice. The class during a recitation must have his undivided attention; and it is almost as great an evil for the attention of the class to be distracted.

If a school is subject to so loose a discipline that such interruptions are unavoidable, the teacher had better discontinue all recitations until order can be restored, or resign his position that it may be filled by some one more competent. Slight interruptions, however, will occur under the best management, when recitations are heard in school-rooms where some pupils study while others recite. It is only in recitation-rooms that the teacher and his class are wholly free from noise and interruptions, and it is only then that the best recitation-work can be done.

4th. *Sufficient Time.*—Theoretically, the recitation should be sufficiently long to enable the pupils to tell what they know about the lesson, and to enable the teacher to add what further concerning it it is well for them to know. Practically, the length of recitations will depend upon the amount of work to be done in the school where they are conducted, and the circumstances which control its distribution. In most schools, practice cannot be made to conform to theory; and if placed in circumstances wherein he cannot obtain all the time he desires for his recitations, the teacher must obtain all the time he can, and then make good use of it. Skill will enable a teacher to greatly economize time in conducting recitations. With suitable blackboards, a teacher can have some pupils write out parts of the lesson while others recite orally; and, if the whole lesson cannot be recited, the most important parts of it should be considered, and the rest omitted.

3. THE METHODS OF CONDUCTING THE RECITATION. —All recitations should be so conducted as to effect the object for the attainment of which they are designed; but as the attaining of some of these objects depends upon the personal character, manner, and skill of the teacher, we will consider here only those methods of conducting recitations which relate to the following points:—

1st. *Imparting Knowledge.*
2d. *Testing Knowledge.*
3d. *Proving Knowledge.*
4th. *Correcting Errors.*

It will be seen, however, that these topics embrace the chief work of the Recitation.

1st. *Imparting Knowledge.*—Four modes of imparting knowledge will be named,—that by *lectures*, that by *text-books*, that by *dialogues*, and that by *catechization.*

Knowledge is imparted by lectures where the teacher speaks and the pupils listen in silence. As a mode of instruction, the lecture is used in all kinds and grades of schools, and it has certain advantages over every other mode.

One of these advantages is that oral instruction is more impressive than that of books. We attend to what we hear more closely than to what we read. Knowledge communicated orally, too, seems more new and fresh than knowledge gained in any other manner, and, consequently, is more attractive. Besides, in the lecture, knowledge is presented with all the auxiliaries of voice, gesture, expresssion of countenance, and words. These aid the thought in making an impression.

Another advantage is that the knowledge communicated in lectures is more apt to be original than that which is found in books. A lecturer cannot repeat merely what others have said or written; he must think for himself; and, thinking for himself, he will have something original to present to his pupils at every recitation. The most eminent scholars the world has ever seen were lecturers, and their scholarship may, in some measure at least, be attributed to the circumstances of the lecture-room.

Young children who cannot read must be taught orally. A formal lecture before them would be out of place; but they can be taught much by simply talking to them. It is sometimes desirable to impart to pupils a knowledge of subjects upon which no proper text-books have been written; and in such cases resort must be had to the lecture-method of instruction. The higher classes at our colleges and universities are supposed to be familiar with the text-books which treat of the subjects that engage their attention; and the professors in these institutions use lectures to make them acquainted with new matter and to awaken their interest in original investigations. In connection with all the methods of imparting knowledge, a teacher must give much oral instruction,—sometimes make a simple suggestion, sometimes state a fact, and sometimes discuss a principle, as the occasion may demand.

If a teacher confine himself to lecturing, he will not be able to estimate very fairly the progress of his pupils, he will furnish them little opportunity of telling what they know or of having their mistakes corrected, and he will render impossible that repetition of what is learned which is necessary to fix it firmly in the mind; and these, we have seen, are important objects of the recitation. Something can be done, however, to obviate these objections, by requiring pupils to take notes of the lectures they listen to, and undergo periodical examinations with respect to their subject-matter.

Knowledge is gained from text-books when we read or study them. The books used for study in school-classes are usually outlines of the subjects upon which they treat; but it is generally expected that students will read, in connection with them, other books containing full information. Text-books, rightly used, can be made a valuable auxiliary in the work of imparting knowledge.

The knowledge contained in text-books is generally more reliable than that which is communicated by lectures. "Writing makes an exact man," says Bacon; and all experience shows that men will use hasty expressions in speaking that they would discard in writing. Text-books, too, are apt to present a subject in a more methodical manner than is the case when it is presented orally.

Text-books enable pupils to prepare their lessons at all times. If the instruction in a school is wholly oral, pupils must wait until they hear the lecture before they can study it; but if they have text-books, no time need be lost. This is a great advantage in a school composed of several classes.

When pupils are compelled to rely for information concerning particular subjects upon the impressions they receive at a lecture, or the hurried notes they may be able to take of it during its delivery, their knowledge is apt to be inaccurate, incomplete, and wanting in method. To obviate such difficulties, text-books may be made useful to students.

The fixed arrangement and the fixed expressions of a text-book enable learners to stop and think; but the "winged words" of oral discourse must be caught as they fly; and thus the connections of the subject may be lost or its points be misunderstood.

Text-books, however, may be used to the great detriment of learners; but their general uses and abuses are discussed elsewhere in this volume.

Knowledge may be acquired by means of a conversation or dialogue carried on between two or more persons. The dialogue is used for the purpose of communicating and obtaining information in the family, in the social circle, and in scientific associations. Its use is more appropriate, doubtless, among equals; but a teacher can greatly benefit his pupils by sometimes relaxing the forms of the recitation, and permitting his pupils to ask him questions. He can also take them with him upon excursions, and on the way engage in profitable discourse with them.

It was principally in the form of dialogues that the learned men of ancient Greece taught in the porches and gardens of Athens. Their disputations were not carried on, as is generally supposed, for the purpose of concealing the truth, but mostly to help one another find it. It was thus Socrates conversed with his friends and with the Sophists, though his method became sometimes more catechetical than dialogical.

Knowledge may be imparted to pupils by catechizing them, or asking them questions. Questions may be asked to enable the teacher to find out what his pupils already know, and also to enable him to lead them to find out for themselves something that they do not know. It is only when the latter of these objects is aimed at that the mode of catechizing will be noticed here.

Teaching has no higher art than that of leading a pupil to the discovery of a truth by questioning him. A truth gained by oneself is of much greater value than the same truth gained by the help of another. An English author, in speaking of the method of Socrates, says, "He found those with whom he conversed ignorant of some important truth, and, instead of professing to instruct them, he sought to know their sentiments upon some other truth with which he knew they were acquainted, and which he knew was connected with the one he wanted to lead them to. By familiar interrogatories, he conducted them, step by step, through the intermediate principles, till they were at length surprised with the perception of what they had never observed before. He found them under the influence of some dangerous error, and, instead of professing to correct them, he led them on, by successive questions, to discern an absurdity in which they unexpectedly found themselves landed by their own principles. And thus he avoided all that resistance to conviction which often renders the most conclusive demonstration ineffectual to persuade." This extract expresses the spirit of what is meant by the catechetical method of imparting knowledge. It simply consists in putting questions in such a manner as to lead the pupil to answer them for himself. Its great advantages are that it makes teaching *exact*, *thorough*, *methodical*, and *animated*. Of course, it can be used in connection with lectures, text-books, and dialogues.

2d. *Testing Knowledge.*—A skilful teacher first endeavors to induce his pupils to tell what they know, next to find out what they can, and then adds whatever else he may deem proper. In examining pupils as to what they know, questions, either expressed or implied, are used; and I have called the process of questioning, testing knowledge. In teaching pupils to find out what they can by catechizing them, questions are also used; and most of the principles to be observed in questioning in one case are equally applicable to the other.

What can be said in reference to the questions used in testing knowledge will regard *the matter of the questions, the form of the questions, the mode of questioning*, and *the teacher in questioning.*

In matter,—

The questions should relate to the subject under consideration.—Pupils will not long continue to make careful preparation of lessons they are not required to recite. The concentration of the mind of a class upon the subject studied is much more profitable than a rambling discussion of topics foreign to it. It is sometimes very proper, however, for the teacher to ask questions which relate to the subject under consideration, but which may not be answered in the text-book used. The questions asked may relate to the facts or the principles of a subject, or to the language used to express them.

They should be well defined.—Nothing tends so much to confuse an intelligent pupil as to be asked questions which are obscure in language or wanting in point. The whole subject-matter of a lesson should lie clear in the teacher's mind, and each element or part of it be so separated from the rest as to admit of definite statement; for otherwise no thorough teaching can be done.

Their degree of difficulty should correspond to the capacity of the pupils for whom they are intended.—If the questions put to a class are too hard, it will discourage its members, and if too easy, it will create habits of idleness among them. The former is the more common error; for teachers are apt to think that what seems easy to them is easy for their pupils. Where the members of a class are all equally studious, but unequal in ability, the teacher may adapt his questions to their several capacities, if he do it with an eye single to the interests of the whole. It is well that the poorest scholar in a class be assigned questions that he can answer; and it is well that the best scholar in a class be sometimes assigned a question that he cannot answer.

They should follow one another in a logical order.—Disconnected, fragmentary knowledge is of comparatively little value, and little discipline can be obtained from its acquisition. Except to very young pupils, knowledge should be imparted as bound together by its associations and its laws, and all mental development should be made systematic. It follows that the questions by which knowledge is tested, or by which it is evolved from something already known, must follow one another in a logical order, —must be like the links of a chain fastened together. When the object is to review what has been learned, this order need not be so closely observed; indeed, it is sometimes an advantage in reviews to ask questions miscellaneously without regard to any order.

They should be exhaustive.—Lessons cannot be considered as recited until the pupils have shown their ability to answer all the questions that can be put with respect to the subject-matter of which they are composed. These questions, therefore, should be exhaustive. With advanced classes, they should exhaust the subject; with those less advanced, they should exhaust the subject so far as the pupils are able to comprehend it.

In form,—

The questions should be concise.—To answer well, a pupil must see clearly the point submitted in the question; and this he cannot do, if the question is long and complicated. Allusion is here made to oral questions; when the questions are written, they may be longer, but not less compact.

They should be clear, precise, and correct.—In addition to the task of answering questions, pupils should not be troubled to make out their meaning. Few students have not found it difficult to understand certain problems in Mathematics and certain rules in Grammar, owing to the faulty language employed by the authors of the text-books used; and still fewer have not been puzzled by the thoughtless expressions used by careless teachers in putting questions.

They should be varied.—I have heard teachers ask questions who always ended them with the word *what;* as, "Geography is, *what?*" and sometimes other forms of framing questions are so strictly adhered to as to become exceedingly tiresome. Questions at recitation, therefore, should be varied as a matter of taste. But there is a better reason. The same form of question cannot be used in presenting facts and principles in all their aspects and relations; and, besides, properly varied questions are necessary to secure properly varied answers.

They should not contain the answer.—Some teachers so far relieve their pupils from the trouble of thinking, as to frame their questions so that they require only a *Yes* or a *No* for an answer; and others intimate the answer less plainly, but always give a pretty broad hint as to what it should be. In examining a class, such hints are entirely out of place; but, in an effort to lead a pupil to find out for himself something that he does not know, they may be quite proper. This distinction the student-teacher will do well to bear in mind.

They should be adapted to the subject under consideration, and to the circumstances of the class.—Lessons consist of letters to be learned; words to be spelled, pronounced, and written; facts to be remembered; rules to be committed; sentences to be analyzed; inferences to be drawn; demonstrations to be made; exercises to be performed; &c. &c.: all of which require forms of questions adapted to test the knowledge of them which pupils may possess, and these necessarily are somewhat different.

A teacher ought to consider the forms of questions best adapted to the subject assigned for a lesson before the recitation takes place; but the varying circumstances of the class may necessitate changes in these forms. A general shows as much skill in providing for the exigencies of a battle during its progress as he does in making his arrangements for it before it begins. With young pupils especially, constant changes are necessary in the forms of the questions put to them.

In mode of putting them,—

Questions may be elliptical.—This mode of putting questions cannot be used at all in many studies, and can scarcely ever be made a very efficient way of imparting knowledge. When conducting a recitation according to this mode, the teacher reads the text and makes a short pause wherever a word, a clause, or a sentence occurs which he desires the pupils to supply. It may be rendered serviceable in instructing young children, if used in connection with other modes of questioning; but by itself it can be seldom employed to advantage. It is most applicable to lessons containing statements of facts, as History, Scripture Lessons, &c. For example, the teacher may read, "Columbus discovered—*America*—in the year 1492. He was born at the city of —*Genoa*—in—*Italy*." Or, "Now Peter sat without in the—*palace:* and a—*damsel*—came unto him, saying, 'Thou also wast with—*Jesus*—of—*Galilee.*'" Here the pupils supply the words printed in italics. In teaching young pupils to use words properly and to construct sentences, the elliptical mode of questioning may be made to answer a good purpose. A good exercise of this kind consists in assigning to pupils a piece of easy composition, omitting certain obviously implied words, and requiring the pupils to supply them.

They may be Heuristical.—The word Heuristical is derived from a Greek verb, *εὑρισκω*, which means "to find out what is sought for." I adopt it from Rev. W. Ross, an English writer on education. By the Heuristical mode of questioning is meant that mode by which the object-matter of instruction is presented in the form of precomposed questions, such as problems to be solved, sentences to be parsed, exercises to be written, &c. It is very evident that such questions may consist of wholes to find parts or of parts to find wholes, and thus may be either analytical or synthetical. The parsing of a sentence is an example of the former, and the writing of a composition is an example of the latter.

This mode of questioning can be more advantageously employed with advanced pupils than with beginners, and it is better adapted to some studies than to others Its chief advantages are that it requires great self-effort on the part of the pupil, that knowledge acquired by it is deeply impressed upon the mind, and that it allows the student time to put forth his whole strength.

They may be Categorical.—I mean by categorical questions such as are direct and positive, or such as require direct and positive answers. This mode of questioning is applicable to all studies, and is that which is most commonly used. It may be employed in imparting knowledge, as well as in testing what is already known. No other mode is so well calculated to create life and interest in the recitation, especially with young pupils. It leaves the teacher more at liberty in the selection of questions, in varying them, and in distributing them among the members of a class. Whatever other mode of questioning it is best to adopt in particular cases, this one must be used in connection with it.

They may be Topical.—Instead of asking direct questions or putting them in the form of problems, the subject-matter of instruction may be arranged in the form of topics, and these be given to the members of a class for discussion. For example, in Geography, in referring to a particular country, a teacher may say, "Boundaries," "Surface of the Country," "Internal Waters," "Soil and Climate," &c., instead of asking in particular all the individual questions that may be embraced in these topics. This method devolves upon the student much of the work which by the categorical method is performed by the teacher. He is required to analyze his topic into its several parts, place those parts in their proper order, and make a connected and exhaustive discussion of the whole. For advanced pupils, this mode of questioning has advantages possessed by no other; and it can be used to some extent with the youngest pupils in our schools. It is well adapted to reviews. Care must be taken in distributing the topics to give all the members of a class something to do at each recitation. Necessity will generally be found, after the discussion of each topic, for asking particular questions, and these may be answered by different members of the class, thus securing the undivided attention of all; or all the members of a class may be made responsible for the mistakes of the one who is speaking, unless they correct them.

The teacher in asking questions,—

Should make them proper as to matter, form, and mode.—How this should be in particular cases will depend upon various circumstances, such as the age of pupils, their scholarship, the kind of study in which they are engaged, whether the study is being first introduced to them or they are reviewing it, what apparatus is at command, the length of time which can be devoted to the recitation, &c. The most important general principles relating to the matter have already been stated, and for the rest the young teacher must rely upon himself. No two teachers can conduct a recitation in the same way; and any attempt to learn to teach by merely imitating another's work will be a failure. Teaching has principles which all must observe, but the application of those principles will be as various as the tastes and dispositions of men.

Should assume a graceful posture, and adopt a becoming manner.—A standing posture before a class is more graceful than any other, and gives the teacher a better command of his class. In this posture, he can secure better general attention, and, by casting his looks about the class, he can better detect the careless and idle. Men do not often sit to make speeches or to command obedience. A sitting posture may imply dignity, it does not denote animation or energy. For these reasons, it is considered best that a teacher should generally stand while hearing a recitation. There may be some necessary modifications of this rule. A teacher who is compelled to hear classes for several hours in succession would be likely to grow very much fatigued, and should probably sit a part of the time. Small classes, too, can be heard as well sitting as standing. Besides, whether the teacher sits or stands does not make so much difference to advanced pupils as to beginners. Under no circumstances, however, should a teacher suffer himself to recline on his seat, to place his feet on his desk, or to assume any other ungraceful posture which he would not like to see his pupils imitate.

A man possessing a cold, phlegmatic temperament, whose imperturbable feelings are never excited whether things go well or ill, is not fit to be a teacher. Recitations conducted by such a person must always be dull, heavy, dragging. There is another extreme. The Scotch teachers described by Horace Mann seemed to be during the recitation almost incapable of hearing or seeing any thing else. They walked rapidly in front of their classes, gesticulated violently, and indulged in loud vociferations. The recitation thus became a scene of the greatest excitement, a perfect hurricane of questions and answers and words of approbation and reproach, with all the accompaniments of din and noise. Both of these extremes should be avoided. More teachers, however, err on the side of indifference and dulness than on that of an excess of interest or activity.

In questioning, the voice should not be too low and soft, nor too loud and shrill. Its pitch and force should generally be as in ordinary conversation. If properly varied in tone, it will do much to preserve the attention of the class and add much to its life.

A teacher may use gestures in hearing a recitation; but those which are calm, dignified, and expressive seem most appropriate.

A teacher's manners in the class-room should be those of the finished gentleman or lady,—those of a model man or model woman.

3d. *Proving Knowledge.*—A pupil can only prove what he knows by answering the questions put to him; and the nature and conditions of those answers will constitute the present subject of inquiry.

As in testing knowledge, what can be said in reference to proving knowledge will regard *the matter of the answers*, *the form of the answers*, *the mode of answering*, and *the pupil in answering.*

In matter,—

Answers should contain nothing not implied in the questions.—A proper answer to a question has always a logical relation to it. Systematic mental discipline and thorough knowledge are impossible acquisitions to pupils who are habitually suffered to wander from the point presented in the question, and to introduce extraneous matter which has little or no relation to it.

They should contain all implied in the questions.—Partial answers may be better than no answers; but teachers should endeavor to secure those which are full and complete. All the great errors of the world are the result of the partial answers men have given to the problems of life. Children must be trained to delight in that which is exhaustive, systematic, perfect; and then, when grown to manhood, they will not be apt to be deluded by the baseless theories of superficial thinkers. The teacher should not forget that the highest aim of education is *to make men.*

They should be correct and explicit.—Without being correct, what is meant for an answer can be no answer; and without being explicit, it cannot be understood as one. Correctness and clearness are the two most essential characteristics of the contents of an answer as it lies unexpressed in the mind of a pupil.

They should be logical.—When the answer is composed of several parts, those parts should be arranged in a logical order. The object of a recitation is not only to ascertain whether the members of a class possess a knowledge of individual facts and principles, but whether they understand their relations. The latter, indeed, is much the surest test of scholarship.

They should be given understandingly.—A pupil may present an answer to a question which is faultless as tested by the preceding rules; and yet it may have been merely committed to memory without being understood. There are many things that the young may be told, the reasons for which they are unable to comprehend; but the teacher ought never to forget that our noblest mental faculties are judgment and reason, and that one of the great purposes of education is to develop them. Besides, there are wanted independent thinkers, original investigators; and they are not made by simply storing away in the memory masses of indigested facts or multi tudes of formal expressions.

In form,—

Answers should be made to suit the nature of the questions to which they are a response.—Questions may relate to facts, to definitions, to words, to principles, to methods; and as they cannot be always alike, so like answers cannot be given to them. Besides, the filling up of an ellipsis, the solving of a problem, the answering of a direct question, and the discussion of a topic, must all necessarily differ. In short, the answer should be an appropriate response to the question.

They should be concise.—Most men use more words than are necessary to express their ideas; few have the power of crystallizing thought. Pupils should be trained to express themselves in sentences which are compact and close. I do not object, as some have done, to stating the answer in a single word, when the sentence of which it is an abridgment is sufficiently obvious.

They should be correct and clear.—This has already been said respecting the matter of questions; it is not less true in respect to their form. Ungrammatical or inelegant, obscure or ambiguous language, when used to express answers to questions, should never be allowed to pass unnoticed. All recitations should be considered as in part linguistic exercises.

They may be original, or derived from authority.—As a general rule, pupils should be required to give their answers in sentences of their own forming, because it is a good discipline in language, and a sure test of their knowledge of the subject. This course is not always the best one, however, and it is very proper for pupils to commit definitions and rules in the words of those who have carefully considered the forms in which they can be best expressed. It does not follow because a thought is expressed in the language of another, that it is not understood. The young learn to use language skilfully by noticing how others use it.

They should not be monotonous.—It is very unpleasant to hear children drawl out their answers; it is almost as much so to hear them repeat them in the same form of words. Both faults are readily corrected, however, if the teacher attend to the rules for putting questions.

In mode,—

Answers may be given consecutively.—This mode requires the answers to be given by turns. The first question is usually put to the pupil who stands at the head of the class; the second, to the next; and so on to the foot, when the same order is observed with the remaining questions. If an incorrect answer is given by any one, the question is passed to the next, and if he answers it, he takes the place of him who failed to answer. If the question is missed by several, he who answers it correctly takes the place of the one who first committed the error, the others retaining the same relative position.

Common as is the use of the consecutive mode of answering questions, it is open to several objections.

When it is known that a certain order is to be followed in assigning the questions, some pupils cannot resist the temptation of preparing only those parts of the lesson which they expect to be called upon to recite. I have known pupils to count the number of members in a class and the number of questions in a lesson, and shrewdly calculate in the revolution of the wheel what questions would come to them, and prepare accordingly. When this can be done, it need scarcely be added, that the purpose of a recitation is in great measure defeated.

The consecutive mode of answering does not tend to secure that close attention to all the questions addressed them, on the part of pupils, which is necessary to insure their rapid progress in study. When a pupil has answered a question, he is quite sure he will not be called upon to answer another until all have answered; and he may spend the interval in idly looking about, in play, or in mischief. A Superintendent once corrected this faulty mode of conducting a recitation, in the following manner. A large class was reciting a lesson in reading. The lesson was divided into paragraphs, and each pupil read a paragraph, commencing at the head of the class; but having read he made the necessary calculation to enable him to ascertain the number of the paragraph he would be required to read next, and then, placing his finger upon it or marking it, he occupied the time others were reading in perfect indifference as to what was passing in the class. After the recitation had proceeded for some time in this way, the Superintendent was permitted to take charge of the class. He immediately gave each member of the class a number, not knowing the names of the pupils, urged attention to the lesson, stating that he would consider himself at liberty to call upon any one, either to continue the reading, or to answer a question concerning the matter or the language of the lesson. When all were ready and intent upon the work before them, he called upon them promiscuously. The change was magical. Life and interest took the place of dulness and indifference. After some time, one forgot himself and looked aside, but at once his number was called, and he found he was caught. This illustration exhibits the imperfections of the mode of answering now under consideration, and suggests a better one. This method, however, may be used advantageously in connection with other methods, and it is well adapted to small classes. The system of "trapping" or place-taking in class can be more easily applied when the questions are assigned consecutively; and it can scarcely be doubted that with young pupils some good may result from it.

They may be given simultaneously.—This mode requires the answers to be given by the whole class in concert.

One of the principal objections to this mode of answering, is that the answers must be given by all the pupils in a set form of words and in a certain order, or the concert will be spoiled; and these mechanical conditions are wholly at variance with independent thinking.

A second objection to it is that it lessens individual responsibility among pupils at the recitation. The class as a whole is responsible; but if two or three lead the concert, the rest can easily join it in such a way as to render it difficult to distinguish him who leads from him who follows. Teachers, even, are sometimes deceived in regard to the amount of knowledge possessed by classes that recite in concert; but the deception can be readily detected by a few well-directed questions put to individuals. It may be stated as a general principle that no mode of answering will be successful that does not compel each member of a class to think and speak for himself.

The simultaneous mode of answering, however, has its uses. A few questions answered in concert, now and then, will enliven a class and tend to increase the interest in the recitation. Any lessons or parts of lessons that are intended to be committed to memory in a certain order, as the Tables, Declensions, and Conjugations, may be recited in this mode with considerable advantage. The same is true to even a greater extent with the training exercises in Reading and Vocal Music. Still, even in these cases the teacher must frequently address questions to individuals in order to ascertain that all are making sure progress, and to guard them from the danger of forgetting that each is responsible for himself.

They may be given promiscuously.—When conducting a recitation according to this mode, the teacher calls upon the different members of his class to answer, without regard to any particular order. If there is reason for it, he may assign more questions, or harder ones, to some pupils than to others; but he must treat all with the most strict impartiality.

For the ordinary purposes of a recitation, and for general reliability, this mode of answering is undoubtedly better than those which have been previously named. It concentrates the attention of the class upon the work of the recitation, it compels pupils to study all parts of the lessons with the same care, it makes each one responsible for his own work, and enables the teacher to make the most advantageous distribution of his questions. If it be desirable to have a head and a foot to a class, or places of honor, the records of the recitations which should be kept by the teacher will enable him to assign places to its members according to their relative scholarship.

There are several modifications of the promiscuous mode of answering questions which must be noticed.

The first modification is that in which the question is stated without designating any one to answer it, but with the expectation that all who think they can do so will raise their hands, and then the answerer is selected from among them. If pupils always would or could report their knowledge correctly, this mode might enable a teacher to see at a glance who could answer and who could not; but, in most classes, teachers will find, upon experiment, some modest and conscientious pupils who think they can answer but who are afraid they cannot, and do not therefore raise their hands; and others who raise their hands without having the most substantial data upon which to base the conclusion that they are able to give the correct answer. Besides, it is not best for a teacher to seem to take it for granted that any member of a class is not prepared to recite.

The second modification is one in which a question is put and the answerer selected from among all the members of the class. This mode gives the teacher more freedom in the distribution of his questions, and obviates the objections just named as applicable to the preceding mode. If the first one called upon fail to answer, it may be well to permit all others who feel prepared to raise their hands.

There is a third modification of the promiscuous mode of answering questions. In this, the teacher calls upon a member of the class, who responds by rising or taking a designated seat, when the teacher proceeds to put a series of questions to him, or to assign him a topic for discussion, and, being satisfied, calls upon another. This mode is thorough and searching. It is well adapted to reviews and examinations. The objection to it is that it does not sufficiently distribute the work of the recitation to secure the highest interest in the class.

Following a fourth modification, the teacher puts no direct questions, at least in the beginning, but calls upon some one to state the subject of the lesson, another to commence the recitation, a third to continue it, a fourth to follow, and so on until the matter under consideration has been exhausted, each being stopped, criticized, and corrected at any point where the teacher deems it expedient. Such a class is almost a self-working machine, the teacher merely mentioning the names of those who recite and those who volunteer comments or criticisms. It is very evident, however, that this mode strictly applied would prevent a class from receiving any help from the teacher during the recitation, and that it is only adapted to advanced classes under peculiar circumstances. It answers a very good purpose in reviews.

They may be given in writing.—In all that has been said in regard to modes of answering questions, pupils have been supposed to give their answers orally. It is proper to add that the answers may be written, and given consecutively, simultaneously, or promiscuously, with only those changes which are necessitated by the difference between writing and speaking. For example, in a Mathematical recitation, each pupil in turn may be assigned a problem to solve, all may be required to solve the same problem at the same time and to announce the result together, or any one may be called upon to solve a particular problem.

When the principal object is to examine a class, the whole subject-matter intended for the examination may be submitted to each member, and all be assigned the same task with respect to it. The work when done should be handed to the teacher. To make the result a fair test of knowledge or skill, each member of a class must perform his own work. When thus done, there is no other method by which a class can be examined with so much accuracy. It gives time for thinking, and time to find fit words by which to express the thought.

In ordinary recitations, the Written mode of answering questions is open to some objections. It requires too much time to write the answers, the teacher cannot so readily explain difficult points or make suggestions, the pupil loses the opportunity of practice in speaking, though he gains in the opportunity of practice in writing, and the recitation itself is necessarily devoid of that interest and flow of feeling which go so far to secure its objects. These objections only apply to this mode when used by itself; for in connection with the oral methods of answering, it is highly valuable. There is no lesson that does not contain questions the answers to which cannot be written on blackboards, and many lessons can be most conveniently recited in this way. Blackboards can be used in spelling, in solving problems, in writing definitions, and in giving analyses of subjects, forms of paradigms, and lists of examples. Teachers can often economize the time of a recitation by having some members of a class use the blackboard in answering questions, while others recite orally.

The pupil, in answering questions,–

Should make them proper as to matter, form, and mode.—What is proper in the matter, form, and mode of answers has already been indicated, so far as it could be done by the statement of the general principles relating to the subject. Detailed directions are left to the teacher, as they must be varied by the varying circumstances in which recitations take place.

Should be attentive, respectful, and adopt a becoming position.—No pupil can recite well who does not have his mind occupied with the subject. He is in danger of misapprehending the questions asked him, or of saying things in answer which have no bearing upon them. It needs only to be stated, to secure universal assent, that a pupil while reciting should be respectful towards his teacher and classmates. A pupil in answering questions should generally stand. To sit may be proper in some cases; but no ungraceful posture should be tolerated.

4th. *Correcting Errors.*—Answers to questions may be either wholly wrong or partly wrong. In both cases they should be corrected. A pupil who commits an error in reciting may have it corrected by his classmates or by the teacher. This necessitates a twofold division of the subject: first, *the correction of errors by the pupils;* second, *the correction of errors by the teacher.*

If a pupil who is reciting makes a mistake, several advantages arise from allowing his classmates to correct him if able to do so. It enlists the attention of the class more closely. It creates more interest in the recitation. It gives opportunity for industry to exhibit its fruits, and for ambition to distinguish itself. It enables the teacher to distribute more equally the matter of the recitation, and to test more accurately the power of the class. The teacher may hold all the members of a class responsible for the mistakes of any one of them; that is, he may count the question missed by one as missed by all unless they volunteer a correction.

The danger of class-criticism is that it may create ill feeling among the members of a class; but against this a judicious teacher can always guard by promptly checking any approach to it.

If his classmates cannot correct a wrong answer given by a pupil, the teacher must do so; and, besides, it is his duty to inquire into the causes which induced the mistake. It might be remarked, however, that it is sometimes useful to refer questions, or to postpone an answer to them, until the pupils have made some additional investigations. Such is particularly the case when the inability to answer arises from either a want of time or a want of inclination to study.

When the teacher corrects an answer, he should give no more of it than is sufficient to suggest the rest to the pupil's mind. His language should be plain, and his manner pleasant. A wrong answer may result from an improper question, or an improper manner of putting it; and, if so, the teacher must correct his own fault before he can expect to correct the fault of his pupil. It may result from timidity; then the teacher must endeavor to strengthen the pupil's confidence in himself. It may result from an unwillingness to answer; and in that case, such a course should be pursued as to cause the pupil to change his mind. It may result from a want of disposition to study; the proper remedy then is to apply means to increase that disposition. It may result from inability; and, if so, the teacher must render judicious help. To know exactly when and how to correct the answers of pupils at a recitation, requires much judgment.

4. THE PREPARATION FOR THE RECITATION.—With a knowledge of the Objects of the Recitation, the Requisites of the Recitation, and the Methods of conducting a Recitation, we are ready to make inquiry concerning the preparation necessary to effect these objects, supply these requisites, and conform to these methods. We shall want to know—

1st. *The Preparation the Pupil needs for the Recitation.*
2d. *The Preparation the Teacher needs for the Recitation.*

1st. *The Preparation the Pupil needs for the Recitation.—The pupil must study the matter of the lesson.*—This is the main purpose for which lessons are assigned. It is necessary in order to give correct answers to questions concerning it. This matter should not always be confined to that which is contained in the text-book, but may extend to that which is to be found in other books, or that which may be obtained by original investigations. The relations of one lesson to those which have preceded it can never be safely overlooked in preparing for a recitation. Something may be gained by the pupil from suggestions by the teacher in reference to the manner of preparing a lesson. I have always succeeded best by first securing a general view of a subject or a general understanding of it, and then a mastery of its details. The subject-matter usually assigned as lessons for pupils consists of facts, axioms, definitions, or reasonings. Facts can be learned best by classifying them according to the laws of association. Axioms and definitions impress themselves more deeply upon the memory when applied or illustrated. Processes of reasoning must be understood to be remembered or to serve any useful purpose. The statement of facts or the evolution of principles should be given in the pupil's own language.

It may be proper to say a word here in regard to the propriety of the teacher's giving assistance to a pupil in preparing his lessons. More mistakes have been made by teachers in giving too much help at such times than too little. It economizes time to render such help at the recitation; for in all probability the same difficulty will occur to more than one member of the class. In this way, too, the class may be made to teach itself,—a thing always desirable. But pupils sometimes need assistance in preparing a lesson. A point in the solution of a problem, a word in the construction of a sentence, may effectually block the pupil's pathway in the preparation of his lesson; and the teacher may remove the difficulty, or, what is better, aid the pupil in removing it. For this purpose a time should be provided in the school-programme. It should be remembered, however, that whatever a pupil can do for himself in a reasonable amount of time, he should be allowed to do.

The pupil must prepare to place his answers in proper form.—Elsewhere the forms of answers have been considered, and it is very evident, from what is there said, that these forms require study. True, the questions are often unknown; but then they can be pretty easily imagined. When topics are assigned for discussion, problems for solution, or definite exercises for preparation, the forms of the answers can be fully studied. The pupil cannot be too careful in the work of acquiring the use of good language.

The pupil must prepare to assume a becoming position, manner, and deportment during the recitation.—What is proper in these respects was mentioned in another place. I speak of the matter in this connection only in order to say that these requirements cannot be generally complied with unless some preparation is made. Gracefulness of person, politeness of manners, and propriety of deportment, may be natural to some; but many, if not all, can acquire them. Pupils should avoid rudeness, roughness, and awkwardness everywhere; but these faults appear to most disadvantage in the recitation, and there, at least, all should endeavor to regulate their appearance and their conduct according to the principles of good taste.

The pupil must go to the class-room in a teachable spirit.—The value of a recitation depends greatly upon the spirit with which pupils receive instruction. If they attend the recitations reluctantly, listen to the teacher impatiently, be restless while classmates recite, and reckless as regards the manner in which they recite themselves, and, when the recitation-hour has expired, hurry away to some scene of pleasure or place of mischief, progress in learning will be an impossibility. Pupils' likes and dislikes, in the same way as the likes and dislikes of other people, are very much under their own control. If they do not like study in general, or a study in particular, they can make themselves like it. The spirit was intended to control the flesh. What is often attributed to a want of ability is a want of will. The receptivities of our mental nature, no less than its activities, need culture. Preparation to receive a lesson must be made, as well as preparation to recite one.

2d. *The Preparation the Teacher needs for the Recitation.—The teacher must assign proper lessons.*—It is evident that a lesson ought not to be too difficult nor too easy for the pupils who are expected to prepare it. To assign it properly, the teacher must consider the capabilities of the class, the nature of the subject-matter of the lesson, and the time the pupils will have for preparation. A teacher can know the capabilities of his class only by close observation at the recitation, he can acquaint himself with the nature of the subject-matter of the lesson only by an examination of it prior to its assignment as a lesson, and the time at the disposal of a class for the preparation of a lesson can only be ascertained when estimated in connection with the time which its members must devote to other objects.

The teacher must make himself familiar with the subject-matter of the lesson.—Merely to ask questions from a book, or to depend upon the help of a book to know whether an answer is correct or otherwise, is not teaching. No one can teach another what he does not know himself. The more familiar a teacher is with a subject, other things being equal, the better he can communicate a knowledge of it to others. This knowledge on the part of the teacher of what he attempts to teach should extend as far as possible beyond what is contained in the text-book used. Text-books generally present but a mere outline of the several branches of instruction. The teacher must prepare himself to fill up this outline,—to explain, illustrate, and add to the lesson. Mental growth depends more upon what is suggested by the text-book than what is learned from it.

The teacher must arrange the subject-matter of the lesson into proper questions, both as regards matter and form.—From what was previously said, it can readily be seen that some preparation is necessary in order to frame such questions. A teacher ought not to trust to the inspiration of the moment or to his general knowledge of the subject he is engaged in teaching for the selection of matter for his questions or for their expression in verbal forms. Clumsy, unmeaning questions confuse the pupils and vitiate their taste. The shrewd lawyer prepares himself with reference to the *points* of law and fact involved in his client's cause; the wise clergyman makes his sermons bear *specially* upon the weaknesses, the follies, and the sins of his congregation; the skilful physician would be ashamed not to study the *peculiar* symptoms of a disease submitted to him for treatment: so the teacher who is awake to the interests of his class makes like preparation as regards the questions he proposes to ask, and the manner of asking them.

The teacher must choose a mode of reciting, and select the necessary apparatus for conducting the recitation.—The mode of reciting will depend upon the nature of the lesson; and no teacher can afford to allow it to be determined by chance. Apparatus is frequently needed for conducting recitations,—maps, charts, models, cards, philosophical and chemical apparatus, &c. All this ought to be procured and set in order before the recitation begins.

The teacher must observe the proprieties of person and manner during the recitation.—What these proprieties are has been stated in another place: here it is only proper to say that the teacher must make preparation to observe them. Nowhere else does the teacher come in such close contact with his pupils as at the recitation, and nowhere else can his example in dress, in position, in manners, in habits, have so great an influence. Let the teacher prepare to meet his class like a gentleman, and the silent influence of his cultured manners will teach lessons as valuable as those gained from books.

III. Exercise.—In every well-regulated school, the pupils are allowed to employ a part of their time in taking exercise. No lengthened argument will be entered upon here to show the value of such a provision; but it may be stated—

That exercise is necessary to health.—The results of common observation, as well as the investigations of physiologists, attest the truth of this proposition. Confine a child, forbid him exercise, and sickness is almost inevitable. Without exercise, all the organic functions of the body are impeded in their action. The digestive organs are weakened, the circulation goes on slowly, the nervous system becomes deranged, the vital forces are diminished; and, as a consequence, disease may fasten upon the body and cause it to sink under its effects. It needs not that instances be given when all have witnessed them.

That exercise is necessary to strength.—We need physical strength to enable us to work efficiently. Work must be done; forests must be cut down, roads must be opened, mountains must be tunnelled, canals must be dug, bridges must be erected. cities must be built, shelter, food, and clothing must be obtained, our country must be defended; and all this requires strong arms. Vigorous, healthy men are necessary to make a great nation; and such cannot be had if the young enjoy no opportunity of exercising. "Only a *whole* man is capacitated to perform in the best manner the tasks of life." Exercise toughens the muscles, hurries the blood with its freight of rich nutriment through the arteries, enlarges the lungs, and invigorates the whole system. What length of hair was to Samson, exercise is to common men.

That exercise is necessary to study.—Good health and strength of body are necessary to study; and therefore exercise, which is essential to both, must be so. A sound mind can be found only in connection with a sound body. Some of the plainest facts of Physiological Science are those which exhibit the sympathy between mind and body. A weak or diseased body affects the mind, and a weak or diseased mind affects the body. It follows that the exercise of the body tends to promote success in study. The same principle might be proven by other facts. Experience has everywhere shown that students who confine themselves closely to their rooms, who take no exercise, make in a series of years less progress than others who, at proper times, and in a proper manner, relieve their minds weary from study, and refresh their spirits by exercising the body. The body does not need rest more than the mind, and physical exercise renews mental strength.

Exercise as taken at school consists of two kinds; and the discussion concerning it may be divided into two parts:—

1. Unregulated Exercise.
2. Regulated Exercise.

1. Unregulated Exercise.—By Unregulated Exercise is meant those games or plays which children contrive for themselves, or in which they engage of their own accord. Plato said, "The gods are the friends of amusement;" and any one who studies the nature of children will find that play is almost as necessary to them as breathing. The young of all animals are fond of play. It is a common instinct. Through the air, upon the earth, and in the waters, they have their sports and gambols, and make of the beginning of life its mirth-time. Children, at home and at school, must be allowed to play. God did not implant within them the strong sportive instinct which they manifest, without a purpose. Its gratification is necessary to health, strength, and intellectual and moral development. It is wonderful how much children learn from one another in play. An afternoon spent by a child with fit companions is worth more to him than days passed alone with teachers and books. From his playfellows a child takes his manners, acquires

his habits, adopts his opinions, and imbibes his principles. Mothers who notice sudden changes in the disposition and character of their children will probably find this to be the cause. Children must play. It is cruel to deprive them of it. But a watchful care must be exercised as to where, when, and how they play. What it is desirable to say further upon this subject may be embraced under the following heads:—

1st. *The Place for Play.*
2d. *The Times for Play.*
3d. *The Manner of Play.*
4th. *The Teacher at Play-time.*

The Place for Play.—Connected with every school, there should be places for play. Elsewhere, school-grounds adapted to this purpose have been described. In good weather, all playing should be done in the open air; but a place for play in bad weather should be provided. This provision can be best met by having in our country school-houses a basement story arranged for the purpose. The grounds connected with Boarding-Schools should be sufficiently large to admit of games of ball, cricket, sliding, skating, swimming, rowing, &c. Pupils will furnish themselves with much of the apparatus needed in play; but it is not at all amiss for the school-authorities to assist them.

The Times for Play.—In Primary Schools, or Ungraded Schools which are attended by pupils under the age of ten years, one-third, if not one-half, of the school-day should be devoted to play. All schools should devote a considerable time to the same purpose. The authorities of Boarding-Schools and Colleges sometimes permit certain days to be set apart for particular games, or games between particular parties; and it is my opinion that they do wisely. I am sure that a well-contested game of cricket or base-ball, now and then, does more to make men than the few lessons that might be recited during the playing. The exact hours or days that should be devoted to play must be determined by each teacher for himself. The only principle that need be stated is that periods of work should alternate with periods of play.

The Manner of Play.—The word play is used here to denote all kinds of games, sports, and amusements in which the young engage; and they constitute a very great number. It is not necessary to distinguish the different kinds, or to describe in detail the manner of playing. Play is unrestrained activity the end of which is a delight in itself; it therefore must be left free. It is best for school-children to engage in plays that require physical exertion, since after sitting in the school-room the body needs exercise. Plays at school should always be so conducted as not to annoy those who live neighbors to the school, either by unpleasant noises or trespasses upon property. Good taste can be shown in play; and this will banish from the school play-ground all sports and games that are rude, rough, or unchaste. All plays that endanger the morals of the young, or that are apt to lead them into bad habits, should be prohibited. In this category are found games of chance, such as card-playing, matching or pitching pennies, and even marbles, when each party engaged in the game keeps what he wins. I am well satisfied that a play-ground properly managed may be made an excellent school for character. What is wanting in the discipline of the school-room may be supplied here. It is society in miniature; and plays can be so directed as to make pupils energetic, manly, polite, generous, honest, and truthful. Indeed, the weeds that are so apt to spring up in the untilled garden of the childish heart are here best rooted up, and their place supplied with good seed; but it must also be remembered that evil companions, enemies, are ever present to sow tares among the wheat.

The Teacher at Play-time.—I think it is no less a teacher's duty to be with his pupils while at play than it is to meet them at the recitation. I know that some schools are so organized that the discharge of this duty is impossible; but in that case the authorities who control the organization are responsible for its non-performance. Whenever a teacher cannot be with his pupils at play, he should still exercise as much supervision over them while thus engaged as may be practicable.

On the play-ground the teacher should so act as to make his presence welcome. He should not be a restraint upon the play. The fun should be greater because he is by. The merry frolickers should fee that they enjoy his hearty sympathy. His presence may elevate and chasten; but stiff dignity and crusty criticism are wholly out of place.

The teacher may take part in the plays of his pupils. In no other way can he study their character so advantageously, and I am led to think that in no other way can he do them so much good. There is scarcely a better test of a good teacher than that his pupils like to play with him. When thus taking part, he will naturally make suggestions as to the direction of the play, but should never assume privileges not accorded to his position as a participant in it.

A teacher will find it bad policy to reprove or punish on the play-ground. It may be necessary to stop a play, or to deny a pupil the privilege of participating in one; but this will occur very seldom. It is best for the teacher on the play-ground to appear in an unofficial capacity. He may direct and advise, but should seldom command. He may teach there by his presence, by his example; but precepts are generally better suited to the school-room. His principal object ought to be to observe, to study the character of his pupils, for the purpose of turning the information obtained to good account elsewhere. If he notice any thing wrong or improper, the offenders should be treated with privately.

2. Regulated Exercise.—In addition to the exercise which is voluntarily taken at school in the form of play, there is, many times, a necessity for a course of systematic physical training. This necessity arises from the fact that many pupils among those who most need it will not take exercise of their own accord; and from the fact that regulated exercises can be made better to secure an equal and harmonious development of the different organs of the body. The moral advantages arising from play

are of higher value than any which can be derived from systematic gymnastics; but the latter are better calculated to give perfection and strength to the body and quickness and grace to its movements. Both seem indispensable.

I do not advocate the introduction of physical training into our schools for the purpose of developing the human body to its greatest strength, for the purpose of making men like Dr. Windship, who can lift a ton or more,—for the time and trouble required to do it might be devoted to a better object,—but for the purpose of keeping the body in a healthy condition and fitting it for its highest uses. For want of such training, a large proportion of the human family are weak and sickly, unable to perform the work of life, and subject to an early death.

Without going into detail, the subject under consideration will be treated of in the following order:—

1st. *The Place for Exercising.*
2d. *The Times for Exercising.*
3d. *The Manner of Exercising.*
4th. *The Teacher at the Exercises.*

The Place for Exercising.—When instruction is given in skating, swimming, rowing, riding on horseback, &c., nothing more definite can be stated with reference to the place for exercising than that it should be suitable for the purpose.

In fair weather the school-grounds may be used for various gymnastic exercises. Military drills, when deemed proper for introduction into schools, are best conducted out-of-doors; and, indeed, most of the apparatus of our gymnasiums can be erected and used almost as well in a yard as in a room. The difficulty in the way is that it soon decays when exposed to the weather; and rain, snow, and cold prevent the use of it in exercising, many times, when exercise is most needed.

The school-room may be used as a place for exercise, if care be taken to engage only in such exercises as do not raise the dust from the floor or disturb the furniture. In most of our ungraded country schools, teachers have no other resource; but, by stationing their pupils properly about the room, they can have them go through with vocal gymnastic exercises, and exercises calculated to expand the lungs and strengthen the muscles of the neck, chest, back, arms, &c. The employment of such simple apparatus as dumb-bells and wands will occasion no inconvenience. No one who has not used them can estimate fully the value of such exercises, when taken at proper intervals during days when pupils would otherwise be confined to the school-room.

A room specially arranged for the purpose and supplied with suitable apparatus is, of course, the best place in which to conduct the exercises necessary in systematic physical training. No detailed description of such a room can here be given; but it may be said that it should be amply large to accommodate those who are to practice their exercises in it, well lighted, well ventilated, and properly heated. Great care should be taken to keep it free from dust. Many of the most appropriate exercises for schools admit the accompaniment of music; and a school-gymnasium would be very incomplete without a piano. As to other apparatus, if the gymnasium be intended for both sexes, the bags, dumb-bells, wands, rings, &c., as arranged by Dr. Lewis, are decidedly the most appropriate; but if for boys alone, it may be well, in addition, to provide some of the apparatus used in common gymnasiums, for leaping, climbing, lifting, balancing, &c. &c.

The Times for Exercising.—Every good teacher has a fixed time for hearing the recitations of each class; and if he intends to subject his pupils to a systematic course of physical training, he will find it equally necessary to appoint regular times for doing it. Weak muscles cannot be made strong, stooped shoulders cannot be made erect, narrow chests cannot be made broad and deep, without going through a regular and methodical series of exercises. The exact hour of the school-day when such exercises should be engaged in must depend upon the circumstances of the school. For a day-school, perhaps the middle of the forenoon and the middle of the afternoon sessions would be the most appropriate times; and for a Boarding-School, in the morning before the school regularly opens, and in the evening after it regularly closes. It is unwise to engage in violent exercises immediately after meals; and the exercises ought never to be prolonged beyond a reasonable length.

The Manner of Exercising.—To describe in full detail the various kinds of exercises practiced in gymnasiums would require volumes, and, of course, no attempt will be made to do so here. A few general remarks only will be made; and those who would investigate the matter further must have recourse to books which treat specially upon this subject.

The principal object of physical training is to secure strength of body combined with quickness and grace of movement. An increase of mere animal strength is not what is wanted: horses, oxen, steam-machinery, are designed to do our heavy pulling and lifting. Nor is it ability to perform wonderful feats: a circus-rider cannot be regarded as the highest type of a man. All our energy should not be spent in training the body, any more than in developing the mind. The body must be made strong and tough, but not at the expense of beauty of form or of quickness and grace of movement; and no corporeal perfection ought to be coveted, if its attainment tends to weaken the mind. These principles admitted, the manner of exercising should be controlled by them. Light apparatus that admits of quick handling is more appropriate for school-gymnasiums than that which is heavy and can be moved only with effort.

Gymnastic exercises for beginners should be very simple, and such as require little exertion to perform them. As soon as these can be performed with ease, others more difficult may be introduced. A series of exercises should be progressive in difficulty. It should be remembered, also, that over-exertion is more hurtful than a neglect of exercise.

A system of gymnastics should comprehend means for the training of all the muscles of the body. The most perfect system, probably, is that of the Swedish gymnast Ling. Dr. Dio Lewis has done more than any other American to invent apparatus suitable for persons of all ages, and especially for pupils of both sexes in our schools. If I were selecting apparatus for a school-gymnasium, I would procure almost all the articles he has invented, with perhaps a few of those used in ordinary gymnasiums. By means of such exercises as are described in the works of Ling, Lewis, and others, it is practicable for a teacher to conduct his pupils through a systematic course of physical training; at least, methods of physical education are not more difficult to understand than methods of mental education.

Exercises in a gymnasium should be taken, as far as possible, in the form of games or play. Profit may be derived from these exercises when taken by oneself, but much more if in company with classmates or friends, and accompanied with music, conversation, and merriment. Dancing, when properly regulated, is no less useful than beautiful as a school-exercise.

The dress worn by persons exercising should be such as to permit the free movement of every part of the body and the unimpeded handling of the apparatus. Good taste would dictate that all the members of a class should dress alike; but, of course, this adds nothing to the value of the exercises.

The Teacher at the Exercises.—Mere practice in a gymnasium without end or method will prove very dull and quite unprofitable. In nothing is there more need of system than in physical culture; and to have system in a school-gymnasium, the teacher must direct the exercises. He must adopt a plan, select articles of apparatus, and determine the methods of using them. He must make preparation as he would do to teach some branch of learning, and must require his pupils to attend the class as regularly and hold them as well in command as at an ordinary recitation. Indeed, the teacher in the gymnasium should evince the same qualities that give him success in the school-room.

CHAPTER IV.

THE GOVERNMENT OF THE SCHOOL.

GOVERNMENT is that system of laws or principles by which a sovereign controls his subjects; and it is founded upon the relation existing between them. For the existence of a government of any kind, a ruler, those who are ruled, and reciprocal duties growing out of these relations, are necessary conditions.

In Divine government, the Sovereign is God, and the subjects are mankind; in state governments, the sovereign is the authority in which are vested the Legislative, Judicial, and Executive powers, and the subjects are the inhabitants of the state; in family government, the sovereigns are the parents, and the subjects are the children and servants; and in school-government, the sovereign is the teacher, and the subjects are the pupils.

The end of Divine government is primarily to secure to the Sovereign the love and reverence of His subjects. We cannot for a moment suppose that God would be satisfied with an outward obedience to His laws. He desires that we should act from pure motives,—should give Him our hearts,—should leave all and follow Him.

The end of state government is to secure public order. If a citizen commit no overt act against any other citizen or against the state, no matter how bad his thoughts or intentions may be, the state is satisfied; for it does not aim to purify men's hearts, but only to punish their unlawful deeds.

The end of parental government is to secure order in the family through affection. A good parent seeks to be obeyed, but he wants that kind of obedience which springs from love. The aim of parental government combines that of Divine government and that of state government. In the family are designed to be trained good citizens and good men.

School-government is family government transferred to the school. Its end is the same. The teacher takes the place of the parents.

What it is proposed to say on School-Government may be embraced under the following heads:—

I. School-Ethics.
II. School-Retributions.
III. School-Legislation.
IV. School-Administration.

By a close examination, it will be seen that these subjects follow one another in a logical order, and that the classification is exhaustive.

If a teacher is unacquainted with the rights and duties of his pupils or his own, he cannot know how to adjust the affairs of the school, cannot have a basis upon which to establish school-laws or administer school-discipline.

The rights of pupils must be maintained, their duties must be discharged; and to secure these ends, the teacher will need to know what rewards it will be proper for him to bestow, and what punishments to inflict; or, in other words, he needs to possess a knowledge of School-Retributions.

Knowing what is right and what is wrong in school-affairs, and knowing likewise what rewards and what punishments it is proper to use in the school, a teacher must be able to adjust rewards to duties performed, and punishments to duties neglected or wrongs done,—must find means for preventing and correcting disorder,—and thus legislate for the school.

It is one thing to make laws, it is another to administer them. The teacher must promulgate and defend his school-laws, he must decide what constitutes offences under them, and inflict punishment upon the guilty. In a higher sense, he must train his pupils to delight in good order, and to do right because it is right.

With any part of this work undone or badly done, the government of the school will be just so far mere guess-work. With all of it well done, school-government can be reduced to a system which is as complete as it is beautiful.

I. School-Ethics.—Ethics is the science which treats of human rights and duties. School-Ethics relates to the rights and duties of persons connected with the school. The several classes of persons thus engaged may be named as follows:—

1. The Teacher.
2. The General School-Officers.

3. THE COMMUNITIES THAT FOUND AND SUPPORT SCHOOLS.

4. THE PUPILS.

The ethical relations of the teacher, the general school-officers, and the communities that found and support schools, will be found discussed elsewhere in this work; so that it is proper in this connection to speak only of the DUTIES OF PUPILS. Besides, since it is the main object of school-government to secure on the part of pupils the performance of their duties, the statement and discussion of these duties must be made specially prominent.

The school-duties of pupils may be comprehended under the following classification:—

1st. *Duties to Themselves.*
2d. *Duties to One Another.*
3d. *Duties to the School-Property.*
4th. *Duties to the Teacher.*
5th. *Duties to the General School-Officers.*
6th. *Duties to the School as a Whole.*
7th. *Duties to Visitors at the School.*
8th. *Duties to Society.*
9th. *Duties to God.*

This classification is adopted for the sake of convenience. It might be more or less general. When well understood, indeed, a pupil's duties to himself include all his other duties; and a specific enumeration of all these duties would make a very long list.

It ought to be remarked that school-duties have

the same ethical basis as other duties; but this is not the proper place to enter upon an investigation as to what is the *standard of right.*

Some general remarks will be made upon each class of duties, without attempting to find all the special duties included in the class.

Duties to Themselves.—A pupil has duties to himself which the teacher must see that he discharges. Generally considered, these have respect to his person and his property. Without being fully aware of the consequences, the young may do that which will impair their health, impede their progress in learning, or corrupt their morals. They are very apt to injure their books and clothing. All such acts are violations of their duties to themselves.

Duties to One Another.—Pupils have no right to take away, destroy, or injure the property of others; nor have they any right to commit with respect to them an act of personal wrong. On the contrary, it is their duty to respect the rights of others both with regard to persons and things.

Duties to the School-Property.—The pupils of a school should feel an interest in protecting and improving the school-property. Too often, however, it is purloined, destroyed, or injured by them.

Duties to the Teacher.—A pupil owes to his teacher the same duties he owes to a fellow-pupil; and in addition he should respect and obey him. What treason is in a state, disrespect and disobedience are in a school.

Duties to the General School-Officers.—The general management of schools is mostly intrusted to bodies of men, called School-Directors, School-Trustees, School-Committees; and though their relations to the pupils may not be so intimate as those between teacher and pupils, yet the duties of pupils towards them are the same as to the teacher.

Duties to the School as a Whole.—It is the duty of the pupils of a school to be regular in their attendance, to observe all its rules, and to honor it abroad both by word and deed.

Duties to Visitors at the School.—Visitors at a school may be either friends or strangers; and, in either case, they should be treated with kindness and respect. A want of such treatment on the part of pupils will always show a want of good breeding, for which teachers and parents are most in fault.

Duties to Society.—All persons have certain social duties which they ought not to neglect; but a more perfect discharge of these duties is reasonably expected from those who are educated. If scholars do not make better citizens than ignorant persons, endowments for Colleges and Academies, and taxes for Common Schools, are greatly misapplied. Scholars ought to elevate society by precept and example, and be the foremost advocates of social order. Pupils should be careful not to commit a wrong with reference to the persons or property of those who live near the school.

Duties to God.—The plain interpretation of the parable of the talents is that all persons will be held accountable for the proper use of their natural abilities, and for the opportunities of rendering them available in the work of life. Those who enjoy the privileges of learning, therefore, owe special thanks to God for them, and have resting upon them special duties towards Him. Education increases knowledge, and increased knowledge brings with it increased moral responsibility. We should expect from scholars more than from others a full discharge of their religious obligations.

This brief summary of the school-duties of pupils will be followed by a statement of the offences which they are most likely to commit. These will be arranged in classes corresponding to the classes of school-duties. The use that will be made of this classification in the further treatment of the subject, renders it expedient to state it conspicuously.

OFFENCES AGAINST THEMSELVES.

1. Injuries to their own property.
2. Injuries to their own persons.
3. Neglect of opportunities of learning.
4. Uncouth manners.
5. Bad habits.
6. Immoral conduct.

OFFENCES AGAINST ONE ANOTHER.

1. Theft.
2. Injury to property.
3. Trespass upon property.
4. Personal injury.
5. False accusation.
6. Usurpation of rights.
7. Temptation to wrong-doing.
8. Defamation.

OFFENCES AGAINST THE SCHOOL-PROPERTY.

1. Accidental injury or destruction.
2. Malicious injury or destruction.
3. Accessory to injury or destruction.

OFFENCES AGAINST THE TEACHER AND SCHOOL-OFFICERS.

1. Disobedience.
2. Disrespect.
3. Conspiracy.
4. Injury to property.
5. Injury to person.

OFFENCES AGAINST THE SCHOOL AS A WHOLE.

1. Speaking evil of the school.
2. A general disregard of the school-regulations in respect to order.
3. A general disregard of the school-regulations in respect to study.
4. Irregular attendance.
5. Wrong or unworthy conduct.

OFFENCES AGAINST VISITORS AT THE SCHOOL.

1. Rude treatment.
2. Mischievous tricks.
3. Injury to property.
4. Injury to person.

OFFENCES AGAINST SOCIETY.

1. Disturbance of the peace.
2. Injury to property, or trespass upon it.
3. Uncivil treatment or injury of persons.

OFFENCES AGAINST GOD.

1. Disregard of the religious observances of the school.
2. Creating disrespect for sacred things.
3. Immoral speaking, profanity, vulgarity.
4. Immoral conduct.

It is not claimed that this classification embraces all the offences which may occur in school, nor that some classes do not include others; but the object had in view in making the classification, is to give point to the discussion, which is to follow, upon the means of preventing and correcting these offences, and of training pupils to guard against committing them.

It is not deemed necessary to enumerate each particular act of offence, because intelligent teachers can readily refer any given act to its own class.

II. School-Retributions.—A sovereign can only make known to his subjects how well it is to obey his commands, and how bad it is to violate his laws, by a system of rewards and punishments. Laws and precepts may of themselves manifest the will of the sovereign; but the rewards and penalties attached to them are the only means of presenting a tangible expression of the strength of that determination. It is possible to understand our ethical relations and make laws respecting our rights and duties without attaching retributions to them; but a government that did no more than this would not subserve the ends for which governments are established, either in state or in school. The sovereign authority must everywhere exhibit an unflinching purpose to carry on the work of the government by rewarding virtue and punishing vice.

It will be convenient to consider—

1. Rewards for Good Conduct.
2. Punishments for Bad Conduct.

1. Rewards for Good Conduct.—Nothing further is contemplated in this connection than to name those means which may be used in schools as rewards for good conduct. The adjustment of particular rewards to particular kinds of good conduct will be spoken of elsewhere.

In the Divine government, every good thought and good deed has its appropriate reward. "Behold, the righteous shall be recompensed in the earth: much more the wicked and the sinner." The state seldom directly rewards the citizen for well-doing, except for some extraordinary service done it, as well-doing is a reward in itself, and the state-machinery is too clumsy to do entire justice in the administration of such a system; but it classifies offences with great care, and has fixed penalties which it imposes upon those who commit them. School-government partakes of the nature both of Divine and state government; and the teacher must have a system of rewards as well as a system of punishments.

The natural rewards of well-doing in the school, as well as elsewhere, are the following:—

1st. *The Approbation of Relatives and Friends.*
2d. *The Approbation of Society.*
3d. *Success in the Attainment of Life's true Ends.*

4th. *An Approving Conscience*
5th. *The Favor of God.*

The rewards which the teacher may cause to follow good conduct are—

1st. *Gifts.*
2d. *Honorable Position.*
3d. *His Approbation.*

With respect to the first class of rewards, it may be said that the teacher has no direct control in determining them. They grow out of relations which he has little power to disturb. But, while these rewards are themselves the fixed results of good conduct in all moral and Christian communities, the most skilful teacher will need all his ingenuity in making them generally operative in the school-room. In this, indeed, consists the whole of moral training,—the most difficult, the most important, but the most neglected, part of education. Something will be said of this training in another place.

In speaking of Incentives to Study, these rewards were mentioned, somewhat more in detail, as Proper Incentives. As they are proper incentives to study, they are so to good conduct; and the reader may understand what was then said to be repeated here. The reasons for desiring to be good are the same as for desiring to be wise; but the imperatives which impel us to seek the former end are stronger than those which impel us to seek the latter. The voice of conscience approves a pupil's industry in study; but its approval is more emphatic when he does his duty to his fellows and to God.

When a teacher desires to reward a pupil for good conduct, he can do so by presenting him a gift, assigning him an honorable position, or expressing approval of what he has done. All of these are merely different forms of expressing the teacher's approbation.

I do not mean by gifts, prizes; though prizes may be presented as an incentive to good conduct as well as an incentive to study, and, under the same circumstances and subject to the same conditions, they may be as useful in the one case as in the other. But I mean by gifts, any object of a material nature, as a book, which a teacher may see proper to present to deserving pupils. To such gifts there can be no valid objection in principle; but they should always be considered not as some thing *won*, but as something *earned*. Pupils should act well, and afterwards receive their gifts,—not merely act well with a view of obtaining them.

Good conduct in school should win an honorable position. The most honorable place in a school should be given to the pupil who stands highest in character and deportment, and not to the one who merely stands highest as a scholar. This position may be indicated by place in class, merit-marks, grade of diploma, or honorable mention in public reports. Teachers have power to bestow the honors of a school upon the most deserving; and, if this was always done, better order would be found in many schools than now prevails. The material value of an honorable position in school is chiefly found in the recommendation it furnishes to the public,—a recommendation which is due from the teacher to all his pupils who deserve it.

A word of approbation from a loved teacher sinks deep into the heart of a pupil. If a teacher enjoys the respect and love of his pupils, and then knows when and how to commend them for good conduct, he needs little else to enable him to govern his school. This commendation may take the form of words of approval, a pleased expression of countenance, or a simple nod of the head or sign of the hand. It may be indicated to a pupil by showing confidence in him, quoting his example, speaking well of him to his friends, or recommending him to some responsible position in business. There are, indeed, a thousand ways in which a teacher may express his approbation.

2. Punishment for Bad Conduct.—The rewards which are given to those pupils who conduct themselves well cannot be accorded to those who conduct themselves badly; and this of itself constitutes one part of their punishment. Besides this, however, there are certain positive punishments which are made use of in school, the most prominent of which are the following:—

1st. *Reproof.*
2d. *Reparation of Damage done.*
3d. *Performance of Duties neglected.*
4th. *Deprivation of Privileges.*
5th. *Acknowledgment of an Offence before the School.*
6th. *Confinement.*
7th. *Personal Chastisement.*
8th. *Suspension from School.*
9th *Dismission from School.*

A teacher is expected to govern his school, and there is vested in him all the authority necessary for that purpose. He is in the place of the parent; and all that a parent can legally do in the government of his children, a teacher can do in the government of his pupils. Teachers frequently inflict all the punishments named in the preceding list, and *they ought everywhere to have the power to do so.* As a matter of fact, they generally have the power; but sometimes a provision is made that a pupil shall be suspended or dismissed from school only after the consent of the General School-Officers shall have been obtained.

A few remarks concerning each form of punishment will place the subject in a better light.

Reproof.—This is the most common kind of punishment, and many teachers seldom find it necessary to inflict any other. It may be mild or severe, according to the nature of the offence. Sometimes a look of disapproval, a shake of the head, or the pointing of a finger, will be sufficient; and sometimes it takes earnest words again and again repeated to arouse the offender to a proper sense of his duties. Circumstances may render it politic to administer reproof publicly; but, as a general rule, private admonition is much more effectual.

Reparation of Damage done.—When a pupil destroys the property of the school or of a fellow-pupil, it is his duty to replace it; and when he injures such property he ought to repair the damage done. If the destruction or injury be wilful, some additional punishment should be inflicted.

Performance of Duties neglected.—Pupils often neglect to prepare their lessons or perform their tasks when they should do so. In such cases, little just complaint can be made if the teacher compel them to occupy a part or the whole of their play-time in the performance of their neglected duties.

Deprivation of Privileges.—In state-government, the abuse of a privilege is frequently followed by its forfeiture. The same principle may be applied with good effect in school-government.

Acknowledgment of an Offence before the School.—Such an acknowledgment ought only to be required when the offence is a grave one and of a public character. When one pupil has wronged a fellow-pupil publicly, or wronged a number of his fellow-pupils, it is appropriate. A mismanaged case of inflicting punishment in this way is calculated to do much harm.

Confinement.—A pupil may very properly, for certain offences, be detained in the school after the school shall be dismissed, or during recesses or intermissions. I have thought that solitary confinement in a small room, suitably prepared, for hours or days, during school-time or during play-time, might be a more effectual and a less degrading punishment for graver offences than that with the rod.

Personal Chastisement.—There are cases in many schools in which force must be used to compel obedience; and in these cases it ought to be used. It is a means of governing, however, that needs to be managed with the utmost care.

Suspension from School.—When a pupil in a school is doing harm to others, and no good for himself, ne should be suspended from school until his reformation shall be effected.

Dismission from School.—In case no reformation is probable, dismission from school may take place. Teachers should remember, however, that the consequences of such a punishment last through life; and it should not, therefore, be inflicted without sufficient cause.

It is maintained that all the kinds of punishment named in the preceding list are proper to be used by the teacher in the government of the school; but some of them may be used in such a way as to do great mischief. A few examples will be given.

Scolding.—A scolding teacher will always have a disorderly school. Reproof when constantly given loses all its good effect. Let a teacher contract the habit of scolding, and he will soon render himself and his pupils unhappy, and the work of the school unpleasant.

Expressions of Contempt.—A thoughtless teacher may use such expressions in reference to the moral condition of the family of a pupil, or in reference to some physical defect or mental peculiarity of his own; but they never accomplish any good, and mostly do harm. Sarcastic remarks, or such names as numskull, blockhead, dunce, &c. &c., do not become a teacher in speaking either to or of his pupils.

Personal Indignities.—There are cases in which a teacher would be justifiable in using corporal punishment; but it ought always to be done in a becoming manner. Good never results from the infliction of such personal indignities as pulling an ear, twisting the hair, snapping the forehead, &c. &c.

Prolonged Tortures.—In the dark ages of the profession, teachers sometimes resorted to punishments like the following: holding a book in the hand with the arm stretched out horizontally from the body, standing on one foot, stooping down or leaning forward so as to touch with the finger a nail in the floor, &c. &c.; but these days have almost passed.

III. School-Legislation.—Having found what duties pupils have, and how these duties can be violated, what rewards may be conferred upon the good, and what penalties may be inflicted upon the bad, we are ready to engage in the work of making laws for the school. Arbitrary and unjust laws are hurtful anywhere, but nowhere more so than when used to control the young. For those proposed here, an effort will be made to establish a philosophical basis.

The ends of School-Legislation may be stated as follows:—

1. To find Means of preventing Disorder in School.
2. To find Means of correcting Disorder in School.
3. To find Means of inducing Pupils to discharge their Duties of their own Accord.

Much of the disorder in school may be prevented by judicious regulations. The most judicious regulations will not prevent all disorder; and such as cannot be prevented must be corrected. It is not enough simply to secure good order in a school, either by preventive or corrective means, or both; the pupils must be induced by the process of training to which they are subjected to discharge all their duties freely and of their own accord. It is the perfection of good government in a school to make the pupils capable of governing themselves.

1. MEANS OF PREVENTING DISORDER.—Disorder in a school is owing to certain causes which can often be removed before they produce any bad results. These causes may be generalized as follows:—

1st. *Unsuitable Accommodations.*
2d. *Unqualified Teachers.*
3d. *Bad Management.*

So much either has been, or will be, said on each of these points in other connections, that no long discussion is needed here.

Unsuitable Accommodations.—These have reference to unsuitable school-grounds, school-houses, and school-furniture. If play-grounds are too small, trespasses will be committed in the neighboring fields or on the adjacent highway. It is impossible to have good order in a room badly lighted, poorly heated, or ill ventilated, or in one into which a hundred pupils are crowded that was designed to accommodate but fifty. With seats too close together or so arranged that the movement of one pupil always disturbs a number of others; with desks too low or too high; with impure air to breathe, limbs shivering with cold or burning with heat; with the glaring sun streaming his dazzling rays full in their faces; with school-room dark, dull, and dirty, it is no wonder that children are restless. The school-authorities ought to provide means of removing such causes of disorder.

Unqualified Teachers.—Some persons seem born to command. They naturally take the lead in affairs. Napoleon among his schoolmates at Brienne, and Washington with the comrades of his youth in Virginia, both exhibited those traits of character which eminently fitted them to lead the armies of their respective countries. Let a person who has a natural capacity for governing take charge of a school, and the pupils at once instinctively understand that they must obey, and act accordingly; while the commands of another possessing no such capacity would be unceremoniously disregarded. A school taught by one who has the gift of governing seems to govern itself; but in reality it is governed by the unconscious working of the peculiar energies of the teacher. On the contrary, no effort can preserve order in a school if such a gift be wanting in its head. Between those who can govern without effort, and those who cannot govern with all the effort they can make, there will be found a large number of persons who, if they could never learn to manage large bodies of men, can at least acquire the power of governing a school successfully. Such persons must cultivate the talent for governing. A disorderly school is *prima facie* evidence of incapacity on the part of the teacher, and he must either adopt a rigid course of self-discipline, or give place to another better qualified. The teacher, who is to a great extent the source of law in the school, must be himself subject to law.

It may be proper to name some of the most important qualifications which a teacher must possess in order to govern well.

He ought to have *polished manners;* for, if he is rude and noisy, it is not likely his pupils will be polite and quiet. He should have no *bad habits,* for the young are both good critics and quick imitators. He should be a *scholar;* for otherwise his pretensions will eventually be discovered, and create towards him disrespect, if not contempt. He must *plan judiciously,—wisely adapt means to ends,*—or his pupils will first be led to question his ability and afterwards to disregard his authority. He must exhibit *self-confidence* and *self-control;* for these qualities are necessary to initiate authority, and almost equally necessary to maintain it. He must have *firmness;* for a fickle-minded teacher, who does to-day what he will undo to-morrow, who makes laws and fails to execute them, who prosecutes nothing to the end, can never inspire confidence among his pupils or command their respect. He must be *consistent,*—regulating the affairs of the school upon well-settled principles of justice and policy; for if it is suspected that his enactments are arbitrary, his rewards and punishments the results of whim, caprice, or prejudice, there will be an end to all voluntary obedience, and a virtual revolution in the school. He must be *courageous;* for every school has crises which the weak and timid will be unable to control. He must be *just;* for favoritism and partiality will do much to undermine his authority He must have *sympathy* with children,—entering easily into their joys and sorrows, loving their company, and taking an interest in what interests them; for otherwise his government will be cold and formal, and secure at best but a cold and formal obedience. He must be *tolerant;* for party-feelings and party-interests will exhibit themselves in the school-room, and he must know how to temper all without taking sides with any. He must be *kind,*—for kindness is the solvent to which all that is wrong in the human bosom yields most readily,—and *patient;* for patience is necessary to enable him to wait while kindness works.

Bad Management.—Bad management is one of the most fruitful sources of disorder in a school. If a school be well organized, its classes well arranged, its work well systematized; if pupils be properly employed in study, in recitation, in exercise; if school-government be well understood and wisely administered, a large proportion of the offences which now occur in school will disappear.

To give details on these points, however, would be to repeat what has already been said; and a few remarks only will be added concerning provisions which may be made to prevent much disorder, and which have not been spoken of elsewhere.

Rules.—A few plain rules, informing pupils as to their duties and obligations, will tend to promote good order in a school. There must be rules, either written or unwritten; and I think it is decidedly better to have the most important of them written,—better, because the pupils can frequently read them for themselves, and because the teacher in enforcing them does not seem to act arbitrarily.

Plenty of Work for Pupils.—Mischief is mostly

done by idlers. There should be no unoccupied time in school-hours; and even the exercises of the play-ground may be to some extent regulated.

Close Inspection.—A pupil who knows that his work will be closely inspected will be more apt to take pains in doing it. If he feels that the watchful eye of the teacher follows him everywhere, he will hesitate longer about engaging in what is wrong. A military officer is not satisfied with the general appearance of his men along the line, but he examines the condition of every man and every musket. The teacher must be equally close in his inspections. He must remember that the good conduct of a school is made up of the good conduct of the individuals who are members of it. If a teacher cannot make such inspections himself (and this may be the case in a large school), he must require very strict reports from his assistants.

Co-education of the Sexes.—The regulated intercourse of the two sexes in the school, as in the family, tends to the good of both, intellectually and morally. It brings the restraints of public opinion into the school, and thus prevents disorder. It raises the moral standard of the school, and the teacher can always be sure of large sympathy among the pupils in enforcing necessary discipline.

2. Means of Correcting Disorder.—It is hardly necessary to say that the same means which tend to prevent disorder in a school will also tend to correct it; but, however skilfully these means may be applied, however convenient and pleasant the accommodations of the school may be, whatever qualifications the teacher may possess as a discipli-

narian, or whatever judgment he may show in his school-management, there are still pupils in almost every school who will neglect their duties or be guilty of misconduct. This fact at once brings before us one of the most difficult branches of inquiry connected with school-government, and it must be considered at length.

The question is, How shall that disorder in the school be corrected which the teacher is not able to prevent or to overcome by making the circumstances of the school-room favorable to good order?

In answering this question, I propose to consider—

1st. *The punishment of those who offend.*
2d. *The pardon of those who repent.*

1st. *The punishment of those who offend.*—It is scarcely suspected by many teachers that school-punishments can be regulated by any principle. Offences occur, the offenders are punished, much or little, sometimes in one way and sometimes in another, and justice seems satisfied. Very few teachers trouble themselves to inquire into the reason for the mode or degree of punishment which they adopt. Even the same teacher punishes similar offences in different ways, according to his mood, fancy, or caprice. There seems to be a general conviction that wrong-doers should be punished; but, judging from the practice in our schools, nothing has been settled as to why or how. Sad as is the confusion in methods of teaching and in plans of managing schools, there is no department relating to education in which reform is more needed than in that of school-government

In the Divine government there is punishment for wrong-doing. God has done all that could be done to prevent sin. He has given man a habitation every way suited to his wants. All the circumstances by which he is surrounded are calculated to elevate and ennoble him. Wisely as God could plan it, the universe is so ordered as to prevent wrong-doing.

But the human will was made free, and it was foreseen that man would lose sight of his highest interests, forget God, and commit sin. To correct these evils, to win men back to purity of thought and uprightness of life, a system of punishments was instituted. No one can doubt the existence of such a system, for, although he may not have studied its philosophy, he has witnessed its operation.

If now the principles that underlie the system of punishments in the Divine government can be ascertained, among them will be found those which should be applied in school-government. The Divine Mind, indeed, can make a perfect adjustment of punishments to offences, which no human skill can do; but all forms of government among men, whether in the state, the family, or the school, will subserve the ends for which they are established in proportion as they pattern after the beautiful system of retributive laws by which God governs His moral universe.

Punishments in the Divine government are designed to accomplish three ends,—viz.: *the reformation of wrong-doers; the warning of those who are in danger of becoming wrong-doers;* and *the manifestation of the Divine displeasure with respect to wrong-doing.* A man eats too much, and gets the dyspepsia. He learns in consequence to eat more moderately; others profit in eating by his example; and the Creator, in the emphatic language of sickness and pain, shows His displeasure at the violation of His laws. The upbraiding voice of conscience ofttimes turns the guilty back in their downward course, warns those who have not fallen so far into wickedness by example, and expresses God's exceeding great hatred of sin. It is believed that such instances as these fully exemplify the ends for which all punishments of Divine origin were established.

The objects of school-punishments are the same as those of Divine punishments. If a pupil commits a fault, his punishment should tend to prevent his repeating it, serve as a warning to his school-fellows, and, at the same time, manifest the teacher's disapprobation of the act. I do not hesitate to say that all school-punishments that are not calculated to effect these objects are either improper in themselves or improperly applied.

It follows, from what has been said, that school-punishments are identical in design with the Divine punishments, and, consequently, must be controlled by the same principles. The task remains of pointing out and applying these principles.

From careful observation in respect to the workings of Providence in the affairs of men, I infer that the leading principles according to which God regulates the penalties He imposes for wrong-doing are the following:—

1st. *That punishments invariably follow offences.*

2d. *That all offences are punished in proportion to their magnitude.*

3d. *That each class of offences has its own kind of punishments.*

4th. *That all punishments are connected to the offences as effects to causes.*

Some statement of the grounds upon which these principles rest will be given.

That punishment invariably follows an offence appears from history, from observation, and from personal experience. In a just government, it could not be otherwise. Every page of history tells the story of the punishments inflicted upon wicked men and wicked nations; and this story, when well understood, reveals the fact that no such men or such nations escaped it. Common observation teaches the same lesson. The murderer is always wretched, and may be imprisoned or hanged. The liar is not believed when he tells the truth. The dishonest man is not trusted. The drunkard dies in want and misery. The miser hardens his heart and is despised. The sinner, no matter what may be the nature of his sin, is upbraided by his conscience,—a fire that is never quenched. Our own hearts reveal the same truth. We are all conscious that if we sin we must suffer. No man in his senses ever yet thought a bad thought or did a bad deed and remained unpunished, unless his heart had become stone and himself a brute,—which is in itself the heaviest punishment God inflicts upon men. Sin is moral sickness; and moral sickness must be attended with moral pain. Justice demands the enforcement of this law, and God has declared in His Word that He will enforce it.

In the Divine government all offences are punished in proportion to their magnitude. Few stripes or many are used, according to the nature of the offence. This principle necessarily results from the Divine perfections; but it is also inferable from experience. Every individual is aware that his health and strength are impaired in proportion as he violates the laws that regulate his organic constitution; and every individual is no less sensible that the moral nature is damaged to the same extent that moral laws are violated. Each one can settle the question for himself by an appeal to his own consciousness.

Each class of offences has its own kind of punishments. Different classes of offences arise from the violation of different kinds of laws, and the nature of the punishment has been made to correspond to the nature of the offence. We may obey a law of one kind and disobey a law of another kind; and pleasure will result from our conduct in the former, and pain in the latter case. A man may observe the laws of economy and become rich, and at the same time live in habitual disregard of moral and religious duties; and, on the other hand, good men do not always prosper in business. A leaky ship with pious, self-sacrificing missionaries on board might founder in a storm, while a strong, stanch vessel manned by a crew of lawless pirates would safely outride the dangers of wave and wind. Health and strength may be enjoyed by those who use them in injuring their fellow-men, while ill health and physical debility are the portion of such as go about doing good.

These seeming contradictions and inconsistencies of the Divine government admit an explanation. The Divine laws as they operate upon men have been divided into three great classes,—viz.: first, *physical laws*, or those which govern the material world; second, *organic laws*, or those which relate to vegetable and animal structures; third, *moral laws*, or those which were designed to control intelligent and responsible beings. This classification is sufficiently correct and exhaustive for my present purpose; and little is risked in saying that those who obey the laws of one class will be rewarded, and those who disobey them will be punished, entirely irrespective as to whether they obey or disobey the laws which belong to the other classes.

If a man leap from a house-top, ride upon an unsafe railroad, embark in a leaky vessel, expose himself to the cold with the thermometer twenty degrees below zero, risk his life beyond his depth in water when he is unable to swim, he will render himself liable to be punished for his temerity; and in such cases, without miraculous interference, there can be no respect of persons.

Let any individual disregard the laws that govern his corporeal nature; let him neglect to attend to the light that was intended to shine about him, the heat that was designed to warm him, the air he breathes, the food he eats, the clothing he wears, the exercise he takes, and it matters not if in himself he possess the sum of human virtues, he will become weak and sickly, and perhaps will die.

A man may violate all of the ten commandments, and it is possible he might still enjoy a good degree of health and strength. The wicked may flourish, may obtain wealth and honor, but they cannot escape punishment. God does not punish moral evil by the infliction of bodily pain, unless some physical or organic law be broken at the time of the violation of the moral law. The penalties imposed in this world upon those guilty of wrong-doing are the stings of conscience, the sense of unworthiness, the loss of the respect of the good, and the conscious forfeiture of God's approbation,—penalties incomparably more severe than any other class of punishments.

In this independent operation of the physical, organic, and moral laws, may be found an explanation of what is sometimes called the mysterious ways of Providence, in giving health and prosperity to the bad and afflicting the good with sickness, misfortune, and death. There will be punishments in the future world, but they are not designed in any way to compensate for defects in the providential ruling of this one. God is just to all His children here; and from this we may conclude He will be just hereafter.

All punishments are connected to offences as effects to causes. Nature's discipline is a discipline of consequences. If any individual breaks a law, he must pay the penalty, and this penalty results directly from his conduct. Ignorance does not excuse one. A child may not know the effect of heat;

but a hot stove will burn its hand nevertheless. A mother may with the best intentions administer poison to her child instead of medicine; but, while her conscience may approve her well-meant kindness, she is sorely punished for her ignorance in the loss of her child.

If a careless mechanic falls from a building and is injured, an ignorant miner is killed by the explosion of the gas which sometimes accumulates in mines, thoughtless children are drowned while bathing, does any one fail to see the connection between the violation of these physical laws and the punishments that follow? Are not the laws good, and the punishments right?

If a man eat too much, he will get the dyspepsia; if he take poison, he may lose his health or die; if he overwork or overstudy, expose himself to too great a degree of heat or of cold, obstruct the growth or the healthy action of any of the vital organs, he will experience suffering and pain; and all of these punishments are the just consequences of his conduct, known to follow it as effect follows cause.

If moral laws be broken, the consequences will be different but no less certain. The murderer, thief, liar, slanderer, drunkard, gambler, he who is dishonest, and he who passes by while his brother-man suffers for want of help,—all carry in their own bosoms the pain consequent upon their wrong-doing. The prodigal wastes his substance, and must live on husks; the sluggard will not work, and in harvest he has nothing; the miser gloats over his gold until his soul shrivels up; and the hardened sinner con verts his very heart to stone, and dies worse than a brute.

Examples need not be multiplied. In Nature's punishments there is nothing arbitrary, nothing unjust, nothing unkind, no partiality. Each individual who suffers punishment will know hereafter, if he does not here, that it is the just consequence of his own wrong-doing or the wrong-doing of those for whom he was responsible.

An application must now be made of the great principles just explained, to the punishments of the school.

Punishments in the school must be made invariably to follow offences. The teacher may not always find it necessary to administer these punishments. Real sorrow may follow the commission of a fault, and that may be a sufficient punishment. Nature's laws are inexorable. Those who break them must abide the consequences; and yet these laws are entirely compatible with Divine love. So those who violate the laws of the school must be punished, and proper punishment will be to them the greatest kindness. Any escape from the consequences of bad actions only tempts to further crime. This is emphatically the case with children. A teacher's indulgence begets contempt for his authority. A timid administration encourages a spirit of rebellion among pupils. Let punishments be just but certain, and children will show little disposition to disturb the order of the school. "A less punishment," says Beccaria, "which is certain, will do more good than a greater which is uncertain." God punishes wrong-doing in the school as elsewhere, and it is the teacher's duty only to intensify and make manifest the design of those punishments, or to adopt and administer others in the same spirit and according to the same principles.

That all offences should be punished in proportion to their magnitude in school, as elsewhere, is a principle so obvious that little need be said to enforce it. Motives must be taken into consideration in determining the magnitude of the offence. A pupil may do a good act from a bad motive, a bad act from a good motive, or the act and the motive may both be bad,—all of which a teacher must carefully consider before he is prepared to determine the punishment that is deserved.

It hardly seems questionable that each class of school-offences should have its own kind of punishment, but, if true, the practice of many teachers is sadly at fault. The treatment of a pupil who injures the school-property should be very different from that of one who tells a falsehood, or rebels against the teacher's authority. A pupil who fails to prepare his lesson, one who quarrels with his school-fellows, and one who plays truant, all ought to be punished, but surely not in the same way.

One of the most important principles which should control all school-legislation is that punishments should be connected to offences as effects to causes. It is presumed that all those who inflict punishments upon the young, if they think at all, intend them to be understood as the effects of misconduct; but almost everywhere, in adjusting punishments to offences, wide departures are made from the laws that express the relations of causes and effects.

I unishments are generally felt by pupils to have no firmer basis than the will of the teacher, which they have frequent reason to suppose is moved by caprice or passion. In place of this arbitrary mode of punishment, there is needed a system of discipline in schools, founded upon well-established principles,—the principles which characterize all natural punishments.

I have said that school-punishments are mostly arbitrary in their character. The truth of the assertion may be shown by facts. It is not uncommon in school for children to be whipped for breaking a pane of glass, making a bad recitation, or being tardy in coming to school. Threats, scoldings, blows, pulling the hair, snapping the forehead, cracking the hands, personal indignities, and bodily tortures, are used to punish offences without discrimination and without any regard to principle. One pupil does not know his lesson, and his ears are boxed; another tears his book, and his hands are slapped with a ruler; still another talks too loud, and he is made to stand on one foot or learn some difficult task. Teachers whip, threaten, scold, almost at random. Without the recognition of any principles governing the matter, they choose punishments and the manner of inflicting them much according to the mood they may be in. At any rate, the children thus punished cannot see any logical connection between the offence and its punishment, and all sense of moral distinctions becomes obliterated in their minds. A child can only be made better by punishment when he feels that it is just.

That school-punishments may be connected to

offences as effects to causes—that they may be made their natural results—will appear from a statement of examples. If a pupil injure some part of the school-property, the natural punishment would be that he should repair the damage. One who comes to school late may be detained just as long as he was behind time during recess or noontime. One who does not know his lesson should learn it over. One who disturbs his neighbor may be made to sit out of his reach. One who throws dirt upon the floor should clean it up. One who quarrels on the play-ground should be deprived for a time of the privileges of play, except by himself. One who tells a falsehood may be compelled to feel that he cannot be so implicitly trusted. One who uses profane or vulgar language ought to be kept away from his school-mates, lest his example do them harm. One who openly disobeys the teacher or conspires against him may be overcome by force or sent away. In all these instances, the consequences are plainly the results of the offences, and any child will so understand them. Other consequences will also follow,—the loss of the good opinion of the teacher, the loss of standing in the school, the loss of self-respect, &c.; but the dull senses of evil-disposed pupils do not so easily appreciate them. The teacher should in all cases endeavor to make his pupils feel the wrong they have done, and to awaken a desire on their part to avoid the committing of like errors in the future; but of this in another connection.

The advantages of such a discipline of consequences over a system of punishments which are inflicted arbitrarily are very great. As the administrator of such a system, the teacher has no occasion to lose his temper. He can be both firm and kind. His personality is in great measure removed from his administration of the school-affairs, and like a judge he announces the offender's sentence, who feels that it is just. If a pupil is quarrelsome and disturbs the enjoyments of the play-ground, the teacher may say to him, "I am sorry to deprive you of play, but you annoy others, and must forfeit your privileges in this respect." To another, who whispers much and loud, he may say, "James and you are great friends; I would like to have you sit together; but you disturb others with your loud talking, and spend time in conversation during which you ought to be at work; I must separate you." To still another he may say, "I have done for you what I could: I have always been ready to assist you in your studies, have tried to treat you kindly, and have warned you of your faults; but you continue to break the rules of the school, you mock at my authority, and must leave school." No one can fail to see that a teacher who governs a school according to such a system will be able to do his pupils much more good, and do it with much more satisfaction to himself, than if he practised the method of controlling his school by arbitrarily threatening, scolding, and whipping.

In addition to this, such a system of training is well calculated to make good citizens and good men. They will become accustomed to trace the consequences of their acts, and be ready to render full obedience to the Divine and civil government, seeing that all good laws are designed not for the pleasure of the sovereign, but for the good of the subject.

The principles now indicated enable us to make a general adjustment of punishments to offences. For this purpose, use will be made of the list of school-offences and school-punishments already presented. Details must be left to be arranged by the teacher according to the ever-varying circumstances of school and pupil.

Punishments for Offences against Themselves.

1. *Injuries to their own property.*—When a pupil injures his own property, its loss is the natural punishment. The teacher does not buy books or clothes for his pupils, and if they are injured it is the parents' rather than the teacher's place to correct the evil. The teacher may, however, reprove the child and inform the parent: I think his duty extends no further.

2. *Injuries to their own persons.*—A pupil may be injured at school by eating unripe fruit, by exposing himself to cold or wet, and by going into danger in many ways. If the teacher has not specially forbidden the act by which a pupil injures himself, with appropriate reproof and warning, he may leave him to learn wisdom by suffering the natural consequences of such conduct. If the teacher has prohibited it, the erring pupil should be punished as provided for offences against the teacher.

3. *Neglect of opportunities of learning.*—The natural punishment for the neglect of opportunities of learning is ignorance; and this brings with it many disadvantages. The teacher may do what he can to make

his pupils appreciate these disadvantages. For neglect in preparing his lesson, a pupil may be made to learn it over again during play-time. For inattention in class, he may be punished with a reproof, the loss of position, or dismissal from the class, according to the magnitude of the offence. For the worst forms of laziness the school can hardly be made to furnish the best remedy. The best remedy is either some employment that can be made to interest the person under treatment, or some mechanical business that cannot be discontinued without detection. If the loss of all that ambitious pupils aspire to attain does not arouse a lazy boy to study, he may possibly be reached by shame or ridicule. I doubt whether corporal punishment in such cases can do much permanent good.

4. *Uncouth manners.*—Uncouth manners are the result of defective home-training, or of the example of rude companions. In the presence of the polite and refined, children will soon improve in this respect. The teacher must assist them in the effort by watchful care, kind counsel, and gentle reproofs.

5. *Bad habits.*—Bad habits, in the sense intended here, have reference to such habits as shrugging the shoulders, holding the head to one side, fumbling the hands, spitting constantly, walking heavily over the floor, &c. &c. In general, nothing more is needed than to call the pupils' attention to the habit every time it is noticed, with such a reproof as may be deemed appropriate. If the habit cause the abuse of a privilege, the privilege may be withheld for a time. I once knew a teacher cure a boy of the habit of making a great deal of noise in walking

about the school-room, by compelling him, for two or three days, to take off his shoes every time he left his seat.

6. *Immoral conduct.*—That kind of immoral conduct which consists in injuring others is not referred to here, but only that which is wrong independently of its effect upon others. A pupil may write profane or vulgar language which no one reads, he may form the habit of drinking liquor by himself, he may meditate mischief which he does not execute, he may injure himself secretly in many ways that are immoral; any of which acts coming to the knowledge of the teacher he should not permit to pass in silence. In such cases, however, warning and reproof are the only punishments that can safely be resorted to, unless the conduct be so grossly immoral as to deserve suspension or expulsion.

Punishments for Offences against One Another.

1. *Theft.*—A child may take the property of another without being conscious of the crime he commits. In such a case, the immediate restitution of the property taken must be made to the loser, and an explanation of the nature of the offence be given to the one who took it. Sometimes reproof, more or less severe, is appropriate. When children take trifling things, not realizing that such pilfering is theft, the treatment should be the same as when they are entirely unconscious of the wrong done. If a pupil with a full sense of the offence steal the property of another, he should be made to return it, be confined for a proper length of time where he

cannot repeat the offence, or be suspended or dismissed from the school.

2. *Injury to property.*—A pupil who injures the property of another, whether by accident or on purpose, should be required to repair it immediately. If he injure it on purpose, confinement would seem to be the proper penalty.

3. *Trespass upon property.*—The books and playthings of some pupils are often used by others without any intention of injuring them. If injury should be done to them, restitution must be made; but if not, the teacher may demand the discontinuance of the practice. A few words concerning the rights of property will show that no one should use the property of another without his consent.

4. *Personal injury.*—A slight personal injury may be punished by reproof. Graver personal injuries ought to be punished by confinement. If a pupil's temper be such as to render his presence dangerous to his school-fellows, dismission from school is the proper remedy. For such an offence, I do not see that physical force should in any case be used, except to separate combatants who are engaged in fighting.

5. *False accusation.*—Children sometimes accuse one another falsely. To escape punishment themselves, they accuse others who are innocent. This is a mean and cowardly act, and should be severely punished. I do not think corporal punishment should be resorted to; but the deprivation of all the social privileges of the school would seem to be the natural consequence of such an abuse of them. In addition, the teacher should administer such

reproof as the state of the circumstances seems to demand.

6. *Usurpation of rights.*—Pupils are entitled to the positions which they have won, and to the privileges which have been granted them; and these rights cannot be justly usurped by others. In case of usurpation, the mode of punishment should be much the same as with respect to injuries to persons or property.

7. *Temptation to wrong-doing.*—One of the most potent causes of evil in respect to the young is bad company. Children at school are frequently exposed to very great temptations to wrong-doing presented by those older than themselves. It is not uncommon for a child pure and innocent to contract bad habits, and to become acquainted with much that is evil in its character, in the short space of a few months. A child may thus learn to use profane or vulgar language, to lie, to cheat, and to deceive. How shall children be guarded from such temptations? What punishment shall be meted out to those who tempt them? The answer is given without hesitation. For such conduct in its milder forms, the offender should be excluded for a time from the society of his school-mates; but in aggravated cases, expulsion is the only remedy. Better have a mad dog or a viper among children than one whose example is poison to the soul and whose influence gives it deadly effect.

8. *Defamation.*—Pupils sometimes endeavor to injure the good name of their fellow-pupils by giving currency to false reports concerning them, and in various other ways. A pupil guilty in this

respect may be made to acknowledge the offence before the school, as it is a public wrong, and afterwards he may be denied for a time the social privileges of the school.

Punishments for Offences against the School-Property.

1. *Accidental injury or destruction.*—Pupils may accidentally deface walls or furniture, destroy books or apparatus, and break windows or doors. In all such cases, the reparation of the damage done will be the proper punishment.

2. *Malicious injury or destruction.*—A pupil who maliciously injures or destroys school-property should first be compelled to repair all the damage done, and afterwards be reproved, denied privileges which he has abused, confined, suspended, or dismissed from school, according to the grade of the offence.

3. *Accessory to injury or destruction.*—Those who injure or destroy school-property are often instigated by others more cautious or more cunning than themselves. In such cases both parties should be punished according to their degree of guilt, and no difference need be made in the mode.

Punishments for Offences against the Teacher and School-Officers.

1. *Disobedience.*—There are many grades of this offence. Children often disobey the requests of a teacher from thoughtlessness. They do not clearly apprehend the ground of his requests, and, becoming absorbed in present enjoyment, they forget them

The teacher must not form too harsh a judgment in such cases, but make large allowance for youthful fickleness. A reproof calculated to induce reflection is all the punishment demanded. Children who disobey, however, must in all circumstances suffer the just consequences of their disobedience. For example, the teacher may forbid throwing snow-balls towards the school-house. A thoughtless boy disobeys, and breaks a pane of glass. The punishment should consist in repairing the damage, in being reproved for the disobedience, or in being detained in the school-house when the pupils next engage in the sport of snow-balling.

Graver acts of disobedience must be punished more severely. If the offence be a private one, private reproof and a private acknowledgment of the wrong, accompanied with a promise to try to do better, will be a proper mode of treatment; but if the offence be a public one, the circumstances may require that the acknowledgment and the promise be made before the school.

An open or premeditated act of disobedience may be punished by personal chastisement. A teacher may make a request of a pupil which he will openly refuse to comply with. Indeed, he may have published the fact among his fellow-pupils that he would so refuse. In such a case, the teacher must either compel the pupil to obey, or send him away from the school. If the teacher possess the necessary physical strength, I prefer the former alternative. It is one of the few cases in which the use of the rod will do good. Of course, if a pupil persists in his disobedience, he must be expelled

2. *Disrespect.*—A good teacher will covet the real love and respect of his pupils, and these can only be obtained by loving and respecting them. But bad pupils may offer indignities to the most faithful teacher, which his position will not allow him to submit to in silence. As, however, the nature of disrespect is similar to that of disobedience, the punishments named for the latter offence will be appropriate for the former.

3. *Conspiracy.*—Treason is the worst offence citizens can commit against a state, because it seeks the state's destruction; and conspiracy in a school is analogous to treason in a state. The state rids itself of traitors by imprisoning them for life or hanging them; and so the most severe punishments which a teacher is legally authorized to employ may be inflicted upon those pupils who plot the overthrow of his authority or stir up sedition in the school. They must be either conquered or expelled. A compromise will only postpone the crisis. A rod is for the fool's back, and in such a case I would not spare it; but, unless the conquest can be made complete, the preservation of order in the school will demand the expulsion of the leaders at least of a conspiracy against its authorities.

4. *Injury to property.*—Any injury pupils may do to the teacher's property should be repaired or compensated for. If the pupils do it maliciously, it is disrespect, and should be treated accordingly.

5. *Injury to person.*—It is very seldom that a teacher is personally injured by his pupils. In the case of its being done intentionally, severe corporal punishment or dismission from school seems to be

the only proper punishments proportionate to the offence. Where severe bodily injuries have been received, the matter should be referred to the court of the district for settlement.

Offences against the general School-Officers should be punished in the same manner as those against the teacher.

Punishments for Offences against the School as a Whole.

1. *Speaking evil of the school.*—It is at least as wrong to slander a school as it is to slander an individual. A pupil may speak evil of a school without designing to do it harm; and in such a case the correction of the wrong done, as far as possible, is the obvious penalty. A proper reproof may be administered with good effect.

With respect to a pupil who deliberately speaks evil of a school with which he is connected, or who purposely tries to injure it, no other punishment will be so befitting the offence as expulsion.

2. *A general disregard of the school-regulations in respect to order.*—All disorder in a school is an offence against the school as a whole. It disturbs its work, and lessens its reputation. Most of these offences have other relations, however, and their proper punishment can be found stated elsewhere.

Among the numerous examples of offences which arise from a general disregard of school-regulations in regard to order, may be named, loud talking, rattling chairs or desks, scraping with the feet, heavy walking on the floor, leaving seats without liberty to do so, &c. &c. One of the most effectual means of removing such sources of disorder as these is to cause the offending pupil to sacrifice the privilege he has abused. A pupil who disturbs the school by loud talking may be placed at a distance from others; one who rattles his chair or desk may be made to stand; one who scrapes the floor with his feet or walks heavily over it ought to be required to procure light shoes or wear none at all; and one who leaves his seat without liberty may be denied that liberty when others enjoy it. The same mode of treatment applies generally to this class of offences whether committed in the school-room or on the play-ground.

There are graver offences which disturb the order of the school, that must be punished in a different manner,—among them, quarrelling, stamping on the floor, forced coughing, or any noises made to attract the attention of the pupils or to annoy the teacher. The mildest grade of such offences should be punished by severe reproof, and those of graver character, first by confinement, and afterwards, if necessary, by suspension or dismission.

3. *A general disregard of the school-regulations in respect to study.*—Every good teacher directs his pupils what to study, when to study, and how to study. His regulations in these respects are as far as possible made general, and the disobedience of one pupil has a tendency to affect the whole school; and it is thus an offence against it.

The natural punishments in cases of a general disregard of the school-regulations in respect to study are, first, reproof, and it may be public, as the offence is a public one; the loss of position, the performance of whatever duty was neglected, and the deprivation of such privileges as may be deemed necessary to secure that performance; and when these remedies fail, and where the reputation of a class or a school is at stake, resort may be had to suspension or dismission from school.

4. *Irregular attendance.*—Parents may be to blame for the irregular attendance of their children at school; and in such cases, though the children cannot be shielded from the effects of falling behind their classes, occupying a low position in the school, and making little progress in study, they should receive no further punishment.

When pupils come late to school in consequence of wasting their time on the way, the teacher may deprive them of recess or intermission; and they will readily understand that it is just for them to work while the other pupils play, inasmuch as they enjoyed their play-time in coming to school.

A truant is one who absents himself from school without the consent of his parents or guardians. The teacher, of course, knows who are absent, but he has no means of knowing directly whether they are absent with the leave of responsible parties or without their leave. Some means of communicating such intelligence ought to exist between teachers and their patrons. Supposing such to be the case, all instances of truancy should be at once reported to the care-takers of the guilty parties at home. A little vigilance exercised both at their homes and at their school will, in nearly all cases, be sufficient to correct the evil.

If, however, as it sometimes happens, teachers can

receive no aid from parents or guardians, confinement must be resorted to, or the truant must have his seat declared vacant for a time or altogether. I do not think that personal chastisement is the proper remedy for truancy, although doubtless many teachers have used it with apparently good effect.

5. *Wrong or unworthy conduct.*—The wrong or unworthy conduct of its pupils always injures the reputation of a school. This is true even when the offence is one against the school-property, against one another, or against the teacher; but the injury to the school as a whole is much greater when pupils are known to become intoxicated, to gamble, to destroy or take away property, to disturb neighborhoods by unnecessary noises, or to create riots in streets or highways.

The pupils of a school who participate in such offences may do so thoughtlessly; and, if this be the case, reproof and warning will be sufficient to guard them against such participation in the future. If, however, the offences be committed deliberately and with mal-intent, the teacher who would guard other pupils from the influence of bad example, and who would keep untarnished the reputation of his school, must get rid as speedily as possible of such dangerous characters.

Punishments for Offences against Visitors at the School.

1. *Rude treatment.*—Rude treatment on the part of pupils to visitors at a school is generally owing to ignorance; and reproof and proper instruction from the teacher will be the proper correctives. If

pupils treat a visitor at the school rudely, the teacher should always insist on their making an apology to the person against whom the offence was committed. No teacher should allow his pupils to make sport even of a beggar.

2. *Mischievous tricks.*—Children are fond of fun, and they are sometimes disposed to indulge this passion at the expense of others. I have often seen tricks played by pupils upon strangers who chanced to call at the school, for no other motive. In such cases, the correctives just mentioned in the case of rude treatment should be applied. To compel a pupil to confess himself the author of a trick and to apologize for it, is generally an effectual means of preventing its repetition.

3. *Injury to property.*—The punishment should be the same as that for the injury of property belonging to the teacher or school-officers.

4. *Injury to person.*—The same principle should govern the administration of the punishment here as in the cases of "injury to person" already mentioned. If pupils commit such injuries during play-time, confinement at that time, in addition to the other punishments suggested, will probably cure the evil.

Punishments for Offences against Society.

I have named as offences against society—(1) Disturbance of the peace; (2) Injury to property, or trespass upon it; (3) Uncivil treatment or injury to persons. The punishments for all these classes of offences may be considered together.

School-children may, during play-time, disturb

the peace of the neighborhood by loud noises or rough games; they may injure fruit-trees, tear down fences, or frighten horses or cattle; they may throw stones or snow-balls at passers-by, or otherwise treat them uncivilly or do them injury. In all such cases, they should be made to repair, as far as possible, the damage they may have done, ask pardon of the persons they may have injured, and undergo such confinement during play-time as the teacher may deem proper under the circumstances.

These offences, too, may be committed by pupils in coming to and going from school; and then the teacher, in connection with the parent or guardian, the duty in this case devolving upon both, should require the same kind of restitution for damage done to property or disrespect shown to persons as when such offences are committed near the school during play-time. If the offending pupils be detained some time after school, and compelled to go home alone, the punishment will generally be effective.

The most grave cases of disturbance of the peace of society, or injury of the property or persons of citizens, on the part of students, are apt to be committed by those who board away from home. Students, not so frequently in this country as in Europe, escaping the vigilance of teachers, sometimes engage in bacchanal revels, in riots, in destroying the property and injuring the persons of those against whom they entertain some prejudice or hold some ill will. If reproof avail nothing against such practices, the authorities of a school must either suspend or expel the offenders. Their proper punishment, however, belongs to the state.

PUNISHMENTS FOR OFFENCES AGAINST GOD.

1. *Disregard of the religious observances of the school.*—It is not uncommon for pupils to be inattentive during prayer or the reading of the Scriptures in school; and they sometimes prevent others from paying attention. A remedy I have never known to fail in such cases, is to place the offender where he cannot easily disturb others, and where inattention on his part can be readily observed by the teacher. A special seat can be provided for the purpose.

If the disregard of such observances be persisted in, and come to be an open violation of the teacher's commands, the offence must be treated in the same way as any other act of disobedience.

2. *Creating disrespect for sacred things.*—Prayer may be ridiculed in school, the Bible may be condemned, and the conduct of good men may be unjustly criticized. Boys in their teens assume to doubt the truths of religion and make sport of religious ceremonies. All this is bad in itself, and bad in its effect upon others.

For offences of this kind, reproof may first be tried; next, the confinement of the offenders, in order that the influence of their example may be felt as little as possible; and afterwards, if reformation be not brought about, suspension or expulsion should be resorted to. The rod is altogether out of place as a punishment for offences of this kind. No one was ever yet whipped into respect for sacred things.

3. *Immoral speaking, profanity, vulgarity.*—If the

teacher find among his pupils one who is profane or vulgar, he must first guard the rest from the influence of his example by compelling him to sit and play by himself. If necessary, confinement should be resorted to; for if this kind of punishment, accompanied by fitting reproof, answer not the desired end, no personal chastisement will do it.

4. *Immoral conduct.*—All immoral conduct is an offence against God; and, though it is wrong for other reasons, this consideration ought never to be lost sight of in the punishment of it. Such immoral conduct as is most likely to be committed by pupils at school has already been designated, and the proper course for the teacher to follow has also been indicated: so that nothing remains to be said here, except that in all wrong-doing the pupils should be impressed with the truth that they are offending against God as well as against themselves and their fellows. God will punish in His own way offences against Himself; but no teacher should suffer a pupil to laugh during a prayer, to scoff at a religious ceremony, to utter oaths or blasphemies, to act wickedly, without making him feel, by warnings and by punishments, that he has not only violated the regulations of the school, but committed a sin in the sight of God.

2d. *The pardon of those who repent.*.—The subject now under discussion would be left incomplete if nothing was to be said in respect to the pardon of those pupils who do wrong, but repent of their misconduct.

Into all forms of government which relate to human beings, there is incorporated some provision for pardoning, under certain circumstances, persons who have by their misconduct incurred the penalties of violated law. This is true in all legitimate state governments; the head of every family has felt its necessity; and God Himself has sanctioned it in the grand scheme through which He offers salvation to a fallen world. Indeed, the same principle is recognized every day in social life. Men constantly do wrong to their fellow-men, and ask and receive pardon for their wrong-doing. All men are conscious of the necessity of receiving pardon from persons whom they have wronged, and from God whom they have offended. The principle of pardon must be allowed to operate in the government of the school. There is even more necessity for the exercise of the pardoning power in the school than in the state; for children are more apt to do wrong thoughtlessly than men.

Can a teacher grant pardon to an erring pupil? If the State-Executive can do so to a guilty subject, or a parent to an offending child, the same right undoubtedly is legally vested in the teacher. He is a sovereign in his own sphere, and can punish or pardon, being always responsible for the abuse of his powers. Still, it is evident that the too frequent or inconsiderate exercise of the pardoning power in school, as elsewhere, has a tendency to weaken authority. A teacher must be just as well as kind,—must punish as well as pardon. The pardoning power in school must, therefore, be exercised under certain conditions, the most important of which I name, as follows:—

1st. *That the guilty party give evidence of sincerity in his repentance.*

2d. *That he make good the damage to all property he has injured or destroyed.*

3d. *That he apologize to all persons whom he has wronged.*

4th. *That he ask the forgiveness of God when he has offended Him.*

The guilty party must give evidence of sincerity in his repentance before he can receive pardon. If a pupil commit a fault, and exhibit no signs of regret or sorrow for it, he must incur the full penalty attached to the violation of the law he has broken. Besides, the teacher must satisfy himself that the repentance manifested is not feigned. Pupils are sometimes base enough to profess great sorrow, which they do not feel, for faults, for the purpose of moving the sympathy of teachers and securing their pardon. If in such cases it be granted to one, others will make the same attempt, discipline will be destroyed in the school, and many of the pupils will come to be hypocrites. Let the teacher be cautious, therefore, in pardoning the guilty. He has his pupils with him all the time, and, if he deem it proper, he can readily *suspend* the punishment of an offender until his future life prove or disprove his sincerity. If, for example, a pupil quarrel with a fellow-pupil during play-time, and the teacher consider that he should be confined for the offence and deprived of play for a time, upon his exhibiting repentance the teacher may suspend the penalty until he have an oppor tunity of noticing whether the disposition of the offender has or has not improved.

The guilty party must make good the damage to all property he has injured or destroyed. If a pupil break a window or a chair, no matter how sorry he may be for it, while he may receive free pardon for the moral part of the offence, he must be required in justice to repair the damage done. A third party, indeed, may be allowed to do it for him; but the responsibility of doing it belongs only to him who committed the injury.

The guilty party must apologize to all persons whom he has wronged. If a pupil has been wanting in respect towards, or has injured in any way, a fellow-pupil, his teacher, a school-officer, a visitor at the school, or any other person, his repentance for the act cannot be sincere until he is willing to confess his fault and to apologize to the individual he has wronged. No pardon should be granted him until this apology has been given in a manner that is satisfactory to the teacher.

The guilty party must ask the forgiveness of God when he has offended Him. All bad conduct is an offence against God; but some kinds of conduct of which pupils are sometimes guilty have been pointed out as being peculiarly so. A pupil who has committed an act of this kind must be required by the teacher to ask God for forgiveness before he can be relieved by the teacher from any penalty which may have been attached to his misconduct. Let the pupil have time to report that forgiveness, and, when God forgives, the teacher may safely do so. God requires a reformed life, however; and so may the teacher.

3. Means of inducing Pupils to discharge their Duties of their own Accord.—The end of all government of the young is to make them capable of governing themselves. The highest imperatives to duty must come from within. When a pupil acts well of his own accord, even under unfavorable circumstances, the object of school-government has been attained in him. It is well for school-authorities to provide means for preventing disorder in the school; but it is better to strive to train pupils to be so firm in their character, so strict in their integrity, that they will stand erect, self-poised, even when temptations are held out by false gods to allure them to wickedness. It is well, also, for school-authorities to provide means of correcting such disorder as may occur in the school; but it is better to strive to make the law of conscience of such binding force in the school that punishments and pardons will become unnecessary. Teachers must strive to attain this end,—to induce their pupils to discharge their duties of their own accord; but they must not expect to reach it. This end—the end of human perfection—is the great end of the discipline of life, which God is working out in the lapse of centuries.

To discuss this subject fully would be to open up the whole field of Moral Culture, than which no other educational work could be fraught with more interest; but it is not included within the scope of this volume. A mere outline of the subject is all that will in this place be ventured upon.

In order that a pupil may discharge his duties of his own accord, he must—

1st. KNOW *what is right.*
2d. FEEL *the claims of the right.*
3d. WILL *to do the right.*

The teacher must, therefore, direct his attention to three kinds of moral training, which, if the expressions be allowable, may be named as follows:—MORAL KNOWING, MORAL FEELING, and MORAL WILLING.

Pupils must know what is right.—It is obvious that right knowing must precede right feeling and right doing. A blind man may desire to pursue a certain path, yet if he cannot see it he will be apt to take one which leads in a different direction.

The apprehension of the right is intuitive; but we are not conscious of possessing such a power until we notice right and wrong actions. Our idea of right is not formed by the generalization of the consequences of the acts of responsible beings; but such consequences furnish the occasion of its formation. In expanding this idea and making it clear, *the teacher's duty consists in judiciously multiplying these occasions.*

Many things are wrong in school which elsewhere might be right; as, for example, playing in school-hours, talking, going some distance away from the school-house, &c. &c. For the purpose of making pupils acquainted with their duty in these respects, it is best for the teacher to have a system of written school-rules, or school-regulations, covering this ground. But, in order that pupils may fully understand them, the reasons upon which they are based, and illustrations of the consequences of disobeying them, should be presented.

It is not, however, with regard to the acts of pupils which would be conventionally wrong that the teacher should most concern himself, but with regard to such as are absolutely wrong,—wrong in the school and wrong everywhere else. Pupils must be taught to know good from evil. How? When old enough, they can learn it from the Bible, from works on Ethics, from Nature, and from History: *when young, they can learn it only from specific examples.* The question, whether an act is right or wrong, comes up many times every day in the school-room and in social life. Let the teacher constantly call upon his pupils to decide such questions. The power by which we discriminate right from wrong must have exercise. The teacher must furnish it, —furnish it in governing his school,—furnish it in hearing recitations,—furnish it in commenting upon events transpiring in the world,—furnish it in private conversation with his pupils. *Pupils must be trained to form the habit of appealing to their consciences to guide their conduct.*

The form in which moral questions should generally be presented to the young for decision is the concrete, as examples. Truths presented in a narrative form, or as a story, secure attention and reach the heart. A child cannot discern a truth deep hidden in a proverb or an aphorism. I would prefer using a work on History to a work on Ethics in imparting moral instruction to the young.

Pupils must feel the claims of the right.—Wrong acts are not often owing to ignorance of what is right; they much more frequently arise from the fact that men do not feel the strength of the imperatives to duty. The head is oftener right than the heart. In moral training, the feelings which impel men to the performance of duty must be aroused; —there must be heart-culture. This, indeed, is the most delicate and difficult work incident to the teacher's profession.

Moral truth must be so presented as to awaken moral feeling. To the mature mind nothing can be more agreeable than a great principle when expressed in the most concise form,—when it is crystallized in words. I am inclined to think, however, that the feeling thus arising is more intellectual than moral in its nature. The moral heart throbs only in response to principles expressed in life, in tangible realities. It is the philanthropist visiting prisoners in their cells, the patriot dying for his country, the good Samaritan relieving by the wayside the wants of the man who had fallen among thieves, the expiring Saviour praying for his enemies who were cruelly crucifying him,—these and other such scenes as these,—that most move the better impulses of our hearts. Whether this statement is correct or otherwise, I am certain that the concrete is the only effective form in which the young can be made to feel the claims of the right. A single reading of the story of "George Washington and his little Hatchet" will do more to make a child honest and truthful than the maxim "Honesty is the best policy" repeated to him a thousand times. Taking advantage of this hint, the teacher can find examples of the good, illustrations of noble principles, incidents, anecdotes, stories, with which he can acquaint his pupils and be rewarded by seeing them grow in virtue. Moral acts may be presented in pictures, and these, when properly used, can be made to exert a very powerful influence upon the youthful heart.

There are times when the heart seems hardened. There are times, too, when it seems open to receive impressions from good influences. Let the teacher seize the fit occasion for giving his moral lessons. I have never succeeded well in giving such lessons when I appointed a fixed time and place for doing it. I have succeeded well when I was all alive to the great interests involved, and dropped, now and then, into the open hearts of my pupils, seeds of truth which I have reason to know have grown up producing fruit, some thirty, some sixty, and some an hundred fold. The human heart is a fortress that can be taken better by indirect than by direct approaches.

The influence of example is very powerful with the young. A teacher does his pupil a great service when he induces him to read the biography of a good or great man. Such biographies should fill the shelves of our school-libraries. Pupils would rise from the reading of them with more admiration for noble deeds and a greater desire to do them. The teacher's own example, if a worthy one, will do much to make his pupils love virtue. If they love him, they will insensibly make him a model.

Children learn to love to do what they have formed the habit of doing. If a child has been taught to give a penny to deserving persons asking alms, he will not withhold help from the poor and distressed when he becomes a man. One who is accustomed in youth to always ask forgiveness of those he may have wronged, will always feel like doing it. The habit of prayer formed at our mother's knee is apt to ripen into a love for such communion with God. A boy who has been made to obey parents and teacher will never plot rebellion in the state. Solomon *was* wise in saying, "Train up a child in the way he should go, and when he is old he will not depart from it." Teachers have abundant opportunities of inculcating virtuous habits.

A pure character is exceedingly beautiful. A good "man is the noblest work of God." Let the teacher inspire his pupils with a high ideal of human perfection. Let him spare no pains to make moral excellence attractive. Let him ever hold up before them a model whose perfections they may endeavor to realize in themselves. A high aim and a noble purpose actuating a young man, he can hardly sacrifice his manhood so far as to waste his time in foolish pleasures or ruin body and soul by degrading vices.

To all this it must be added that mere moral culture does not make Christians. The love of God must be shed abroad in the heart before men are secure from the temptations of life. The great truths of our holy religion should be taught in all our schools. The Scriptures should be read, hymns should be sung, prayers should be offered. Let young souls come in contact with the beautiful and ennobling truths of the gospel, and they will be greatly strengthened for the conflicts of life and better prepared for the enjoyments of heaven.

Pupils must will to do right.—We may know what is right and feel an interest in doing it, and still fail in the resolution to begin the work. How many full-grown men there are who lack firmness, determination, executive power, will! Any moral culture is incomplete that does not give this kind of strength to character.

Pupils should be accustomed to do what they undertake. The teacher should carefully measure their capacity and induce them to work up to it. There is much in trying, and, if we fail once, in trying and trying again. If a teacher allow his pupils to give up their tasks because they cost some labor, they will soon be unwilling to do any thing. On the contrary, he should spare no pains to inculcate habits of perseverance,—no pains to teach them to have confidence in their own powers. Thus in general must what we call character be formed. Specifically, the young must be trained to will to do right. This kind of training requires a careful hand; for ten thousand foes watch to destroy the first buddings that a tender soul sends up to the light. As the world stands, there is no harder task than that of forsaking sin and death and seeking purity and life. For the purpose of aiding them most effectually in willing right, the teacher must come close to his pupils; he must prove himself their friend; he must sympathize with them; a common bond of affection must link them together. Thus allied by sympathy to his pupils, the teacher can prompt good resolves, he can foster them, and, Mentor-like, he can proffer proper help while their strength 's tested by the storms of life. Every step taken in the path of virtue must be fought for. Enemies await the approach of travellers in it, and attack them on the right hand and on the left, in front and rear. None but the brave can conquer; but the victory is glorious. Let teachers ever keep in view this great battle which all must fight, feebly or fearlessly, and nerve their pupils to triumph in it.

Nothing is better calculated to inspire courage than examples of it. These examples may be found in both profane and sacred history. Amidst many moral cowards, the world presents some moral heroes. The young will eagerly read or listen to accounts of these, and grow like them.

Both parents and teachers sometimes err in their treatment of children who are called stubborn. As a general thing, it is most unwise to punish them for the purpose of "breaking their wills," as it is called. It is better to make them feel the natural effects of their stubbornness, to *divert* them from their purpose, or *to conquer them with patience.* Every parent who has a child with a strong will should be thankful for it; for the world is now full of tame, weak, irresolute, cowardly human beings, and their further increase is not at all desirable. A strong will in a child may put parents and teachers who do not know how to control it to some inconvenience; but I look upon it as a nobler gift than the gift of genius. The world would stand still but for men of strong will; and the highest virtue is unattainable without it.

IV. School-Administration.—Many things have already been discussed that would properly come under the head of school-administration, were this subject to be treated of by itself. All that remains to be done now may be stated as follows:—

1. THE DETECTION OF OFFENDERS.

2. THE SELECTION OF THE PUNISHMENT FOR OFFENDERS.

3. THE MANNER OF INFLICTING PUNISHMENT UPON OFFENDERS.

1. THE DETECTION OF OFFENDERS.—The detection of offenders in school is often a delicate and difficult duty. The difficulty is not so great in schools for young pupils, or in those where the teacher has the pupils during school-hours under his eye in school-room or on play-ground, and whose time out of school-hours is spent under the control of parents or guardians, as it is in those differently situated. Young pupils are more ready to confess their own faults, are less skilful in concealing them, and talk much more freely about the faults of others, than those who are older. When a teacher is with his pupils all the time, he will be likely to see by whom wrong acts are done; or, if not, he is in much more favorable circumstances for finding out the offender than when the offence is committed in secret and plans contrived to prevent detection. The position of a teacher is far from enviable when he feels that his authority has been disregarded, the interests of his school jeopardized, and yet that he is unable to detect the offender. There is an aversion among students in higher institutions of learning against informing on a fellow-student, however grave his

offence may be; and this increases the difficulty the teacher experiences in tracing mischief back to its author. If, however, in any circumstances, misdemeanors occur in school which are calculated to impair his authority among good pupils and disgrace the school, it is the teacher's duty, if possible, to detect and punish the offenders. The duty is often unpleasant, and requires much time in its performance; but a school without order is like a ship in a storm without a helm. When a nation loses its power to detect and punish crime, it is a sure sign of its downfall; when a similar want is felt in school, all school-government will be a failure.

It is unnecessary here to say any thing of those offences of which the teacher is an eye-witness, or of those—a numerous class—which it is best for him to allow to pass in silence; and we proceed to consider the remaining class of offences, with respect to which the good of the school demands that those who commit them should be detected and punished.

Suppose an offence committed in school, and the offender unknown: what should be the teacher's course?

1st. He may state the facts to the whole school, say that the matter would be investigated, and request the guilty parties to make a private confession of it. He may even name a time when they can meet him for that purpose. If the teacher enjoy the respect of the pupils who committed the offence, if they have reason to think that he will treat them justly and kindly, and if they have been taught that self-confession is honorable as well as profitable, they will be likely to call upon the teacher and make known their connection with the fault. Especially will this be the case if the fault occurred by accident or without any mal-intent. The success of such a method of detecting offences depends, however, almost wholly upon the manner of the teacher in asking for the self-confession, and the confidence reposed in him by his pupils. A pupil who under such circumstances freely confesses his fault, and shows that he is sorry for it, should not be severely punished. The upbraidings of his own conscience are already punishing him; and the teacher may generally with safety grant him a conditional pardon.

2d. If the preceding method fail, the teacher may quietly gather up such facts as he can learn of the circumstances connected with the offence. He, in all probability, already knows that certain of his pupils would not commit such an offence; he will find that others were absent; still others could not have taken part in it, from various circumstances; and some will volunteer such information as will clear themselves, and possibly may be led to indicate at least who are innocent. In this way, the circle among whom the offenders must be found is very much narrowed, and circumstances more or less strong will point to the guilty parties. A private interview may now be had with these, at which the suspicious circumstances should be plainly and directly stated, and the question asked of each how he can explain these circumstances, and whether he is guilty of the fault of which they seem to indicate his guilt. In nine cases out of ten, if the teacher proceed judiciously, a confession will now be made;

and the punishment can be adjusted according to the nature of the offence. I ought not to omit the remark that a teacher should be very careful in accusing a pupil even when circumstances seem to point clearly to him as the guilty party; for I have known very great harm to result from so doing. The principle is a good one, in school as well as in courts of justice, to consider all persons innocent until proven guilty; but no pupil can object to being allowed the privilege of explaining circumstances which seem to indicate his connection with bad conduct; or, if he does, the inference is probably correct that he is either himself guilty or desires to conceal the guilt of another.

3d. If the teacher fail to find circumstances which point to particular individuals as the guilty parties, he may require each pupil, in the presence of all the rest, to answer questions as to whether he was either a principal or an accessory in the misconduct. The justification for such a course of procedure is that the interest of the school demands the detection of the offender, and that, as long as no one in particular can be accused of the fault, its disgrace attaches itself to all. In such circumstances, while many well-meaning pupils might be unwilling to implicate others, they would not hesitate to exculpate themselves; and none but the most hardened would dare to utter a falsehood in the presence of the teacher, and of school-fellows who knew it to be a falsehood. This method of detecting an offence should not be resorted to unless the offence be a grave one, and unless the teacher be sure he will be sustained by the public sentiment of the school. He must manage the matter very carefully, too, if he expects the whole influence to be beneficial upon his pupils. All he does should be done calmly and deliberately. Noise, hurry, and fuss in such cases always do harm.

4th. It may happen that all the pupils in a school will deny being concerned in the misconduct which is charged against them. The guilty may be base enough to utter a falsehood, either in public or in private. They and their friends may refuse to answer at all; they may give a wrong answer with some mental reservation or equivocation; or they may deny the right of the teacher to make them convict themselves, as they may hold he is endeavoring to do when questioning them as described in the preceding paragraph. The creed that some students hold is as follows: never to confess their own guilt, and never to inform teachers with respect to the guilt of others. Such a creed is immoral in itself; and in whatever institution of learning it is generally practised by the students, it will render good government impossible. Students, indeed, sometimes plan the means of escaping detection at the same time they concoct the mischief. In circumstances like these, what must a teacher do? His resort must be to students who value the interests of the school and who do not sympathize with the plans and plots of their reckless school-fellows. Unfortunate the school where such cannot be found! In ordinary circumstances, one student ought not to be asked to inform upon another; but in cases of malicious mischief, wanton destruction of property, theft, conspiracy against the school-authorities, and offences equally grave, it is the duty of every well-meaning student who cares for the reputation of his school or teachers, who wishes well to his fellow-students, to come forward, either publicly or privately, and tell all he knows about the matter. Seeing the position of affairs, volunteers will often bring information that will lead to the detection of the offenders; or, if not, a judicious teacher can quietly obtain it.

5th. It might happen that all the circumstances attending the committing of a misdemeanor at school would be unknown to all except the guilty parties, and that they would refuse to reveal any thing concerning it. In such a case, the teacher can do nothing except to use increased vigilance. Special guards may be appointed, while all the ordinary affairs of the school should go on as if nothing had happened. Those who deliberately do mischief once, if not detected, will most likely soon repeat the offence under circumstances which will render their detection more easy. Besides, to-day, as with Cain, a mark is set upon a guilty person which a keen eye can detect. The teacher must be watchful. If "eternal vigilance is the price of liberty" in a state, it is the price of order in a school.

It is proper to notice, in concluding this topic, a system of self-confession which is practised in some schools, and is called the Self-Reporting System. A few illustrations will show how it operates. Near the close of the school-day, some teachers call upon all their pupils who have in any way violated the school-rules to raise their hands: if there has been one violation, one finger may be held up; if two, two; and so on. The teachers, then, noticing the hands, make such inquiries as they deem necessary, and assign to each culprit the punishment he seems to deserve. Other teachers reduce the offences of the school to a few classes, have them printed on properly arranged cards, which are given to the pupils to be filled out, at the end of a week or some other stated time, with a record of the kind and number of offences each has committed, and then returned to the teachers.

With all due respect to some excellent teachers who adopt the Self-Reporting System, I must be allowed to express my doubts both as to its policy and the principle upon which it is based. I do not object to a pupil's confessing his fault to his teacher, —the furthest from it possible; but a formal, forced, and public manner of doing it must deprive the confession of much of its good effect. Pupils must experience much difficulty in selecting those of their shortcomings which ought to be reported, and in representing the exact extent of their offending, even when disposed to report correctly; and it must be acknowledged on all hands that there would be such a strong temptation to report incorrectly that many could not resist it. Besides, in many cases the teacher would have to make inquiries back of the reports: pupils are not always willing to convict themselves; and, when compelled to punish those pupils for omissions in their reports, he will find his success less than if he had punished them directly for the offence itself. In a few schools, where all, or nearly all, the pupils are actuated by high moral principles, the system may work well; but in the majority of our schools it would produce such complications in their government as must cause it to end in failure.

2. The Selection of the Punishment for Offenders.—The detection of an offence in the work of administrating the affairs of the school must be followed by the punishment of the offender. The kinds of punishment open to the teacher, and the principle by which he should be guided in selecting them, have already been treated of; and it is only necessary to notice here some considerations which the teacher must take into account in determining the *degree* of the punishment.

The degree of the punishment depends upon the nature of the offence. If the offence be a grave one, greatly destructive of good order, it should be punished with more severity than an offence of milder form.

The degree of punishment depends upon the character and disposition of the offender. No wise teacher will treat all children in the same manner. The general principles of school-government must be modified in their application to individuals. Practitioners in Law and Medicine recognize like modifications in applying the principles of these sciences. It would be wrong to punish in precisely the same way pupils who have refined feelings, and those who are insensible to beauty or propriety; pupils who have a high sense of honor, and those who scarcely know when they insult another or are insulted themselves; pupils who can hardly bear a word of reproach, and those whose hearts are hardened into stone. The Proverb says, "A reproof entereth more into a wise man than a hundred stripes into a fool." Girls, too, as a general thing, need less severe punishments than boys.

The degree of punishment depends upon the motive which prompted the misdemeanor. It is probably true that teachers often attribute worse motives to their pupils than those which actuated them. They judge them by their own standard of right and wrong, when they should be judged by one quite different. The young are thoughtless, and, in consequence, often do things which are wrong. They are fond of fun, and frequently engage in tricks, with that end in view, which have bad results. The teacher must carefully distinguish such motives from those which are really bad, and administer his punishments accordingly. Whenever a teacher is compelled to hesitate in deciding whether an act was done from a bad motive or not, he should allow the erring pupil the benefit of his doubt.

The degree of punishment depends upon the circumstances in which the offence was committed. The teacher must discriminate between a wrong act done by accident, and one done purposely; between one committed by an unsuspicious, credulous boy, and one committed by a bold, cunning fellow who plots mischief which he persuades others to engage in; between one done under provocation or while angry, and one coolly meditated and deliberately executed.

The degree of punishment depends upon the difficulty necessarily attending the detection of the offence. The state acts upon this principle; and so must the school. A pupil who commits a misdemeanor openly is not likely to be as bad as one who does it secretly; and one who deliberately plots mischief and contrives plans to conceal it is the worst of all. Some wrong acts, too, in their nature are less easily discovered than others. It is evident that punishments must be adjusted with reference to these facts.

The degree of punishment depends upon the number of times an offence may have been repeated. For a first offence a pupil ought not to be punished as severely as for a second or third.

Such are the most important principles in the light of which school-punishments are to be adjusted. It would be unwise to attempt more than this statement of principles. The judges of our courts have extensive discretionary powers with respect to the infliction of punishment upon those who violate the laws of the state; and these powers are necessary, because the degree in which a criminal act is wrong can only be determined from a full knowledge of all the circumstances which were connected with its commission. Teachers, too, must have discretionary powers. While they should carefully study the kind of punishment which naturally follows school-offences, and carefully estimate the weight of all the considerations upon which the degree of punishment in school depends, no theory should bind them to a fixed mode of procedure. Great general principles must guide the teacher in all his practice; but these principles do not pre suppose uniformity in their application.

3. THE MANNER OF INFLICTING PUNISHMENT UPON OFFENDERS.—A list of school-punishments was given on a previous page; and with respect to the manner

of inflicting some of these, nothing need be said, as they indicate in themselves what it ought to be. A few remarks will be made respecting the manner of inflicting three of them,—viz.: reproof, confinement, and personal chastisement.

Reproof is the most common mode of school-punishment, and, if well administered, it is generally sufficient to secure good order. An erring pupil should be reproved in as few words as possible, and in such a way as to make him feel that the reproof is intended for his good.

Reproof may be administered directly or indirectly. When the offenders are known, it is generally best to speak to them directly. Pupils are not very quick to apply to their own conduct general remarks directed to the whole school. The manner of the prophet Nathan, in his rebuke of David, when he said, "Thou art the man," is the best method for correcting school-offences. A teacher should never shrink from the duty of telling any pupil his faults; and pointless reproof directed to all the pupils, when particular ones are meant, is mostly unproductive of good, and frequently dictated by a cowardly spirit. There are times, however, when a fault has been committed of which some are more and some less guilty, and other participants in it are guilty to an extent not known, or when the school or class generally has fallen into some habit that is leading to unpleasant consequences, at which an indirect exposure of the fault, and an indirect rebuke of all who may be guilty of it, would be good policy. A whole school may sometimes be lifted up at once to a higher moral position by having its general faults or shortcomings judiciously reproved, even though no names are specially referred to.

Reproof may be administered privately or publicly. In a large majority of cases, it is much better to reprove a pupil in private. By so doing, the teacher will avoid the expression of any sympathy for the offender on the part of his schoolmates, he will put it out of their power to accuse him of weakness in making his acknowledgments, and he will enjoy a much better opportunity of leaving good impressions upon his mind or prompting good resolves in his heart. A teacher can come much closer to a pupil when he speaks to him in private. The communication is more free when none are present to listen or criticize. But there are offences which ought to be punished publicly. If a pupil publicly disobey a teacher, he should be made to submit publicly. Whenever the offence is of such a character that it will be condemned by a large majority of the school, no harm can arise from rebuking publicly the person who committed it. Offences against the school as a whole should generally be publicly punished, either by reproof or otherwise.

Confinement is a much more natural, and would prove, if judiciously used, a much more effectual, punishment for many school-offences than personal chastisement.

The confinement may take place in the school-room. It is a species of confinement to seat a pupil at a distance from others. The confinement becomes quite a severe punishment when a pupil is detained in the school-room after school has been dismissed or during intermissions. A long detention after school may be inconvenient on several accounts; and in place of it, as a general thing, I would recommend detention during intermissions.

The confinement may take place in a separate room connected with the school-room; and this is decidedly preferable for such a purpose to the school-room itself. Of course, I do not mean a cell, but rather a pleasant little room specially fitted up for the purpose. A closet, or dark room, is very objectionable. I would make it bear somewhat the same relation to the school that a prison does to society; and I am well satisfied that, with such a room, the graver offences which occur in school could be effectively punished without resort to the rod.

Personal chastisement is considered a necessary punishment in school. If home discipline were what it should be, I would allow that it could be dispensed with altogether. Some forms of applying this kind of punishment were referred to on another page, under the name of Personal Indignities. I speak of the matter here for the purpose of saying again that I disapprove of them all. If a pupil openly disobey a teacher, just force enough, and of a kind best suited to the purpose, may be used to secure obedience; but, under any other circumstances, the best mode of administering personal chastisement is with the rod. The Bible seems to approve the use of the rod as an instrument for inflicting this kind of punishment; and experience has shown that the Bible is right. No form of treatment can be worse for a child than the habit of slapping his hands, boxing his ears, pulling his hair or ears, twisting his nose, &c. &c., for slight offences. If he deserve punishment, and personal chastisement seem best suited to the case, let him be whipped with a suitable rod, and with some severity; for an offender that deserves whipping at all deserves to be well whipped. It is very seldom, indeed, that I would whip a boy before the school. I doubt whether the witnessing of such punishments is ever beneficial to a school. Whenever practicable, personal chastisement should only be inflicted after due deliberation. A little delay will enable the teacher to administer the punishment with more effect. If angry, it will allow time for his anger to cool; and he will then be more likely to make the severity of the punishment proportionate to the criminality of the offence. A few hours of reflection, too, will enable a pupil to see an act of wrong in a very different light from that in which it appeared at the moment of its commission. Let me say very earnestly to all teachers, *Be in no haste to inflict punishments, and especially corporal punishments.*

CHAPTER V.

THE AUTHORITIES OF THE SCHOOL

In treating of the science of Political Economy, the discussion is not considered complete unless it includes the producer, as well as the thing produced,—those who operate upon a thing, as well as the thing upon which the operation is performed; so, in unfolding the subject of School Economy, our work would be but partly done, if we omitted to say any thing concerning the agents who devise, direct, and control the whole machinery of schools, and the source from which all their power and right to do so are derived.

The matter which it seems desirable to present can be most conveniently arranged in three sections, as follows:—

I. The Teacher.
II. The General School-Officers.
III. The People in respect to Schools.

I. The Teacher.—Whatever the topic previously under consideration, the teacher has been ever present in our mind. When speaking of the Preparation for the School, the teacher was the principal agent referred to whose duty it was to make that preparation; and, when treating of the Organization, Employments, and Government of the School, the teacher was constantly before us,—if not in all places the principal figure in the picture, yet always an indispensable accessory to its proper effect. We will now put him altogether in the foreground; and it is our desire to paint him as he should be,—a model man.

The subject will be discussed in the order of the following heads:—

1. The Teacher's Motives.
2. The Teacher's Qualifications.
3. The Teacher's Duties to his Pupils.
4. The Teacher's Duties to his Profession.
5. A Teacher's Life.

1. The Teacher's Motives.—God has intrusted to our care no duty so responsible as that of the culture of our minds. The duties of the farmer, the mechanic, the merchant, the lawyer, the doctor, are necessary to the welfare of society, but all of them relate in practice to what is temporary and perishable; while teaching, in its broadest sense, includes that preparation which must be made by immortal beings to enjoy the highest happiness beyond the grave. If the work of the teacher is so noble, he must enter upon it confident of his ability to discharge well its responsible duties, and with motives the purest that can actuate human conduct. The diverse necessities of society give rise to many kinds of business. Men are born peculiarly fitted for each. But if there is one office more than others divinely appointed, and to which men are

divinely called, it is that of teacher. Men with sensual natures and mercenary aims ought not to be found anywhere, but everywhere rather than in the school-room, where character is in its formative state, and where "every chord that is struck in a tender mind vibrates at the throne of God."

If by any means those who now have charge of our schools could be summoned to state the objects they have in view or the motives by which they are actuated in teaching, it is to be feared that many of them would fail to come up to that standard of duty which is adopted by every true teacher. There may be found, attempting to teach in our schools, young persons who have never made teaching a study, who have no love for it, but who teach merely to put in time until some more congenial employment presents itself, or until they accumulate sufficient money to enable them to engage in a different kind of business. There may be found, attempting to teach, in our schools persons who have failed in other avocations,—broken-down doctors, lawyers, and clergymen, bankrupt merchants, farmers, and mechanics, worn-out clerks and editors: all these and others become schoolmasters from necessity, or because they can conceal more effectually from the public eye, in the school-room than elsewhere, their want of energy or skill. There may be found, attempting to teach, in our schools persons who merely go through a routine of reciting, whipping, and scolding, most irksome to them; who are careful to perform no duty but what they must; who are behind time at the opening of the school, and hurry away as fast as possible after its close; who dislike school and pupils, and are never pleased except when pay-day comes, and never seem interested in any thing connected with their schools except an increase of salary, shorter school-terms, and more numerous holidays. Such classes of persons as these still disgrace the profession of teaching, and good teachers everywhere are growing impatient with the slowness of the process by which they are being got rid of. Speed the day when better men, with better motives, take their place!

A teacher may make his comfort and his pecuniary interests an object. Since teachers are generally so badly remunerated for their labor, he may be even urgent in his claims in these respects, and incur no rightful censure. But, still, all such objects should be subordinate to the great one of doing good to his pupils, and, through them, to the cause of humanity. Selfish as the world is, men can be found who would a thousand times rather labor to spread the glad tidings of the gospel among the heathen in the interior of Africa, deprived of almost all the ordinary comforts of life, than to engage in many kinds of business which custom sanctions, live in a palace, and enjoy an income of ten thousand dollars a year. Called upon to make fewer sacrifices than a missionary, the teacher who does all that he may for the pupils in one of our Common Schools must be actuated by the missionary spirit. Life, indeed, has other and higher ends than that of mere animal happiness; and it is possible to live truly, nobly, without wealth, unknown to fame, unhonored by the world, but with the peaceful consciousness of having been faithful to men and to God.

The grand object that every true teacher has in view, is to so instruct and so train his pupils that they may become a blessing to the world and to be themselves worthy of the blessings of Heaven; and to accomplish this good for humanity is the great moving motive that determines his choice of a profession, and induces him to labor on in the work which he has begun.

Men are true to themselves when they use all their powers in the right way; true to society, when they do it all the good they can,—when they love their neighbors as themselves; true to God, when they love Him with all their mind and strength; and teaching, where it aims to make men true to themselves, true to their fellow-men, and true to God, is noble, and the teacher who faithfully performs his work, must be ranked among the best benefactors of his race.

2. THE TEACHER'S QUALIFICATIONS.—In addition to much that has already been said indirectly elsewhere, in this volume, respecting the teacher's qualifications, something more systematic is deemed important. The discussion will proceed in the following order:—

1st. *The Teacher's physical Qualifications.*
2d. *The Teacher's intellectual Qualifications.*
3d. *The Teacher's moral Qualifications.*
4th. *The Teacher's professional Qualifications.*

The Teacher's physical Qualifications.—The position of teacher is sometimes sought by persons with weak and sickly constitutions. This is a mistake. A teacher should have good health. The mental labor required in a school cannot be performed by one whose physical system is not strong and vigorous; and that kind of cheerful spirit so essential to the well-working of a school is not often possessed by one whose nerves are racked with pain. Persons in ill health, therefore, both for their own and their pupil's good, should seek some other occupation than teaching.

Commencing his work with a strong constitution and good health, the teacher should try to preserve both by a careful attention to hygienic laws.

He must observe the law in reference to work. Hard mental labor is healthful; but to spend eight hours at such labor every day in the school-room, and as many more out of the school-room, will, if long continued, exhaust the energies and destroy the health of any one. Periods of work should be alternated with periods of active exercise and cheerful recreation.

The teacher must observe the law in reference to exercise. Such is the intimate connection between the body and the mind that without the due exercise of the former the latter will not long discharge well its functions. The teacher may join in a game of ball or cricket; he may walk, row, drive, skate, swim, ride on horseback, saw wood, work in a garden, do any farm or mechanical work that may be convenient; but he *must* do something. Where all else fails, he should resort to the use of gymnastic apparatus; but exercising in this way by oneself is not very interesting. He should no more think of doing with out exercise than without food; and one should be taken just as regularly as the other.

The teacher must observe the law in reference to air. He ought to have his school-room well ventilated. Open windows and doors, even, are not as hurtful as poisoned air. He should study, exercise, and sleep, where the air is fresh and pure.

The teacher must observe the law in reference to diet. His food should be nutritive, not much concentrated or highly stimulating, easily digested, taken regularly, and in such quantities only as the system demands. He should abstain entirely from the use of intoxicating liquors and tobacco, both on his own account and on the account of his pupils.

The teacher must observe the law in reference to sleep. There is no employment that more exhausts the nervous energies than teaching. The constant care incident to it will wear out the strongest constitution, unless that can be shut up in the school-house, or at least shut out of the sleeping-chamber. With six or eight hours of good sleep, a teacher may encounter his school-trials and perform his school-work and continue to enjoy good health; but without it, such a result is hardly possible. True, he may not feel the exhaustive drain upon his life-forces for some years; but at forty he will be an old man, and at fifty, most likely, he will be in his grave.

The teacher must observe the law in reference to recreation. He should seek the society of cheerful company. Not that he should throw away his time in the frivolous amusements that often characterize the social party, and still less that he should be found among the loungers at stores and in bar-rooms; but no man more needs cheerful conversation and pleasant recreation. Confined all day in his school-room, keenly feeling all disappointments,—and disappointments there will be,—with all his mental forces enlisted in his work,—and no work calls them into requisition more actively,—he needs to find, when his day's work is done, a home made cheerful by the conversation, reading, fun, music, of dear ones there, or he needs to seek such health-preserving recreations among congenial companions elsewhere.

The Teacher's intellectual Qualifications.—A teacher should have a comprehensive and accurate knowledge of the branches he undertakes to teach. His knowledge should not only embrace a subject as treated of in the text-books used, but reach its more general relations. Any failure in this respect will cripple his teaching, and tend to beget among his pupils a want of confidence in his ability. A man who understands the whole of a subject will teach any part of it better than one who merely knows that part.

A teacher should possess a knowledge of other branches than those which he teaches. He will need to do so in order to make his teaching effective. No one can teach Arithmetic well without possessing some knowledge of Algebra, nor Geography without History, nor Grammar without Rhetoric and Logic. No teacher should be intrusted with the management of a school who does not understand Physiology; and all teaching is little better than guess-work that is not based upon the principles of the Philosophy of the Mind. All this knowledge, and more, can be used by teachers in our lowest grades of Common Schools. Teachers cannot know too much. The philosopher in his humility becomes as a little child, can win the little child's sympathy, and is his best teacher. The simplest forms of knowledge always proceed from the most learned. The sage becomes a child again, and thus the circle of human mental life completes itself.

A teacher should inform himself of current events. Monks are no longer the teachers of the world. We live in stirring times; and a teacher must not be a mere book-worm or a melancholy recluse. He must see what passes in the world, take an interest in it, even if he quietly look on while others play the principal parts in the great social drama. If he does not, he cannot adapt his teaching to the exigencies of the times, or add interest to his instruction by reference to passing events. Teachers, too, ought not to forget that we live in America,—not in Greece or Rome,—live in the midst of a struggle compared with which the internal feuds of those countries were insignificant.

A teacher needs thorough mental discipline. What teachers know is important; but how they know it, is much more so. They may have obtained their knowledge in a loose, illogical manner, and it may be stored away in their minds in confused heaps or scattered fragments. If so, they can never make successful teachers. Only a well-disciplined mind can discipline another mind; and mental discipline is the highest end of education.

A teacher ought to be able to make the knowledge he possesses available for the purposes of instruction. Essential to this end is a clear idea of what it is intended to impart. Many think they understand a subject when they have but a glimpse of it; and, when such assume to be teachers, it is the blind leading the blind. Essential to this end, also, is the ability to communicate what is known. It is possible to possess knowledge and be unable to express it. If the teacher is accustomed to make use of ill-chosen words, badly-constructed sentences, or to indulge in pointless remarks, his pupils will never increase their love of learning under his management. A teacher ought to be a good talker.

A teacher must possess ability to manage and govern his school. This requires ingenuity, skill in adapting means to ends, a knowledge of human nature, good common sense. More teachers fail in managing and governing their schools than in teaching; which shows that the former kind of ability should rank higher than the latter.

The Teacher's moral Qualifications.—It is an easy thing to name certain individual moral qualities which a teacher must possess in order to secure success in his profession; but he who attempts to make a systematic classification of these qualities will find a task most difficult. That the subject may present itself prominently before the mind of the student-teacher who may inquire into this department of pedagogical science, a kind of representative classification will be adopted here, which will possess the advantage of suggesting certain important moral qualities which should characterize the teacher, and at the same time of exemplifying them.

The teacher must be, morally,—

A wise Legislator.
A righteous Judge.
A prompt Executive.
An efficient Workman.
A competent Leader.
A liberal Partisan.
A pleasant Companion.
A warm Friend.
A good Man.

A teacher should be a wise legislator. By the expression "a wise legislator" is not merely meant one who can enact appropriate laws for the management and government of his school. This is an intellectual qualification very necessary to the teacher; but certain moral qualities are now referred to, not less important. The legislation of a school should not consist merely in the cold and formal enactment of school-laws, in the nice adjustment of school-machinery, but all must be done with the view of subserving the great end of moral training. School-laws should tend not only to promote order, but virtue, in the school. The teacher may legislate to secure comfort, order, progress in study, but he must never forget the while, that the grand end in which all these ends centre is the good of his pupils,—the *summum bonum* of the school.

A teacher should be a righteous judge. It is considered unsafe in a state to intrust the power of expounding laws in the same hands that enact them. It has been thought best to remove the judicial as far from the legislative power as possible, that it may be exercised without bias. The administration of justice is considered an interest too sacred to be endangered by partialities which can be avoided. In a school, this division of the functions of government is practically impossible. The teacher administers justice according to laws of his own enactment. His decision is final. Unless, then, he has an eye single to the interests of his pupils, unless he is strictly impartial in his judgments, unless he rewards and punishes fairly, he is unfit to be a teacher. The teacher should weigh all his decisions in well-balanced scales, blind to all motives except those of justice.

A teacher should be a prompt executive. Laws, however wise and just, may be worthless unless strictly enforced. Regulations which are found only in statute-books restrain no evil-doer. The management of a school requires an efficient executive. Plans must be carried out, punishments must be inflicted, the whole working of the school-machinery must be controlled; and no other than an active head-master can do it. As a ship in a storm needs a prompt captain, as an army in time of battle needs a prompt general, so a school needs a prompt teacher,—one who is bold, firm, self-possessed, consistent, and ready for all emergencies.

A teacher should be an efficient workman. The teacher has more to do than merely to make, expound, and execute school-laws: he has to work himself, his position requiring the severest labor. The teacher must, therefore, be willing to work and able to work efficiently. If a teacher is un willing to work, the school must stop; if he is unable to work efficiently, the school can only be partially successful. A slow, plodding, heavy man—one who must think long before acting, and who then acts slowly—is out of place in the school-room. To teach well, requires skill, earnestness, activity,—skill to know what to do and how to do it, and earnestness and activity to make that skill effective. The teacher should be a model workman; for his work is to be imitated, and even his manner of working will be copied by his pupils. A teacher can impress his pupils through his work. If he work skilfully, they, too, will learn to do so; but inefficient teachers make worthless pupils.

A teacher should be a competent leader. Some of the chief characteristic qualities of a competent leader are energy, perseverance, fearlessness, hope, self-confidence, and enthusiasm; and all of these are found as elements in the character of the true teacher. The school-room is no place for a man wanting in energy, for its work was never yet performed without earnest effort; no place for a man wanting in perseverance, for its obstacles were never yet overcome by the fickle or the weak; no place for a coward, for it has its tests of courage, and cowards must fail when such crises come; no place for the desponding, for despair in a teacher deadens the energies of his pupils; no place for such as distrust their own powers, for those who have no confidence in themselves cannot secure the confidence of others; no place for the cold and phlegmatic, for all true love of knowledge and all earnest pursuit of it must be characterized by enthusiasm.

Some men seem born to command. There is an air of authority about them. Other men at once attract the ready sympathy of those with whom they come in contact. There is something magnetic in their very looks. Both qualities are always combined in the successful leader, be he politician, warrior, reformer, or teacher.

A teacher should be a liberal partisan. A school is the world in miniature. Modified in intensity, all the party contests of society appear in the schoolroom. The school itself has a tendency to break up into divisions and parties. From as many of these contests as possible the teacher should stand entirely aloof; but, when compelled to give his opinion or indicate his choice in action, it should be done in the spirit of the utmost liberality to the opposing party. The teacher may have opinions upon questions in politics or religion which he holds with firmness; but in schools where there are pupils whose parents or themselves entertain different opinions, he must be liberal in the largest sense, or decrease his usefulness. Whenever a teacher in a Common School considers his duty to a party paramount to his duty to his pupils, he should resign his position or be removed from it. Besides, the teacher ought not to be a man of extreme views. His judgments should not be harsh and hasty. He should weigh all sides of questions. He should compel all reasonable opponents to acknowledge his generosity. When acting as an umpire or settling a disputed point among his pupils, he should patiently listen to all that can be said, and then give an unbiassed decision according to the evidence.

A teacher should be a pleasant companion. A teacher's success in his profession depends very greatly upon his social qualities. All incentives to study on the part of pupils do not arise from an interest in study. There are other influences promotive of good order in a school than those which arise from the enactment of strict regulations. Among the most effective of these is regard for the teacher; and this regard he can never secure unless he prove himself a pleasant companion. During intervals of relaxation, the teacher enjoys opportunities of conversing with his pupils; and these opportunities may be improved in a manner highly advantageous to the interests of the school. A tsuch times, the teacher can converse without reserve, can make his pupils feel at home in his company or even to prize highly his society. In the presence of his pupils, a teacher should be polite, agreeable, kind, communicative, even mirthful, but never trifling or undignified. A teacher may talk freely with his pupils, play and joke with them, and yet preserve their highest respect; and such a teacher will be able to impart instruction much more effectively than another who is distant, formal, and unsocial. Even when in the discharge of official duties, a teacher should show himself genial in disposition, frank in manner, and always willing to sacrifice his comfort for his pupils' interests. Requests may be refused, and faults punished, without leaving an impression of unkindness.

A teacher should be a warm friend. Between sociability and friendship there is a difference. A teacher should not only be a pleasant companion, but a warm friend. No one can teach well who does not love those whom he instructs. The instincts of children guide them correctly in choosing friends. To some persons they are at once attracted, and from others they shrink away. It is by those with whom they sympathize that they can be best taught. The love of children is easily gained by those who love them; but in the school, as everywhere else, "Love, and love only, is the loan for love." A child will not learn much from a teacher whom he does not love, and what he does learn is of little value. Under such circumstances, intellectual growth is unhealthy, and moral growth is impossible. A friend is one who is devoted to another, who regards his interests with as much solicitude as his own, who will protect and defend him, whose voice cheers him in prosperity and whose hand gives him help in adversity. All this a teacher should be to his pupils. May the day soon come when what was said of a good teacher can be said of all teachers,—that

> "He, where'er he taught,
> Put so much of his heart into his act,
> That his example had a magnet's force,
> And all were swift to follow whom all loved."

A teacher should be a good man. The same obligation rests upon all men to be good for their own sakes; but the position of some renders their example more influential for good or evil than that of others. The teacher's example is all-powerful, as he is surrounded by the young, who are at once unsuspecting and imitative. Who deliberately could do aught to harm the moral nature of an innocent child?

The ruined picture of an artist may be repainted, a broken statue may be resculptured, subsequent legislation may correct the statesman's errors, a supreme court may right the wrong committed in an inferior one, the death of the body can but follow the worst of a physician's blunders, mature minds may counteract the poison of false preaching; but what power is there to reproduce purity in a mind that bad teaching has corrupted? What legislation can be provided to correct the teacher's mistakes? How much more to be lamented is the death of the soul than the death of the body! How much worse his conduct, even, who leads astray innocent, confiding children, than his the influence of whose bad example and false doctrine can be neutralized by the mature intellects and settled convictions of full-grown men! The teacher should be a model man, —a model in manners, a model in scholarship, a model in virtue. Christianity should find in him that union of faith and works which ever characterizes its truest followers. Remember, teacher,—

"Thou must be true thyself,
  If thou the truth wouldst teach;
Thy soul must overflow, if thou
  Another's soul wouldst reach.
It needs the overflow of heart
  To give the lips full speech.

"Think truly, and thy thoughts
  Shall the world's famine feed;
Speak truly, and each word of thine
  Shall be a fruitful seed;
Live truly, and thy life shall be
  A great and noble creed."

The Teacher's professional Qualifications.—A teacher is born, not made. The principles of teaching are as readily reduced to a system, and as susceptible of study, as those of Law or Medicine; but still the elements of character which make a man a successful teacher must be inborn. A professional education can only improve, it cannot create, talent. It follows that the first professional qualification which it is necessary for a teacher to possess is those natural qualities of head and heart which constitute "aptness to teach." With these qualities, all other professional qualifications are readily attainable; without them, success in teaching is impossible.

In addition to this natural aptness to teach, and based upon it, there are other professional qualifications needed by the teacher, among which are the following:—

A correct Idea of the Teacher's Work.

A profound Knowledge of the Human Constitution, corporeal and mental.

An intimate Acquaintance with educational Means.

A full Understanding of Methods of Teaching.

A great Tact in the Management and Government of Schools.

A thorough Discipline of the Powers used in School-work.

A teacher must have a correct idea of his work. This work consists in educating human beings, in bringing body and mind to that state of perfection of which they are capable: than this, no other task which it is our duty to perform can be more important or more difficult. Man was the last made of created things, the master-piece, the crowning glory of the whole, the complement of all the rest. That in man which distinguishes him from the brutes that perish, is his mind; and it is mostly with this that the teacher is concerned. If

> "On earth, there is nothing great but man,
> In man there is nothing great but mind,"

how transcendently great is the teacher's work! The education of a human soul! The training of an immortal being! An angel might well tremble in undertaking such a task. How, then, can weak mortals perform it without at least making an effort to learn its nature, its importance, and its magnitude? As well might a rough stone-mason, with no sense of beauty in his soul, expect to chisel from marble a statue like that of Venus or the Greek Slave, as for an illiterate schoolmaster with no high ideal of human worth, human perfection, or human destiny, to hope to develop the noble powers with which God has endowed mankind.

A teacher must have a profound knowledge of the human constitution, corporeal and mental. A physician finds it necessary, in order to attain professional skill, to study carefully the human body; and, for the same reason, a teacher must study that upon which he is to operate,—the human, mental and corporeal, constitution. Pope said, "The proper study of mankind is man;" and the teacher has much more reason to engage in this study than others, because without a foundation of principles gained in this way, all teaching would be mere guess-work. In preparing to teach, therefore, a teacher should make himself familiar with the facts and principles of Physiological, Anthropological, and Psychological Science.

A teacher must have an intimate acquaintance with educational means. Man and nature are correlatives. The earth yields food fit for the nourishment of the body no more freely or abundantly than it furnishes means for the culture of the mind. But the teacher must know how to search out these means, to embody them into systems, and to adapt them to the purposes of education. If the memory, reason, imagination, conscience, and other mental powers need culture, the teacher must be able to select appropriate means of imparting it. It is sometimes thought that a knowledge of a branch of study is all that is necessary to enable one to teach it; but to show this view to be erroneous, it may be stated that a teacher should know whether a particular branch of learning is the proper one to teach under the circumstances, and in what order its several parts should be taught, as well as the methods of teaching it. In order to select proper studies for a school, a teacher must be acquainted with all the means used in education; and a thorough knowledge of the relations of its several parts is necessary to enable a teacher to discuss a subject in its logical order.

A teacher must have a full understanding of methods of teaching. With a knowledge of the nature of man's educational wants on the one hand, and of the means of satisfying these wants on the other, the teacher must still study the methods of making the application. The physician finds it necessary to study methods of administering his medicines; the farmer, the methods of fertilizing his land; the mechanic, the methods of making coats, shoes, and carriages: and so the teacher, in like manner, must prepare himself for his work. The science of method is not mastered by easy efforts. The great Bacon left incomplete his Philosophy of the method of acquiring knowledge; and the Philosophy of the method of imparting it is not less difficult. Even when the principles upon which methods of teaching are based are understood, much practice is often necessary in attaining skill in the use of them. Teaching is not a lifeless routine. The teacher, unlike an engineer or a pilot, cannot do his work according to mere mechanical principles. He must so teach as to induce thought, evoke power, develop strength, and inspire activity on the part of his pupils. Education is a growth, not an aggregation or a concretion.

A teacher must have great tact in the management and government of schools. Schools are not well managed or well governed according to arbitrary or variable principles. Human nature is the same everywhere, although it disguises itself in so many forms. The kinds of discipline which preserve good order in one school will preserve it in another: the methods of application only should be different. It follows that there is a theory of school-management and school-government which can be learned; and a teacher can no more dispense with a knowledge of it than a captain who manages a ship can dispense with a knowledge of Navigation, an engineer who builds a railroad, with a knowledge of Engineering, or a general who commands an army, with a knowledge of Military Tactics. But theoretical knowledge alone is not sufficient to enable an individual to teach successfully: he must possess the tact to apply it. There are men who naturally assume the direction of affairs, who are abundant in resources, fertile in expedients, who seem to peer into futurity and foresee contingencies which they skilfully provide for. This is what I mean by *tact;* and no man needs it more than the teacher.

A teacher must secure a thorough discipline of all the powers used in his school-work. Teaching is not a dumb show; it is an active life. The teacher is a workman, and must make all his talent and skill available. He should have the forces he is to employ under the best control. He should have a quick-moving body, an active intellect, strong but well-controlled feelings, a determined will, and gifted powers of expression. His stores of intellectual wealth should be abundant, and ever ready for use. His skill should become a habit. His eyes should see every thing, his ears hear every thing, that transpires in the school-room; and his keen discernment of human character should enable him to guard against improper conduct which is only contemplated, as well as to detect the authors of mischief already committed. Thorough discipline of the powers used in school-work is needed to accomplish all this.

3. THE TEACHER'S DUTIES TO HIS PUPILS.—Pupils legally bear the same relation to their teachers that children do to their parents. The teacher is recognized as being *in loco parentis;* and, occupying this position, the law will justify him in any treatment

of his pupils at school that it will justify in parents at home. Parents and teachers thus stand side by side in the work of education; and they should willingly co-operate in the performance of that work. Children are very dear to parents; and teachers ought to be most careful not to lessen their respect for parental authority, or to adopt plans in violation of parental wishes. Admitting that a teacher generally knows best what is for the good of his pupils, it is not well for him to insist upon his methods or plans too strongly against the known wishes of his patrons. Means may be taken to convince them of their error, or a stubborn few may be disregarded; but the odds of an unwilling many are too great for a teacher to expect success from measures of coercion. A teacher's duties to his pupils may thus be modified in practice by his relations to their parents and guardians.

The teacher's duties to his pupils, too, may be modified by his relations to the General School-Officers. If he is employed to do a certain amount and kind of work, he must fulfil the contract or resign his position, whether he thinks he is doing the greatest good to his pupils, or otherwise.

Subject to these modifications, the teacher's duty to his pupils consists in supplying their wants, as follows:—

1st. *Their physical Wants.*
2d. *Their intellectual Wants.*
3d. *Their æsthetic Wants*
4th. *Their moral Wants.*

The physical Wants of Pupils.— The locating of

schools and the building of school-houses do not often come within the province of the teacher; and it needs only to be said here that both should be done with reference to the health and comfort of pupils, and wherever he can he should use his influence to that end. If a teacher cannot choose the location of his school-house or plan its erection, he can often remedy its defects by bringing them before the proper school-authorities; he can keep his school-house clean and neat; he can have it properly heated, lighted, and ventilated; he can give his pupils comfortable seats, and he can grant them sufficient time for exercise and encourage them to take it.

It is the teacher's duty to notice whether any of his pupils are seated in parts of the house which are too warm or too cold; whether any take too little exercise or are becoming precociously developed; whether any are contracting habits which will prove injurious to their health: in short, it is his duty to care for his pupils as he would for his own children or for himself. It is time teachers should know that the physical wants of pupils—their health, strength, and comfort—are among the objects of education.

The intellectual Wants of Pupils.—The objects of study were stated elsewhere to be Knowledge, Discipline, Aspiration, and Efficiency; and these, therefore, are the intellectual wants which it is the teacher's duty to supply. No argument is needed to enforce that duty: all teachers acknowledge it. It ought to be observed, however, that the intellectual want of a child is not satisfied by instruction in branches of learning. It includes the harmonious culture of all the powers of the mind, the awakening of ideals of perfection in the soul and aspirings towards them, and the evoking of that strength of character before which difficulties disappear, and by which man, rejecting error and holding fast to truth, attains the end of his being.

The æsthetic Wants of Pupils.—The American people are wanting in good taste. There are exceptions; but how large a proportion of our houses, grounds, gardens,—dresses, even,—are arranged without any reference to the pleasing effect they may produce! We prefer to fill our pockets with money rather than our souls with ideas of the beautiful. Something may be done to supply this want in our schools.

Many children in our schools are uncouth in their manners and uncivil in their treatment of their school-fellows. They are sometimes impolite to strangers, wanting in respect to the aged, and ready to make sport of the poor or the distressed. All this it is the teacher's duty, as far as possible, to correct.

He should do more: he should teach them to love the beautiful in nature, in art, and in human actions.

The moral Wants of Pupils.—It is much more important that men should be good than that they should be learned. The culture of the heart should always accompany the culture of the intellect. Intellectual efforts ill directed are a curse to the world: they must be guided by moral principles to be a blessing. Besides, our intellectua. nature is influenced by our moral nature. We do not think as we did before, after having experienced some great grief, having been swayed by some wild passion. or having performed some noble deed. The mind of a nation is changed by a civil commotion or a foreign war.

The teacher's duty in regard to supplying the moral wants of his pupils is plain, and has been elsewhere indirectly enforced; but it might be added that it is his duty also, wherever so privileged, to impart religious instruction. Denominational differences may make it proper that this kind of instruction should be mainly imparted by parents, Sabbath-school teachers, or clergymen; but nothing could wrong a child more deeply than to deprive him of it.

If the teacher is precluded from giving direct religious instruction,—and he is nowhere entirely precluded from it,—his example, if he is a Christian man, imbued with a true Christian spirit, will be a constant illustration of religious duties well performed, and must have a marked influence upon the susceptible minds of his pupils who love him. How dear the Good Father would become to many if the teacher loved Him truly! How near would seem His protecting arm if the teacher always relied upon it! Happy the day when our schools shall be taught by such teachers!

It is a sublime sight to see a little child at prayer. What strong faith he has! How confidently he talks in his childish way with God! How sure he is that father, mother, brother, sister, will be safe.

because he has asked it! Parent, teacher, mar not by your coarse methods this opening bud of religious feeling. It is yours to train, to make bloom and ripen, but not to blast. There is no treasure on earth so precious as a human soul.

4. The Teacher's Duties to his Profession.—In order to examine the question as to whether Teaching has just claims to the rank of a profession, it will be well to state the principal conditions and requirements of a profession, and then ascertain how far teaching answers them. A profession must be characterized by the following conditions and requirements:—1st, It must have a noble aim; 2d, Its operations must not be merely mechanical, but scientific in their character; 3d. It must require on the part of its members a learned general education; 4th, Its nature must be such as to render special preparation necessary to success; 5th, It should have provided an authority competent to decide upon the qualifications of those who apply to become members; 6th, There must be some common bond of union and mutual recognition of claims to membership.

Teaching aims to train, instruct, and develop the various powers and faculties of man, to make him as perfect as his nature admits, to cause him to fill worthily the place God designed for him. Than this, earth has no nobler aim.

A science is a systematic arrangement of principles. A certain work is performed scientifically when it is done according to fixed general laws and in virtue of them. Fixed general laws govern the relations of means to ends in education; and these may be learned and applied. If, therefore, there is no science of Teaching, there is no such thing as science. Many teachers perform their work mechanically; but no profession can claim exemption from quackery.

No one can teach what he does not know. Empty granaries do not furnish food. The teacher must be a learned man. He can find use for all kinds of learning. It is through him that others obtain learning; and a stream is not apt to rise higher than its fountain.

Many pages of this book cannot be read by a candid man without his coming to the conclusion that teachers need special preparation for their work. The education of a human soul is certainly a task as difficult as that of making shoes, building houses, or farming land. Success may be attained in any profession by practice; but in none are blind experiments so dangerous as in Teaching.

There is no more intrinsic difficulty in guarding Teaching from the intrusion of the unworthy by the adoption of a proper standard of qualifications for membership, and by providing an authority competent to apply that standard, than there is with regard to the professions of Law, Medicine, or Theology. Knowledge and skill can be as readily estimated in Teaching as in any other profession.

The lines by which Teaching is separated from other kinds of business have not been very well defined, and, consequently, professional feeling among teachers has not been very prominently manifested. Let teachers once know who are teachers, and no other profession will exhibit a better *esprit du corps.* A meeting of intelligent teachers, even now, is a model in this respect.

If Teaching is a profession, as it seems now proven to be, the teacher has certain duties towards it, which are next to be pointed out. Among them are the following:—

1st. *To adorn it by his Skill and Scholarship.*
2d. *To dignify it by his personal Worth.*
3d. *To elevate it by encouraging all Means of Professional Improvement.*
4th. *To render it more united, by showing Respect to his Fellow-Teachers.*

Every teacher should adorn his profession by his skill and scholarship.—In the past, those who have been the instructors of youth in the lower grades of schools have not, generally, been distinguished as learned men. Schoolmasters have been ridiculed in various literary works for their ignorance or their pedantry; and these sentiments, if unjust in particular instances, expressed doubtless the common estimate of their scholarship. A high standard of scholarship is not required, even at the present time, in one who wishes to enter upon the work of Common-School teaching. The vast majority of those now engaged in teaching the Common Schools of this country are in no way distinguished for learning, and it cannot be much wondered at, as long as such is the fact, that many will be unwilling to recognize Teaching as belonging to the learned professions. True, such a conclusion would be unwarranted, if teachers in all grades of schools are ncluded in the calculation; for no other profession, either in the past or at the present, can present a greater array of learned men than Teaching; but it shows plainly enough that the ignorance of its mem bers tends to degrade a profession.

A teacher who properly appreciates his work, who loves his profession, who desires to see it honored, will exert himself to increase his own store of knowledge and to excite a love of learning among his brother-teachers. He will constantly strive to attain skill in teaching, not more for his own honor than for the honor of his profession. Even though his position be an humble one, he will be ambitious to so improve his opportunities of learning and attaining skill in his work, that subsequent generations of teachers will speak his name with praise.

Every teacher should dignify his profession by his personal worth.—The character of a profession is judged by the character of those who practise it. Their standing constitutes its standing. A man of eminent worth dignifies, while a bad man disgraces, a profession. The members of all professions are proud of the wise and good men who have borne their professional name; and they are ashamed to acknowledge as fellow-members those who are weak, dishonorable, or selfish.

"Every man," said Webster, "owes a debt to his profession." Upon entering a profession, an individual receives from it position, fellowship, honor, means of emolument; and for this service he owes it a debt which he cannot pay without leading a life of integrity. He is a robber who takes from his profession what he does not return to it.

The standing of the teacher's profession depends, perhaps more than some others, upon the personal worth of its members; for it is universally felt that a bad man should not be a teacher. I have said elsewhere that the teacher should be a model man,—a model man in order to be a man, a model man in order to present a good example, a model man in order to dignify his profession.

Every teacher should elevate his profession by encouraging all means of professional improvement.—It will not be denied by any that improvement in teaching can be made, or that it is greatly needed. It will be questioned by as few that the members of a profession are respected in proportion as the profession to which they belong is respected or subserves the interests of society. Every member of a profession, therefore, ought to assist in the work of improving it. Besides, a man is judged by the company he keeps; and if teachers generally are ignorant and inefficient, each particular teacher will suffer from their incompetency.

Teaching is making rapid advances at the present time, and it may be expected to advance still more rapidly in the future: unless, therefore, a teacher be constantly adding to his stock of professional knowledge, he cannot keep abreast of the spirit of the age, and his method of teaching will become stereotyped and unsuited to the condition of things around him. In addition to this, such a teacher is apt to become captious, and to attribute the causes of his failure, which exist in himself, to the bad designs of cotemporaries or the corruptions of the times.

The means of professional instruction generally

open to teachers are Normal Schools, Teachers' Institutes and Associations, School Visitations, books on education, and educational journals.

Normal Schools exist now in many States. They have everywhere sustained themselves against all opposition; and the theory upon which they were established has been proven true by the fruits they have produced. Many good teachers have been made without the agency of Normal Schools, and Normal Schools do not always make good teachers; but these institutions are just as professionally necessary to teachers as Medical Colleges, Law Schools, or Theological Seminaries are to physicians, lawyers, or clergymen. Whenever it is possible for teachers to enjoy the advantages of Normal instruction, they should do so. When properly applied, no other means can meet so well the wants of those who intend to become teachers. Indeed, no other practical agency can be conceived capable of constituting Teaching a regular, well-defined profession.

Teachers' Institutes and Teachers' Associations have done a noble work for teachers, socially, intellectually, morally, and professionally. It was by their means that teachers were first brought together and made acquainted with one another; it was by their means that the desire for professional instruction was first created; and they have been found to subserve so well the purposes of mutual instruction that their number is rather increasing than diminishing. A well-conducted teachers' meeting presents opportunities to teachers of comparing views in regard to teaching, of forming plans for improvement, and of measuring the worth of new principles. They furnish a most agreeable respite from school-duty, break up that feeling of exclusiveness and pedantry which school-life is so apt to engender, and cause those who take part in them to return to their labors with freshened spirit, renewed energy, and higher views of the work in which they are engaged.

Teachers can gain much professional information by visiting the schools of others. Many of the most successful teachers improve every opportunity of making such visitations, and their uniform testimony is that they derive great profit from it. No wide-awake teacher could see a school in operation without learning something. He might learn to avoid errors by seeing their effects in badly-managed schools, and he might learn the value of new methods of teaching by noticing their operation in schools well conducted. What we see generally makes a deeper impression upon us than what we hear described; and in school-visitations the good and the bad are both exhibited in the most striking form.

Teaching can no longer be said to have no literature. The books of a profession are those which discuss its subject-matter or those which relate to its practice. The latter class form a very small portion of professional works. In its subject-matter, Teaching comprehends all works on all subjects. The richest libraries can contain no book that a teacher may not use. With respect to works on the Practice of Teaching, it is not difficult to collect one hundred valuable volumes in the English language; and other hundreds have been published in the various parts of Continental Europe. To a teacher who is ambitious to succeed, a professional library is indispensable.

To keep himself informed of current educational events, every teacher should read educational journals. He will obtain from them valuable facts and important suggestions; and they will keep alive his professional interest.

Every teacher should render his profession more united, by showing respect to his fellow-teachers.—There is much needed among teachers greater professional unity, a better *esprit du corps;* and it can be brought about only in one way,—that of increasing the respect which teacher shows to teacher. Teachers ought to show a proper respect towards all men; but common interests and objects of pursuit should create among teachers peculiar feelings of sympathy and a peculiarly hearty reciprocation of friendly regard. We are all social beings, and find strong incentives to action in the approbation of others. Left alone to work by himself, cheered by no word of approval, encouraged by no friend, stimulated by no hope of gaining a higher professional position, the best of teachers would find his energies weaken and his spirits grow dull. With troublesome pupils and unappreciating patrons, with much work to do and many cares to weigh down his spirit, the teacher more than most men needs kindness and sympathy; and, if he find such feelings among those engaged in the same profession, who have encountered the same difficulties and experienced the same discouragements, he takes heart again, and with freshened energy endeavors to perform his duty. There are pupils who honor their teacher, and parents who thank him, but he needs those with whom he can fraternize. A common bond of sympathy is wanting to bind the members of the profession together in fraternal union.

Teachers are not always even courteous to their fellow-teachers. One teacher sometimes endeavors to establish a reputation at the expense of another. Envy and jealousy now and then find a home in the teacher's bosom. If interests seem to clash, remember, the world has work enough for all good men to do. Let teachers respect one another, and they will be respected.

5. A TEACHER'S LIFE.—In order to show what inducements there are in this country for young men of talents to become teachers, I propose in this place to present a statement of the advantages and disadvantages of a teacher's life.

And first with respect to the disadvantages of a teacher's life: it is alleged that teaching *endangers the health; exacts oppressive duties; yields insufficient compensation; furnishes unsteady employment; spoils the disposition;* and *brings little honor or respect.* While it cannot be denied that there is some truth in these allegations, it is my purpose here to learn to what extent they are true.

Teachers have sometimes lost their health and been compelled to seek other employment. Close study, hard work in-doors, and harassing cares, without physical exercise, without social enjoyment or relaxation, regardless of plain hygienic laws, will inevitably produce ill health. But is this the necessary result of the practice of teaching? May not the teacher regulate his diet, sleep, exercise, and social intercourse in such a manner that his health will not suffer from his employment? Is he compelled to violate the laws of health? If not, then the teacher, and not teaching, is to blame.

The labor of teaching, when faithfully performed, is very great; but not more so than that incident to many other kinds of business. Teachers have preparation to make for their school-duties, but very few are actually engaged in the discharge of those duties more than six hours a day; while mechanics generally work ten hours a day, farmers, twelve or fourteen, merchants are confined behind their counters or at their desks from ten to fifteen, and active physicians and lawyers must be always ready to answer their professional calls. Teaching may be as arduous as any of these occupations; but it requires fewer hours of actual duty per day than any of them, and, consequently, allows the teacher more time that he can call his own. Nor is teaching more wanting in that variety of employment which relieves the tedium of labor than the other kinds of business just named. All of them are in a certain sense mechanical; all of them require the constant repetition of the same processes as is the case in teaching. Besides, the teacher has his holidays and vacations, which come to him as liberty to the prisoner, as spring to the birds, as the green oasis to weary, thirsty travellers in the desert. These are boons enjoyed almost exclusively by teachers, and must be allowed to compensate in some measure for the care and confinement to which their profession at other times subjects them.

Teachers have been, in general, very inadequately remunerated. The public have not properly appreciated education, and, consequently, have been unwilling to pay largely for it. In selecting a profession, a young man very wisely takes into consideration the question of compensation. He may not make money the only end for which he is willing to labor, but he well knows that life has many comforts that money alone can furnish. Thus considering, he who might have become a teacher chooses a more lucrative kind of business. It is readily admitted that much more money can be made in many other callings than in teaching; but it will be shown directly that teaching has inducements of a different kind, which go far to compensate for its pecuniary disadvantages. Even in a moneyed sense, however, teaching is more remunerative than many suppose. A good teacher, one well qualified to teach the branches usually taught in ungraded Common Schools, can obtain almost anywhere a salary of from $400 to $600 a year; and much higher salaries can be obtained for better qualifications. In every State there are numerous positions open to teachers at from $800 to $1200 a year, and a few at from $2000 to $3000. I speak with the very best opportunities of knowing, when I say that a graduate of one of our Normal Schools, if he distinguish himself as a teacher, need not wait long for a situation with a salary of from $600 to $1000 a year. Such a one can generally commence teaching at once with an annual income of $500. A young man can as easily and cheaply become a teacher as he can become a mechanic; and very few mechanics can obtain, without the investment of capital, four hundred dollars a year; and many work for half that amount. It is true that the average salaries of teachers in our country districts are low,—very low; but it must be remembered that the teachers there employed have not generally made any special preparation for teaching, and do not consider themselves permanently engaged in the business. At the worst, however, they are as well paid as ordinary mechanics; and the times betoken a more enlightened liberality towards the deserving. God speed the day! To a young man desirous of becoming a teacher, no fortune can be insured; but all who do their duty can secure a safe and comfortable competency.

Complaint is made that teaching does not furnish constant employment. It is, unfortunately, true that the length of time for which our Common Schools are open in rural districts does not average more than from six to eight months in a year; but it is equally true that competent teachers can almost everywhere find employment in teaching private schools during the vacations of the public schools. Besides, there is such a demand for well-qualified teachers in towns, villages, and enlightened populous rural districts,—in private schools and academies,—that no such teacher need be idle for want of work to do. The demand for industrious, energetic, thoroughly trained teachers much exceeds the present supply. It ought not to be expected, however, that the highest positions in the profession are at once attainable. These will be filled, as in all other professions, by those who win them by success in inferior positions. Aspiring teachers must work and wait.

There is danger, it is said, that the teacher's disposition will be spoiled. Constantly annoyed, he is apt to become captious and irritable. Unaccustomed to hear his word questioned, he is in danger of becoming dictatorial. Familiar only with those who know much less than himself, it is not unlikely he will become conceited and pedantic. Monarch in the school-room, he is apt to be tyrannical towards inferiors, rude in the presence of his equals, and rebellious when commanded by his superiors. A man's vocation always has a marked influence upon his disposition and conduct. Teaching is no exception. The danger is a real one; but it may be guarded against by mingling in general society, by becoming interested in public affairs, and by keeping abreast of the times by reading, study, and travel. The teacher must not forget that he is a citizen and a member of society. Thus guarded against, the influences of teaching upon the disposition are not more offensive to the general taste than those produced by other kinds of business. There are neighborhoods in which teachers are admitted into the most refined society, and in which they are honored guests in every family.

Teaching is not a showy profession. Its work is, for the most part, quiet. Its grand effects are the results of long-continued effort, not of one master-stroke of policy or one electric flash of genius. A lawyer may make a name by one able forensic effort; a general, by the conduct of a single battle; a statesman, by a great oration in the councils of the nation; a surgeon, by a skilful operation which saves the life and brings back the health of some poor victim of disease; but the teacher can win a position or a reputation only by long and hard work. The fruit of his toil slowly ripens. The faithful teacher is not borne about in triumphal chariots, the rapturous huzzas of millions never greet his ears, cities do not drape themselves in mourning when he dies, nor do proud mausoleums grace his last resting-place. For this reason, teaching is less attractive to the ambitious than some other kinds of business; and it is not to be much wondered at that the aspiring youth should rather take a chance in the great lottery that offers the glittering prizes of place and power, though ten thousand blanks be drawn to one fortunate venture, than to engage in the quiet work of rooting out evil from the human heart and training the mind to a just appreciation of the true, the beautiful, and the good. But, while the popular gaze is turned towards those who occupy the high places in the old professions, who stand at the helm of our national ship, who lead our armies, the true teacher needs not fail in an effort to secure a gratified ambition. The teacher who nobly performs his duty is in this country, by discerning men, not less honored than are the members of the other professions. Those who are accustomed to look beneath the surface for the causes which operate in human affairs easily recognize the moulding, guiding hand of the teacher in much that, with the unthinking, passes to the credit of others. The approbation of one thoughtful man is worth more than all the senseless plaudits of a crowd; and to such, and to posterity, the teacher may look confidently for a full appreciation of his deserts. The names of such teachers as Pythagoras, Socrates, Seneca, Pestalozzi, Francke, De Fellenberg, Arnold, Hamilton, Fenélon, Page, and Mann, will not perish, but be preserved among the choicest treasures of history. And, to-day, in France, in Germany, in England, in America, the most profound thinking is done by teachers, and nearly all the great works in science and philosophy are written by them. They now occupy the vanguard in the march of human thought, and the laurel waits to deck the brows of the noble and the brave.

Having seen that the disadvantages of a teacher's life are not so great as they seemed, let us examine what may be its advantages. It is more pleasant, too, to look upon the bright side of a picture; and I gladly turn to it.

It is claimed that a teacher's life *enables him to arrange fixed hours for his work; necessitates no investment of capital; gives freedom from the dangers and temptations incident to many other kinds of business; presents good opportunities for acquiring knowledge;* and *allows great privileges of doing good.*

The teacher has his regular hours for work; and, when that work is done, he can generally have the balance of his time at his own disposal. The lawyer, the physician, the merchant, must always be ready when called upon. They may do nothing all day long, but they must wait, fearful to engage in other serious labor, lest they may be interrupted, or lest some client, patient, or customer be disappointed. Mechanics, too, often work under the whip of their employers. But the teacher can generally devote his t me out of school-hours to the quiet preparation of his work, to self-improvement, to recreation, exercise, or social enjoyments. He has advantages of this kind that few other employments admit, and social regulations are such that he can enjoy them without constraint.

With comparatively few exceptions, teachers find it unnecessary to invest capital in their business. School-buildings and school-property of all kinds are generally owned by communities or by companies. In most cases, teachers receive stated salaries; and when their salaries are due, they get their money, subject to few contingencies. If they desire to change locations, they necessarily sacrifice little property; they are in danger of making no bad bargains, and safe calculations can always be made with reference to the relations between income and expenditures. Teachers, of course, must expend considerable money in preparing themselves to teach; but they cannot lose their knowledge by ill-advised purchases or wild speculations.

Some kinds of business have certain temptations and moral dangers from which teaching is free. No one can doubt, who has had opportunities of judging, that there is much deceiving, cheating, and lying among business-men. They are tempted to do it in order to succeed in business. The teacher has few such temptations to resist. True, teachers sometimes present false statements to parents concerning the progress of their children, and as often attempt to deceive the public by examinations and exhibitions contrived for effect; but such conduct is so easi y exposed that those who resort to it as a means of obtaining patronage are not numerous. Circumstances constantly tempt the lawyer to undertake the justification of wrong, the merchant to overcharge his customers, the physician to make unnecessary visits to his patients, and the mechanic to promise what he cannot fulfil. It is not claimed that teachers are better than other men, or that good men are not found in all vocations; but it is claimed that teaching harmonizes more nearly with other interests than most kinds of business, and that the quiet walks of a teacher's life subject him less than most men to the temptations arising from clashing interests and social wrongs, or the dangers of monetary panics, the turmoils of active business, or the disappointed aspirations and unsubstantial honors incident to power and place.

Teaching presents very favorable opportunities for acquiring knowledge,—first, in furnishing leisure time and that mental state necessary to study, and, second, in being of such a nature that the teacher, in communicating knowledge to others, learns himself. There are few teachers whose time is so occupied with school-duties that they cannot find several hours each day to devote to private study; and this time, well improved, must make scholars.

A teacher's professional duties, too, are well calculated to induce that mental condition which fits the mind for successful study. Busy on the farm, at the shop, or in the office, most men are so absorbed with other cares and duties that few can sit down and summon their mental energies to the task of systematic thinking. With the teacher, it is so directly in the line of professional duty that he generally finds little difficulty in laying aside his school-cares and devoting his leisure hours to communion with books, or to meditation.

The teacher himself learns in communicating knowledge. New thoughts are often evolved when surrounded by sympathizing or opposing hearers. They are struck out, as it were, by the union or concussion of mental forces. A large audience is a necessary condition for the delivery of a great oration. Every teacher feels that the presence of his class inspires him, and that he understands the subject of a lesson better after the recitation than before it. In teaching, he feels the necessity of closer, clearer views of a subject, and uses his best efforts to obtain them. If our object is merely to know a thing, we are satisfied with a much looser knowledge of it than if what we know is to be imparted to others. Every one has experienced the truth of this statement who has selected a familiar theme and sat down to prepare an essay or a lecture upon it. His first impression will most probably be one of surprise that the amount of knowledge respecting it in his possession is so limited, and that he has so much difficulty in availing himself of that which he does possess. To show that our habits of thinking are greatly influenced by the necessity of communicating, I may be allowed to quote the opinion of Sir William Hamilton, and a few authorities named by him. Sir William Hamilton says,—referring to the preparation required to communicate with skill,—"In this case, no man will ever fully understand his subject who has not studied it with a view of communicating; while the power of communicating a subject is the only competent criterion of his fully understanding it." "The one exclusive sign," says Aristotle, "that a man is thoroughly cognizant of any thing, is that he is able to teach it." "To teach," says Plato, "is the way for a man to learn most and best." "*Homines dum docent, discunt*," says Seneca. "*Doce ut discas*," was a maxim among the Schoolmen; and the celebrated logician, Dr. Sanderson, used to say, "I learn much from my master, more from my equals, and most of all from my disciples." I extract the following from an article in Blackwood's Magazine:—"Teaching was formerly a part of the education of students at the universities. In the olden time it was necessary to the obtaining of a degree that the graduate should give evidence of his capacity as a teacher; and in the very titles of his degree as a *Magister* and a *Doctor*, he was designated as a teacher." Such authority and such reasons cannot be questioned; and nothing more need be said to prove the fact, before stated, that teachers are and must be the best scholars in the world.

There are open to all men, who desire to take advantage of them, opportunities of doing good. The greatest good of society can only be attained through the united exertions of all its members. Each in his sphere must do all he can for the common weal. But it is equally true that certain vocations and certain positions in society furnish more opportunities of doing good than others; and the teacher in this respect is peculiarly favored. The most important condition necessary to bring about the highest and happiest state of society is that its members be good men and good women; and if a child trained up in the way he should go will not depart from it when he is old,—and I heartily endorse the sentiment,—and teachers do much of this training, it would seem to follow that good teaching lies at the bottom of all social reform. The population of the United States is not less than thirty-three millions; and of this number at least six millions are attending school. Very soon, those who are now engaged in the various occupations of life will give place to their younger and more vigorous successors, now receiving an education in our various institutions of learning. Trained here to be intelligent and good, they will discharge their duties as citizens and men wisely and well. The patriot may find by this that his country's schools can be made the best nurseries of patriotism, and the philanthropist can discern that his reforms, to be most effectual, must be based upon the virtuous education of the young.

The teacher has a wide field in which he may do good. He has the care of children. He can mould their mental nature almost as he will. They are in his hands as clay in the hands of the potter. They are his plants to watch and care for, and make bloom, and bud, and bear fruit. Let him take care that no weeds choke their growth, or no wrong culture mar it. Let him remember that as the great oak retains the scar which marks the wound received centuries ago, when a tender sapling, so the youthful soul, hurt by a careless hand in teaching, may never heal. A teacher whose pupils have grown to be men and women and engaged in active life, may have the proud satisfaction of reflecting that his was the influence that gave strength to their weak mental activities and guided their tottering footsteps along the pathway which conducted them to honor and success. The farmer is pleased in contemplating his growing crop, or the fruit of his industry well harvested; the mechanic experiences a just pride in gazing upon the results of his own cunning workmanship; the artist feels a thrill of joy as he communes with the forms of beauty he has traced upon the dull canvas, or the beating pulse and heaving bosom he has evoked from the cold, dead marble; but none of these can realize that high pleasure which the teacher enjoys who properly educates men and women and sends them out to bless mankind. Harvest-fruits will pass away, the most imposing structures of human ingenuity will crumble to the dust, forms of beauty will die out on the canvas, and the tooth of time will eat away the hardest marble; but the teacher's work is for eternity; "every chord he strikes in the tender mind vibrates at the throne of God," and vibrates ever.

The faithful teacher, I repeat, enjoys more than most others the high privilege of doing good. As a rich reward, he will receive the grateful thanks of those whom his instruction may have benefited, and he surely cannot lose the smiles of approving Heaven.

II. The General School-Officers.—Under the head of General School-Officers it is intended to embrace the officers who, by the names of Superintendents of Schools, School-Trustees, School-Di rectors, and School-Committees, exercise general care over schools and school-interests.

In speaking of the duties of these officers, no long discussion will be needed here, for the greater part of them have already been described; and the task I proposed to myself will have been completed, when I point the officers to their work.

The General School-Officers select school-sites and provide school-grounds. Their duty in this respect is an important one; for their choice will not only have an influence upon the present, but upon future, generations of children. Let no false notions of economy prevent the selection of such sites and the purchasing and arranging of such grounds as evince at once good judgment and taste and show a proper regard for the welfare of the children who are to use and enjoy them.

The General School-Officers grade the schools and fix their courses of study. The well-working of a system of schools depends much upon the manner of grading them, and the kind of studies that are pursued in the different grades; and no man is qualified to make the necessary regulations concerning these matters, without giving the subject careful consideration. If School-Officers do not possess the requisite knowledge and experience, they should call to their aid some one who does possess them. Nowhere else is guess-work more fatal. A very large number of so-called graded schools are clogged and crippled in their operation by mismanagement.

The General School-Officers build and furnish school-houses. A school-house should be so constructed and so furnished as to answer in the best manner the purpose of its erection, to promote the health and comfort of those who occupy it, and to be in accordance with the principles of good taste. Few of our country school-houses, few school-houses anywhere or of any kind, fully meet these conditions. School-Architecture is yet in its infancy; and its progress will be slow until more liberal opinions prevail among the people respecting the kind and character of the education needed by the young. General School-Officers often have it in their power to change this state of things for the better; and whenever they are willing to improve the school-buildings and school-furniture intrusted to their care, skill can readily be found to do it.

The General School-Officers provide apparatus for the schools. The teacher works at as much disadvantage without tools as the farmer, mechanic, or surgeon; and yet the duty of providing them is often neglected. Indeed, the time is not very far distant when many teachers themselves considered that a penknife, a ruler, and a *birch*, were about all the tools they needed. The articles of school-apparatus mentioned elsewhere in this book are really indispensable to good teaching, and the proper authorities ought to procure them. It is always bad economy to pay men for working with inferior implements.

The General School-Officers desire to preserve the statistics of the schools under their charge, and, of course, they must furnish suitable school-records for that purpose.

The General School-Officers employ teachers; and

this is the most important part of their duty. It is the teacher that must give movement to the whole school-machinery. As the teacher is, so the school will be. No school-officers can know without danger of mistake whether the persons they employ as teachers will prove in every respect qualified for the work, until they are tried; but every effort should be made to obtain this knowledge to the greatest extent practicable. The man into whose hands the young minds and tender hearts of the children of a neighborhood are intrusted, ought to be selected with the greatest care. If damage be done by an incompetent teacher, the authorities that employed him are in great measure responsible for it. Before employing a teacher, the School-Officers should inform themselves,—

First. As to his appearance, manners, tastes, and physical constitution. Some questions may be asked him concerning some of these points; but safe conclusions can generally be reached by close observation while in conference with him.

Second. As to his intellectual qualifications. The intellectual qualifications of a teacher can be approximately determined by a well-conducted examination. The officer who conducts such an examination should be himself a teacher.

Third. As to his moral character. If the applicant for a school be a stranger to the School-Officers, they should require him to produce recommendations, as to moral character, from responsible parties. A teacher ought to be a good man. It is better to leave children untaught than to expose them to the influences of teachers who either entertain bad principles or are guilty of bad practices.

Fourth. As to his professional requirements. A teacher's knowledge of the Theory of Teaching can be learned by an examination, if it be conducted by a competent examiner; but his skill in the practice of his profession must be learned from the testimony of those who have witnessed the operations of his school-room.

General School-Officers visit schools. The value of school-visitation by intelligent School-Officers can hardly be over-estimated. Such visitations are necessary to secure the care-taking of grounds, buildings, furniture, and apparatus; necessary to secure the most rapid progress in study on the part of the pupils; necessary to encourage competent teachers and to detect incompetent ones; in short, necessary to secure the well-working of the whole school-machinery. A railroad or a factory does not need the watchful care of superintendents more than schools require the frequent visitations of their School-Officers.

III. The People in Respect to Schools.—That every child is entitled to an education is a proposition the truth of which at this time, in this country, few will deny. The main facts which prove it are, first, that without education the end of our being, *human perfection*, could not be attained; second, that without it, since God made us capable of being educated, His purpose in our creation would be defeated; third, that without it the noblest truth ɪr science, philosophy, and religion, and the highest beauty in nature and art, could not be appreciated, or even conceived; fourth, that without it the work allotted us as individuals, as citizens, or as members of society, could not be performed.

The right of each individual to an education acknowledged, it seems proper to speak—

1. OF THE RELATIONS OF EDUCATION IN SOCIETY.
2. OF THE AGENCIES BY WHICH AN EDUCATION CAN BE OBTAINED.

1. THE RELATIONS OF EDUCATION IN SOCIETY.—The people who found and support schools ought to understand the social influences of education. Without this knowledge, all provision for education must be made blindly, and, according to well-known principles of human nature in such cases, reluctantly. I desire to discuss, briefly,—

1st. *The Relations of Education to Labor.*
2d. *The Relations of Education to Wealth.*
3d. *The Relations of Education to Crime.*
4th. *The Relations of Education to Happiness.*
5th. *The Relations of Education to Religion.*
6th. *The Relations of Education to Government.*

The Relations of Education to Labor.—Education renders labor more effective. A man who is intelligent and skilful can perform more work of any kind than one who is ignorant and awkward. This fact is made manifest in every shop and on every farm. It is shown, too, by the invention of machinery. In ancient times, much strength was wasted in carrying water from distant springs, brooks, or rivers; but when wells were dug in convenient places and water drawn from them, one step was taken to lessen labor; when pumps were placed in these wells and the atmosphere made to do some of the lifting, further progress was made in the same direction; and when siphons and hydraulic rams came into use, water could be procured almost without the expenditure of muscular strength. A sharpened stick might serve a savage to plant a few hills of corn; a spade would enable him to plant much more; with a plow and the skill to use horses or oxen, one man may do the work of many; and when steam can be made to take the place of animal strength, a still greater breadth of land can be worked with a still less amount of labor. If all the grain now raised in the United States could be thrashed out only by the simple contrivances of the primitive ages and ground by hand in mortars, the whole people of the country might engage in the work and scarcely accomplish it. But while the simplest kinds of labor, such as the cutting down of forests, excavating earth, and quarrying stone, are rendered more effective by education, the more difficult kinds would be impossible without it. This fact appears most conspicuously in the arts of manufacturing and mechanics. There must be labor directed by intelligence to erect bridges, construct railroads, and build steamships; to make watches, pianos, and printing-presses; to manufacture paper, cloth, or cannon. As a question of economy in money, a state will act wisely in educating its laborers.

Education dignifies the laborer. In all mon

archies, at least, if not in all republics, there are two classes of society, the intelligent, ruling class and the ignorant, servile class,—the Patricians and the Plebeians; but in all countries the fact is apparent that the latter class are held in low estimation, not because they work, but because they are ignorant. A good education is everywhere a passport to good society. It everywhere dignifies the laborer and makes freemen of slaves. Cincinnatus could plow his lands, Franklin could wheel home his paper through the streets or set his type, Hugh Miller could work in a stone-quarry, and lose nothing in the esteem of any man whose esteem was worth possessing. I once met, half a mile under ground, in a coal-mine, a Scotch miner. His hands were hard with labor, his face was as black as coal could make it; and yet he could talk to me of strata and formations, of fossil plants and animals, of Locke and Reid and Stewart, of Campbell, Scott, and Burns. I realized then, in conversation with that sooty miner, that learning may dignify the lowliest toil, and that earth has nothing ignoble but sin and ignorance. Man working as a man is respected; but working as a mere animal he is despised. Whenever laborers learn to think, labor will be dignified. The common feeling seems to be that man was intended to work more with the head than with the hands,—that, having the power to make animals and the inanimate forces of nature do his heavy lifting, pulling, and other work requiring muscular strength, he is unworthy of himself if he does not use it. This feeling is the source of the difference in the degree of respect with which the various employments of men are regarded. Intelligence commands a higher price in the market than mere muscle, or the services of a horse would be worth more than the services of a man; and the price, not only in money but in respect, will always be in proportion to the degree of intelligence.

But it is said that education will create a distaste for work, and, consequently, diminish the number of laborers. I think it is true, as before intimated, that education has a tendency to make a man feel that his special work is to think, to plan, and to manage. It does not make him less industrious, but it disposes him to use animals, water, wind, steam, electricity, to help him work. An educated man may not be very willing to pull at a weight with his hands; but he will contrive a capstan and do the work of many men. He does not thrash grain with a flail, but with a thrashing-machine. He does not pick cotton with his fingers, but with a cotton-gin. He might grow weary spinning with a distaff or weaving with a hand-loom, but he will build great factories, and set machinery in motion that will make more cloth than the whole world could do if all were weavers. Education does not make people dislike men's work; it only makes them want to work like men. It may diminish the number of mere hewers of wood and drawers of water, but it provides ample means for hewing all the wood and drawing all the water the world needs. "If all persons were educated, who would do the work?" asks one. A harder question would be, If there were no educated men to economize labor, where could a sufficient number of laborers be obtained?

God, when He made man capable of thinking, did not intend that he should starve himself in exercising this privilege. All needed work will be done, and better done than now, when all men shall have become educated. Most of it will be done by machinery; but no one will object then, more than now, to doing necessary hand-work by hand.

The Relations of Education to Wealth.—Education increases the wealth of a nation in several ways. It makes labor more effective, as previously shown; with a less expenditure of time and strength, it enables men to accomplish vastly more work than they could do without it, and consequently adds to a nation's wealth.

"Wealth consists," says Henry C. Carey, "in the power to command the always gratuitous services of nature." If this is true (and it seems to me to be in good part true), the wealth of a nation must be greatly increased by the education of its citizens; for it is education that gives the power to command the services of nature. A rude, uncultivated people work almost altogether with their hands and a few simple tools or instruments which they acquire the skill to make and handle; later they learn to tame the ox, horse, dog, or reindeer, and make use of animal strength in their labors; but it is only in highly civilized communities that the wind is made to grind corn and propel vessels, that water is used to turn mill-wheels and drive the machinery of manufactories, that steam is forced to lift heavy weights and pull heavy loads, or that electricity is sent on our errands through the land. In this sense knowledge is truly power, and power is wealth.

The resources of a country could not be developed without education. Vast forests of timber would decay if they could not be converted into buildings, bridges, and ships; the mineral masses of coal, iron-ore, limestone, granite, marble, that underlie our valleys and form great beds beneath our mountains, were of little value to the wild Indian who placed his wigwam above them, unconscious of the wealth under his feet; vegetable fibres have been found and fashioned into fabrics with a skill and a rapidity that add immensely to their value; and even the earth is made to increase its yield a hundredfold under the hand of skilful tillage. It is thus that national wealth is developed by education; and further illustrations are deemed unnecessary.

The Relations of Education to Crime.—It is a question of much interest to a people, before making costly provision for education, as to the relation education bears to crime. Does it make society more virtuous or less so?

We do not find the moral quality of an act in its intellectual part. The reason enables us to know what is right; but virtue does not consist in knowing the right, it consists in doing it from a proper motive. It is clear, therefore, that if intellectual culture promotes virtue in a people, it must do so indirectly. But indirectly its influence must be on virtue's side. Right-knowing is a necessary condition for right-doing. Besides, crimes are frequently committed by persons who do not realize the wrong they do; but this can hardly be the case with the educated. Crimes are frequently committed by those who are suffering from poverty or for want of employment; but an educated man need not often suffer on these accounts, and this lessens his temptations to wrong-doing. Crimes are frequently committed by the ignorant during the hours when, released from work, they seek pleasure in animal indulgences; but educated men have tastes and sources of amusement that sometimes at least keep them from the company of the low and depraved. Crimes are frequently committed by those who have lost all self-respect; the educated have a better appreciation than the ignorant of the dignity of the human character and what is due to it. All these circumstances evidently tend to render indulgence in vice and wickedness less common among the educated than among the ignorant. Still, it must not be claimed that education wholly prevents crime. Some men intellectually very great have been morally very bad. Education, indeed, has been used as an instrument of crime. Facts prove that a mere intellectual education is not a sufficient safeguard against the commission of crime: the only safeguard is an education broad enough to reach the moral nature,—the heart as well as the head. But it is claimed that intellectual culture when imparted by itself—if that is possible—tends to diminish crime, and that the education imparted in our common schools, comprehending as it does both intellectual and moral instruction, is greatly promotive of that end. That this claim is not unwarranted, sufficient proof has already been given; but a few facts in the form of statistics will confirm its justice

During seven years the criminal statistics of Europe show that in France, among the persons a cused or convicted of crime, the proportion of the well educated to those imperfectly educated or not educated at all was 227 to 9773; in Scotland, 188 to 9812; and in England, 91 to 9909.

Joseph Bently some years since arranged a chart showing the moral condition of the different counties of England as compared with their means of education. From an inspection of this chart, Bishop Potter, in the "School and Schoolmaster," draws the following conclusion:—"If you take the four best-instructed counties in England, as exhibited on this chart, and the four worst-instructed, it will be found that the average amount of crime is almost exactly in the INVERSE ratio to the average amount of instruction."

Of 9979 criminals committed to the jails and houses of correction in Massachusetts in 1850, only 3175, or less than one-third, could read and write; of 9705 committed in the same State in 1862, 1965 could neither read nor write. Of 445 convicts in the Ohio Penitentiary in 1847, 248 could not read and write when they entered. In 1843, of 1778 convicts in the Eastern Penitentiary of Pennsylvania, 906 could not read and write; of the 646 who were in the same prison in 1862, 112 were entirely illiterate on admission, 106 could spell and read a little, 421 could read and write, but only 7 had a good English education.

The number of commitments to the prisons of New York City in 1850 was 21,299, of whom 9449 could not read, 1646 could read only, 7284 could read and write, and 2737 were pronounced well educated. There were tried in the year 1861 in the principal cities of the State of New York 36,662 cases, and of these 21,158 could not read and write, 11,745 could read and write, and the education of 1156 could not be ascertained. In the California State Prison in 1863 there were 589 criminals, of whom 375 could read, 341 could read and write, and 214 could neither read nor write. The chaplain of the Connecticut State Prison says that at one time out of 190 prisoners not one was liberally educated. Now, when it is remembered that but a very small proportion of the population of the States and localities referred to cannot at least read and write, these facts show with overwhelming force that ignorance is one of the most potent causes of crime.

The statistics above given are quoted because they exhibit the influence of education briefly and in the most convincing form. Multitudes of the same kind of facts are readily accessible; and a careful examination of the inmates of every jail and penitentiary in the whole country would exhibit the same results as those named. Counter-statements, indeed, have been made by M. Guerry in France, and by Sir Archibald Alison in England; but their statements were afterwards found to be based upon a partial knowledge of the facts involved in their calculations.

The Relations of Education to Happiness.—Happiness is defined by Webster as "the agreeable sensations which spring from the enjoyment of good; that state of being in which one's desires are gratified by the enjoyment of pleasure without pain." Does education tend to increase or diminish happiness as thus defined?

That it tends to increase it will appear from the following reasons:—

Education multiplies the sources of enjoyment. The happiness of the ignorant must consist mainly in mere animal gratification. They can derive little pleasure from the contemplation of the works of nature. That pure pleasure which comes from the study of the various sciences is wholly unknown to them. They do not appreciate works of art, except those of the rudest character; and the beauty of painting and sculpture and the charms of poetry and melody never can arouse to rapturous enjoyment their dull senses. They do not see the footprints of the Creator upon the earth, and His handiwork in plants and animals and the stars of heaven. The mysteries of their own bodies they have never essayed to understand, and the whole world of soul is to them a *terra incognita*. The ignorant may be contented; but contentment is not always happiness. Brutes are contented with their condition; and Shakspeare says,—

> "What is man,
> If his chief good and market of his time
> Be but to sleep and feed? a beast, no more."

Education increases the power of enjoying. Agreeable sensations may arise from the proper exercise of the organs of the body; from the lawful gratification of the animal senses, appetites, and passions; from the use of the various intellectual powers; from the discharge of moral and religious duties. The lowest form of happiness arises from the first source named, the next lowest from the second, and the highest from the exercise of the intellect and the conscience. He is the happiest man who derives pleasure from the play of his whole nature, and his power of enjoying is much diminished who suffers his higher mental faculties to remain unused. Besides, the pleasures of the educated are not only of a higher order than those of the ignorant, but they are more intense. A well-cultured intellect is quick to perceive truth and beauty, and well-trained feelings are quick to respond to such perceptions; while the chief care of the ignorant is "to sleep and feed."

Education removes many causes of unhappiness. All the benefits society derives from those who train the young, relieve persons afflicted with disease, or heal the sin-sick spirit, are attributable in great measure to education. Much suffering has resulted to humanity from various forms of superstition. Eclipses, comets, meteors, have struck with terror whole communities. Witchcraft, like a fell spirit, has caused much misery. People have been frightened by ghosts and apparitions. Great inconvenience has been occasioned by belief in charms, spells, and magical cures. Humbugs of all kinds have misled the ignorant. Wicked delusions have been practiced upon the superstitious, and many have been robbed of money and time, and some have lost their lives, in consequence of them. Ignorance seems to have been the great hotbed from which has sprung, like rank weeds, all that is sinful and wicked. Designing men have made use of the superstitious fears, fierce passions, and strong prejudices of the ignorant to forward their evil designs against social order, religion, and liberty. If it were possible to sum up the curses that have burdened mankind with vice, misery, and grief, a large proportion would be found to have a common mother, —ignorance.

The Relations of Education to Religion.—The maxim that "Ignorance is the mother of devotion," if not uttered in irony, must have had its origin when religion was little understood. If by devotion is meant unquestioning obedience to the authorities of a church and a blind compliance with prescribed religious forms, ignorance *is* the mother of devotion; but if devotion means enlightened faith, or free and full sacrifice of self to the ends of piety well understood, the maxim is most erroneous. It is well to state here, in view of the great interest the people have in the matter,—

First, the complaints science makes against religion. Science complains that religion ignores the higher faculties of the mind and requires men to believe when they should reason. Science complains that religion fixes certain doubtful creeds or dogmas by authority, and thus blocks up progress. Science complains that religion is illiberal and persecutes men for honest differences of opinion. Science complains that religion too often degenerates into superstition and faith too often has no firmer basis than fiction.

Second, the complaints religion makes against science. Religion complains that science is proud, and claims to reason of things whereof to reason is impossible. Religion complains that science overlooks certain great truths which God has revealed, and which must be believed and practiced or all progress leads to destruction. Religion complains that science in its toleration of error would sacrifice the truths of God's word, which must be preserved amid all the mutabilities of human affairs. Religion complains that science too often leads to skepticism and reason too often assumes to occupy the place of God.

History, it is to be feared, might show cause for both these classes of complaints; but to the believer in the perfections of God, no antagonism between science and religion is possible. God does not contradict Himself. The truth in His works cannot invalidate in the least particular the truth of His word. Both coexist in the most beautiful harmony. Science has attacked religion because men assumed to have wisdom which they did not possess, and religion has attacked science because men have constructed creeds which they came to regard as the work of God and not of men. Let both "labor and wait," and eventually all seeming differences will meet their reconciliation. Education has no nobler end than that of aiding in bringing about this reconciliation; and happy the teacher who in training a scholar makes a Christian!

Religion, as I understand it, is educational. God gave men the capacity to become religious. "That was the true light that lighteth every man that cometh into the world." Certain conditions must be fulfilled, the strivings of the Spirit of God with our spirits must be heeded, and the converted soul begins its growth in grace, at first like a tender plant, afterwards like a great tree that the storms of life cannot uproot.

All true education is religious. Systems of science

are but the thoughts of God. Kepler uttered but the sober truth when, enraptured with the discovery of his planetary laws, he exclaimed, "Great God, I think thy thoughts after thee!" All science, therefore, leads to God. Its laws all converge and unite in Him; and the student cannot reach his journey's end until he rests safe on the Saviour's bosom.

The Relations of Education to Government.—The first form of government was patriarchal: the father ruled his family: there was no state. Next came the monarchial form: the patriarch became the head of several or many families; or, in times of danger or distress, some one stronger or wiser than others was made chief, and in the course of years, by conquests or affinities, a number of tribes united under one sovereign whose rule was absolute. The form that probably followed the monarchial was the aristocratic: some of the principal men of a nation, great in ability, wealth, or arms, demanded a share in the sovereignty and obtained certain concessions from the monarch, and became a check, more or less strong, upon his power. The form that was the last to be adopted is the republican, in which the people govern themselves by electing their own rulers.

If, then, amidst all the mutations of nations, we can see governments ripening into democracies, it follows that forms of government are the result of education. A republican is the form toward which all highly civilized countries gravitate, and which the most highly civilized ones adopt; but such kinds of government have always failed and will always fail where the masses of the people are ignorant.

Where universal suffrage is enjoyed, there must be universal education.

A republic is endangered by ignorant rulers. It requires great wisdom in the men who make the laws for a great nation and adapt them to the varied circumstances of the people; great wisdom in the men who expound these laws and adjust the rights and redress the wrongs of individuals and communities under them; great wisdom in the men who support the authority of the government by a faithful execution of the laws thus framed by legislators and expounded by judges.

A republic is endangered by ignorant voters. What the Palladium was to ancient Troy, what the Ark of the Covenant was to the Jews, the ballot-box is to Americans. Whenever it does not express the voice of intelligent freemen, republican institutions are in danger. Many other things are necessary to the well-working of the governmental machinery of a republic, but a pure ballot-box is vital. It is the nation's heart. But what shall we say of the ballot-box that expresses only the voice of unthinking, ignorant men? Does it need a prophet to foretell the fate of that republic whose voters are such men? May God put it into the hearts of our American people to provide an education—a right education—for all, that the republic may not perish!

A republic is endangered by unprincipled demagogues. It was by the contentions of parties and party factions that Rome and Greece lost their liberties, and these contentions were fomented by ambitious men who sought their own interests at the expense of the state. The same class of demagogues, not yet grown quite so bold, may be found in America. They pretend to be great friends of the people, flatter them, excite their prejudices, secure their votes, and, when necessary to their purposes, stir up the spirit among them that leads to mobs and violence. Success attends such efforts only among the ignorant. The trade of demagoguism does not flourish among intelligent men. Universal education is the antidote for this evil, and will save our country from the fate of the great republics of the past.

2. THE AGENCIES BY WHICH AN EDUCATION CAN BE OBTAINED.—Taking the term "school" to signify any place where instruction is imparted, the means in present use for the purposes of instruction may be classified as follows:—

1st. *Family Schools.*
2d. *Church Schools.*
3d. *Private Schools.*
4th. *State Schools.*
5th. *People's Schools.*

The Family School.—The work of education is first commenced in the family, and parents are the first teachers. Some care must be taken of children during infancy, or they would perish, and some instruction must be imparted to them by parents, or they will be unfit to become members of even the rudest society. The wild savages of Africa and America do not wholly neglect this duty; and as civilization advances, more care is taken to instruct children in the family, and in some countries, as in Judea, education was almost altogether of a domestic character. The family indeed is a state in miniature, the unit of society; and both reason and revelation devolve upon the heads of a family the responsibility of educating its younger members. An education received from parents in the bosom of a family must have certain advantages over an education received from teachers in a school. Parents can commence the education of their children in their infancy, when they are most susceptible to educational influences; they can continue it without interruptions in time or change in system; they can adopt studies and regulate their family discipline with no one to question their authority or to interfere with their plans; they can commingle in practical application, and vary when desirable, the different kinds of education, physical, intellectual, æsthetical, industrial, moral, and religious; they can unite both paternal and maternal influences in their modes of instruction; and they can shield their children from the temptations to which they would be exposed away from home, even when most watchfully cared for. These advantages, however, it is evident, can only be attained under the most favorable circumstances. In even the most enlightened neighborhoods in this country, it would be found upon trial that parents are not, except in few instances, capable of imparting a complete education to their children, and that, when competent, their business interests would prevent it. The cost of employing private teachers with the necessary qualifications can only be paid by the wealthy. These causes have operated to remove children from the family to receive their education, and if the loss has been great, it will be seen in the sequel that the gain has also been considerable.

That parents cannot in the present state of society fully instruct their children is a proposition which few will doubt; but it is very certain that they might accomplish much more in this direction than they now perform. They are apt to shift the responsibility of the education of their children altogether from themselves, and throw it upon private teachers, or upon Church or State. This is most sadly wrong. Parents can have no higher interest than the education of their offspring, and nothing but the most pressing circumstances can excuse them from the performance of the duty of teaching these offspring so far as they may be able to discharge it. "Schools are a necessary evil," says a writer; and there is much truth in the sentiment. There can be no question that society in all its parts, government in all its functions, must feel the evil effects of defective home-training. Education is the more potent the earlier it is imparted. "Every new educator effects less than his predecessor." Parents cheat their children of their birthright when they leave their whole culture of head and heart to others.

The Church School.—The Church has done much for education in all ages, though its object at times may have been more to increase its membership than to benefit the people. Priests in different countries of ancient times were the chief educators. This was the case in Egypt, Hindostan, and Judea; and during the long night of the Middle Ages, what little intellectual light was disseminated came from the cold cloister or the dark cell of the monastery.

At the present day the Church has everywhere its institutions of learning, and may justly vie with the State in the munificence of its contributions to their support.

Knowing the power of early influences, it is not unnatural that Church authorities should contend for the right of education; nor is it unnatural that parents who are members of particular Churches and solicitous for the religious interests of their children, should desire to place them in circumstances most favorable to the promotion of those interests. All the right the Church can have in the matter, however, in my opinion, is acquired from parents. There is nothing in the constitution of the Church itself that gives it this right; but, if parents or those having the control of children willingly select the Church as an agent to do their work, no valid objection can be made to it. God gave children to parents, and they are responsible to Him for their training and instruction. The Church may advise; but I can find nothing in the Bible nor in the nature of the case to warrant its use of force. I mean that what I have said shall apply to countries in which Church and State are united, or to those in which State authority is subordinate to Church authority; but it is intended to be more directly applicable to the state of affairs in governments like ours, —the only form of government consistent with individual liberty.

The Private School.—The parents of several families have the right to educate their children together, and they may freely appoint teachers for that purpose. If several, then many may do so, and thus

Private Schools, larger or smaller, may be established. Or a teacher may collect about him as many children as choose to attend his instruction, and teach them, and, as far as I can see, he commits no offence. If the Church may be selected as an agent in the work of education, so may an individual, parents being the primary source of educational power in both cases.

The Private School differs from the Church School in this: the latter is necessarily denominational, if not sectarian, in its character, while the former may be composed of children from families belonging to different religious denominations, or to none. In such a school, religious instruction must consist of those broad principles which are recognized as true by the patrons of the school, or be entirely left to other agencies. It is a curious fact in the history of educational progress in America, that these Private Schools as organized in villages and rural districts suggested the necessity of our general Common School systems, and formed the basis, in principle, upon which they are founded.

THE STATE SCHOOL.—In ancient Sparta the State virtually took their children from parents and educated them wholly with reference to its own ends. It prescribed their clothing and food, as well as appointed their teachers and dictated their course of study. Nowhere else has the State arrogated to itself such absolute power respecting education; for the school systems of modern Europe are State institutions in a very different sense from those established by the laws of Lycurgus. These systems, it is true, are under the control of State authority, but this authority is exercised with reference to the interests of individuals and communities, as well as for that of the government. The people do not build their own school-houses, provide their own school-furniture or text-books, or appoint their own teachers or pay them; but the school-authorities commissioned by the governments under which they act generally show much respect for their circumstances in life, their peculiarities of opinion, and their religious belief. Against the sternest despotism in Europe, the people vindicate their right to some show of liberty in matters of education. In America there are no State schools, properly speaking. Here the State merely makes regulations according to which the people establish and support schools.

The question as to the right of the State in the matter of education will depend very much upon the theory of government which may be adopted. If rulers are God-appointed, if the doctrine of the "Divine right of kings" can be substantiated, it follows that the will of the sovereign must be the law of the land, and systems of education may be established by the State as well as navies or armies. But if, on the other hand, the true theory of government is that which vests all power in the people,—makes the people the State,—then, in my judgment, the people can only delegate to officers chosen by them those powers which cannot be conveniently exercised by themselves as individuals. To do otherwise would be incompatible with the spirit of democratic institutions. As a Democracy, the French people had no right to elect Louis Napoleon Emperor; and, as a Democracy, no American State would have a right to usurp power respecting education which could be efficiently used in the hands of the people. The best policy in a Republic is for the government to encourage the people to do their own work as individuals and as communities. Its functions are more to adjust and regulate. In accordance with this policy, our State governments have not imitated the school systems of the Monarchies of Europe. When the people want school laws, they are made by representatives elected by their vote, and they are subject to repeal at their will. Good care is taken to place the working power of their systems of education in the hands of officers chosen directly by them, whose interests are identical with those whom they serve, and whose official acts are open to their criticism and subject to their revision. Even the Prussian system of education, the best in the Old World, could not be adopted in this country without sacrificing the principle which underlies our whole form of government. We might have better school-houses, better teachers, longer school-terms, larger appropriations to schools, if our State authorities provided them independent of the popular will; but such an exercise of power would in so many other respects prove hurtful that it can never be tolerated while we remain faithful to the principles of Republicanism.

THE PEOPLE'S SCHOOL.—Every child that comes into the world has a right to an education.

Under the most favorable circumstances, an education might be received in a family; but to extend the benefits of a good education to all children .r this way, as society is now constituted, is simply impossible.

In some respects the Church could perform the work of education better than any other agency; but in this country denominational differences would utterly defeat any attempt to organize a general system of education embracing the whole people subject to its control. If each denomination should undertake the work of educating the children of those who belong to it, the task would be found very difficult and expensive among scattered families; and immense numbers of children whose parents belong to no denomination would be left uncared for. Besides, in a larger view, it is not desirable, either for the cause of Religion or Republicanism, that sectarian prejudices should be increased; and this would inevitably be the case if each religious denomination should establish schools for the exclusive benefit of its own membership.

Unaided by other agencies, private means would probably, in the present condition of society in this country, supply, in good measure, higher institutions of learning, such as Colleges, Academies, and Seminaries, and provide schools for young pupils in towns and thickly-settled rural districts; but no system of charity could be instituted that would furnish the advantages of an education to the children who live in sparsely-settled sections of country, or to the poor who are found everywhere. It might be objected to Private Schools, also, that they would be so managed as to subserve more the interests of individuals or corporations than the larger interests of communities or states. The end of education cannot be answered in a nation without the adoption of a broad, generous system of schools that will bless with its advantages all sections of the country and all classes of men.

Great as is the interest of the State in the education of its citizens, insuperable objections exist against investing it with plenary educational powers, in a Republic. As public interests would be overlooked by private institutions of learning, so private rights would be trampled upon by a system of State Schools. Parents have too deep an interest in the welfare, especially the moral and religious welfare, of their children, to allow the sacred trust of their education, for which God will hold them responsible, to pass from their hands into those of State authorities, who are cold and distant, and who, looking only at the results of their schemes upon masses of children, are apt to be regardless of their effect upon individuals. An educational agency should commence with individuals and go up to masses, for if it commence with masses it will scarcely get down to individuals. That cannot be considered a right system of education which provides a great educational mill into whose hopper all children are thrown, and, when each has been subjected to the same grinding process, hands them back again to society. At the best, State Schools can only educate the head; their machinery is much too clumsy to reach the heart.

Avoiding most, if not all, the dangers and difficulties of other classes of schools, the People's School recommends itself as an agency best calculated to meet the wants of a free State. This kind of school belongs exclusively to America, and is one of the characteristics of the present age. Systems of schools belonging to this class, by a misnomer sometimes called State Schools, are found, somewhat varied in their provisions, in nearly all the States of this Union. They furnish, when well administered, a good education to all,—free both to rich and poor; they encourage home instruction, and resemble family schools in bringing together the children of neighboring families; they protect the individual interests of parents by placing the power of building school-houses, supplying school furniture and apparatus, fixing courses of study, providing text-books, appointing teachers, levying school-taxes, and expending school-moneys, in the hands of officers chosen by them from among themselves; they educate together the children of all denominations, but admit any amount and kind of moral and religious instruction that their patrons may agree to have imparted in them; they satisfy the just demands of the State by providing means for the education of all its citizens, and allow its authorities just power enough to regulate the work by general laws looking to the interests of all concerned; they compel no child to attend the schools established by them, parents being at liberty to patronize any other kind of school or to educate their children at home, but they tax all persons and all property, because there is no other just way of obtaining the necessary funds to educate all the children in a community or a State, and a body of citizens has as much right to tax itself for this purpose as for any other. Such are the principal excellencies which recommend the People's Schools, and which should attract to their support every American citizen. They are a most beautiful expression of the spirit of free institutions; and, when well understood, none will oppose them but those who are blindly selfish or who hate a democratic form of government.

The People's Schools should be cherished and supported by the people. No philanthropy is better than that which carries the light of knowledge as a free gift to the poor, and no patriotism can be higher than that which provides a good education for a whole nation. If the educational results of such schools bring disappointment, the responsibility rests with the people. They provide the machinery, and they must watch its working,—must watch it even if farm, and desk, and shop, and office, be neglected; for *the dearest interest of a nation is the education of its children.*

Most solemnly let me say that without a full and free education of all our youth, our democratic institutions will prove a failure. A Monarchy or an Aristocracy is possible anywhere, but a Republic can never be long maintained among an ignorant people. All the dangers which threaten our government centre in this one. A sovereign, a voter, must know how to rule, how to vote,—or, otherwise, selfish demagogues may govern by his means, and this is death to the Republic.

If we need any stronger motive to induce us to lend our aid to promote the cause of education, we have it in this: GOD DEMANDS IT OF US. The talents of our children are ours to care for, and we dare not hide them in a napkin and bury them in the earth.

VALUABLE EDUCATIONAL WORKS

FOR

SCHOOLS, ACADEMIES, AND COLLEGES.

Selected from Messrs. J. B. Lippincott & Co.'s Catalogue, which comprises nearly Two Thousand Works in all branches of Literature. Catalogues furnished on application. *Liberal terms will be made for Introduction.*

Haldeman's Outlines of Etymology. By S. S. Haldeman, A.M., author of "Analytical Orthography," "Elements of Latin Pronunciation," etc. 12mo. Fine cloth. 90 cents.

"This is a most scholarly presentation of the science of etymology, . . . to which is added an appendix of inestimable value to the student of language. . . . It is a marvel of conciseness."—*New England Journal of Education*, July 5, 1877.

"There is, probably, no man living who has studied and analyzed the English language so thoroughly and so successfully as this distinguished savant of Pennsylvania, and this little treatise is the latest fruit of his ripe scholarship and patient research. No newspaper notice can do justice to the work, for it cannot be described, and must be studied to be appreciated."—*Philadelphia Evening Bulletin.*

Walker's Science of Wealth. A Manual of Political Economy, embracing the Laws of Trade, Currency, and Finance. Condensed and Arranged expressly for Use as a Text-book. By Amasa Walker, LL.D., *late Lecturer on Public Economy, Amherst College.* Student's edition. 12mo. Extra cloth. $1.50.

"I have, during the past year, made use of Dr. A. Walker's 'Science of Wealth' in the new and condensed form he has given it, in giving instruction to the senior class in Political Economy, and have found the book better adapted than any other with which I am acquainted for use in a college class-room. It is clear, compact, and ample in its illustrations."—Prof. Jules H. Seelye, *Amherst College, Massachusetts.*

"It is, in my opinion, the best work on this subject."—W. T. Harris, *Superintendent of Schools, St. Louis, Missouri.*

Berkeley's Principles of Human Knowledge. A Treatise concerning the Principles of Human Knowledge. By George Berkeley, D.D., *formerly Bishop of Cloyne.* With Prolegomena, and with Illustrations and Annotations, Select, Translated, and Original. By Charles P. Krauth, D.D., *Norton Professor of Systematic Theology and Church Polity in the Evangelical Lutheran Theological Seminary; Professor of Intellectual and Moral Philosophy, and Vice-Provost of the University of Pennsylvania.* 8vo. Extra cloth. $3.00.

Prof. A. C. Fraser, of the University of Edinburgh, says of "Berkeley's Principles:" "It would be difficult to name a book in ancient or modern philosophy which contains more fervid and ingenious reasoning than is here employed to meet supposed objections, or to unfold possible applications to religion and science."

Atwater's Elementary Logic. Designed Especially for the Use of Teachers and Learners. By L. H. ATWATER, *Professor of Mental and Moral Philosophy in the College of New Jersey.* 12mo. Cloth. $1.25.

"This manual shows the hand of a master, and will speedily take its proper place as a valuable contribution to the cause of liberal education."—*Congregational Quarterly.*

"I observe in Atwater's excellent Manual of Elementary Logic a disposition to unite the real improvements of the analytic with the established truths of the old logic."—DR. JAMES MCCOSH, *late Professor of Logic in Queen's College, Belfast, Ireland.*

Dr. Blair's Lectures on Rhetoric. Abridged, with Questions. 60 cents.

The want of a system of Rhetoric upon a concise plan has rendered this little volume acceptable to the teaching and reading public. Many who are terrified at the idea of travelling over a ponderous volume in search of information, will yet set out on a short journey in pursuit of science with alacrity and profit.

Samson's Art Criticism. Comprising a Treatise on the Principles of Man's Nature as Addressed by Art; together with a Historic Survey of the Methods of Art Execution in the Departments of Drawing, Sculpture, Architecture, Painting, Landscape Gardening, and the Decorative Arts. Designed as a Text-Book for Schools and Colleges, and as a Hand-Book for Amateurs and Artists. By G. W. SAMSON, *President of Columbia College.* 8vo. Cloth. $3.15. ABRIDGED EDITION. 12mo. Cloth. $1.60.

"Art criticism, boiled down into small doses for amateurs and students, is the function of Dr. G. W. Samson, President of Columbia College, Washington."—*Philadelphia Bulletin.*

"This work should be in the possession of every lover of the beautiful, and the abridgment deserves to be introduced into all our high schools, and made a part of common education."—*North American.*

Malcom's Butler's Analogy. The Analogy of Religion to the Constitution and Course of Nature. To which are added Two Brief Dissertations. I. On Personal Identity. II. On the Nature of Virtue. By JOSEPH BUTLER, D.C.L. With Introduction, Notes, Conspectus, and ample Index. Prepared by HOWARD MALCOM, D.D., LL.D., *President of the University at Lewisburg.* 12mo. Extra cloth. $1.15.

"We fully justify the editor's reasons for offering another edition of Butler, viz., that he had found none satisfactory as a text-book. . . . His Introduction is valuable, but his admirable Conspectus, of nearly fifty pages of fine type, gives a key to the work which will make the study of Butler a new kind of business. We have been surprised and delighted with this new aid afforded by President Malcom. In our opinion this edition will be the text-book used by all intelligent instructors who once give it an examination. Persons who have been repelled from studying Butler by the difficulties both of the argument and the style, will find these difficulties chiefly disappear by the facilities Dr. M. has afforded."—*Southern Baptist.*

Studies in the English of Bunyan. By Prof. J. B. GRIER. 12mo. Cloth. $1.25.

Smith's Elements of the Laws; or, Outlines of the System of Civil and Criminal Laws in Force in the United States and in the several States of the Union. Designed as a text-book and for general use. By THOMAS L. SMITH, *late Judge of the Supreme Court of the State of Indiana.* New edition, revised. 12mo. Fine cloth. $1.50.

This work is designed to enable any one to acquire a competent knowledge of his legal rights and privileges in all of the most important political and business relations of the citizens of the country, with the principles upon which they are founded, and the means of asserting and maintaining them in civil and criminal cases.

Schmitz's German Grammar. A Text-book for the Practical Study of the German Language. By J. ADOLPH SCHMITZ, A.M., *Professor of Modern Languages and Literature in the University of Wooster, Ohio,* and HERMAN J. SCHMITZ, *Instructor of German and French, Newark, New Jersey.* 12mo. Half roan. $1.50.

"Schmitz's 'German Grammar' I have received and examined, and, to my opinion, it is far superior to any other German grammar thus far published—the best ever come to my sight. I can fully recommend it to all teachers of the German language."—PROF. HENRY MARIN, *State Normal School, Oshkosh, Wisconsin.*

Long's Primary Grammar. An Introduction to English Grammar. An easy Method for Beginners. By HARRIETT S. LONG, *Preceptress in English and French, St. Anna's Hall, Brookeville, Maryland.* 16mo. Boards. 25 cents.

Lieber's Civil Liberty and Self-Government. A Treatise on Civil Liberty and Self-Government. New edition, revised and enlarged. Edited by THEODORE D. WOOLSEY. 8vo. Extra cloth. $3.15.

Lieber's Political Ethics. A Manual of Political Ethics, designed chiefly for the use of Colleges and Students at Law. 2 vols. 8vo. Extra cloth. $5.50.

Progress of Philosophy. By Samuel Tyler, LL.D. In the Past and in the Future. Second Edition, enlarged. 12mo. Cloth. $1.75.

Meredith's Every-Day Errors of Speech. By L. P. MEREDITH, M.D., D.D.S., author of "The Teeth and How to Save them." 16mo. Fine cloth. 75 cents.

"If any one flatters himself that he knows how to pronounce the English language, let him buy this thin little volume of less than one hundred pages, and treat himself to a few hundred surprises. He will probably rise up from its perusal a wiser and a better man; for it treats of the common errors of speech made by educated persons, who would be glad to have their attention called to the mistakes that fall unconsciously from their tongues."—*Louisville Courier-Journal.*

SANFORD'S SERIES OF ARITHMETICS.

SANFORD'S ANALYTICAL SERIES.

COMPRISED IN FOUR BOOKS.

The Science of Numbers reduced to its last analysis. Mental and Written Arithmetic successfully combined in each Book of the Series.

By SHELTON P. SANFORD, A.M.,
Professor of Mathematics in Mercer University, Georgia.

FIRST BOOK.

Sanford's First Lessons in Analytical Arithmetic. Comprising Mental and Written Exercises. Handsomely and appropriately Illustrated. 16mo. Half roan. 27 cents.

SECOND BOOK.

Sanford's Intermediate Analytical Arithmetic. Comprising Mental and Written Exercises. 16mo. 232 pp. Half roan. 45 cents.

THIRD BOOK.

Sanford's Common School Analytical Arithmetic. 12mo. 355 pp. Half roan. 80 cents.

FOURTH BOOK.

Sanford's Higher Analytical Arithmetic; or, THE METHOD of making ARITHMETICAL CALCULATIONS on PRINCIPLES of UNIVERSAL APPLICATION, without the AID of FORMAL RULES. 12mo. 419 pp. Half roan. Cloth sides. $1.25.

From Prof. HUGH S. THOMPSON, *Principal Columbia Male Academy, Columbia, S. C.*

"Sanford's Arithmetics are superior to any that I have seen in the fulness of the examples, the clearness and simplicity of the analyses, and the accuracy of the rules and definitions. This opinion is based upon a *full* and *thorough test* in the school-room. To those teachers who may examine these Arithmetics with reference to introduction, I would especially commend the treatment of Percentage and Profit and Loss. No text-books that I have ever used are so satisfactory to teachers and pupils."

From Capt. S. Y. CALDWELL, *Supt. of Nashville (Tenn.) Public Schools.*

"Your Intermediate and Advanced Analytical Arithmetics are among the best I have examined.

"It is contrary to my practice to write testimonials or recommendations, but the high merit of your book certainly justifies it in this instance."

From Prof. B. MALLON, *Superintendent of Atlanta (Ga.) Public Schools.*

"I think they [Sanford's Arithmetics] are the best books on the subject ever published; and I trust it will not be long before they will be introduced into every school in our State. In my judgment they are the very perfection of school-books on Arithmetic."

CHAUVENET'S SERIES OF MATHEMATICS.

CHAUVENET'S GEOMETRY.

A Treatise on Elementary Geometry, with Appendices containing a copious Collection of Exercises for the Student and an Introduction to Modern Geometry. By WM. CHAUVENET, *Professor of Mathematics and Astronomy in Washington University, St. Louis.* Crown 8vo. Cloth. $1.75.

"I am glad to see at last an American text-book on this subject which is not from seventy-five to two thousand years behind the time, and which, without casting away what is good in the old, does not totally exclude the brilliant geometrical discoveries of the present century. I shall recommend its adoption as a text-book in this University."—PROF. J. W. SAFFORD, *Director of the Dearborn Observatory, Chicago, Ill.*

"At a late meeting of the Board of Public Schools in this city, Chauvenet's Elementary Geometry was adopted as a regular text-book in our High School course. Written by one who is so thoroughly a master, it everywhere in its details indicates in a suggestive form their bearings on the ultimate questions of Analysis. In publishing a work of the high character that the Geometry unquestionably bears, you have laid under obligation to your firm the friends of mathematical studies throughout the land."—WM. T. HARRIS, ESQ., *Superintendent of Public Schools, St. Louis, Mo.*

CHAUVENET'S PLANE AND SPHERICAL TRIGONOMETRY.

By WM. CHAUVENET, *Prof. of Mathematics and Astronomy in Washington University, St. Louis.* New and Revised Edition. 8vo. Cloth. $1.60.

CHAUVENET'S METHOD OF LEAST SQUARES.

A Treatise on the Method of Least Squares; or, The Application of the Theory of Probabilities in the Combination of Observations. From the author's Manual of Spherical and Practical Astronomy. By WM. CHAUVENET, *Prof. of Mathematics and Astronomy in Washington University, St. Louis.* 8vo. Cloth. $1.60.

CHAUVENET'S ASTRONOMY.

A Manual of Spherical and Practical Astronomy. Embracing the general problems of Spherical Astronomy, its special applications to Nautical Astronomy, and the Theory and Use of Fixed and Portable Astronomical Instruments. With an Appendix on the Method of Least Squares. Amply Illustrated with Engravings on Wood and Steel. By WM. CHAUVENET, *Prof. of Mathematics and Astronomy in Washington University, St. Louis.* (*University edition.*) 2 vols. Medium 8vo. Cloth. $7.00.

CLASSICAL WORKS OF REFERENCE.

GARDNER'S LATIN LEXICON.

A Dictionary of the Latin Language, particularly adapted to the Classics usually studied preparatory to a Collegiate Course. By FRANCIS GARDNER, A.M. 8vo. Sheep. $3.00.

LEVERETT'S LATIN LEXICON.

A Copious Lexicon of the Latin Language. Compiled chiefly from the Magnum Totius Latinitatis Lexicon of Facciolati and Forcellini, and the German Works of Scheller and Luenemann, embracing the Classical Distinctions of Words, and the Etymological Index of Freund's Lexicon. By F. P. LEVERETT. Large 8vo. Sheep. $5.50.*

This work contains all the words in the Latin language, embracing those used by authors of the classical, ante-classical, and post-classical periods, with words of modern origin coined for scientific and other purposes.

LEMPRIERE'S CLASSICAL DICTIONARY.

Containing a full account of all the Proper Names mentioned in ancient authors, with Tables of Coins, Weights, and Measures in use among the Greeks and Romans; to which is prefixed a Chronological Table. 8vo. Sheep. $3.25.* ABRIDGED EDITION. 12mo. Extra cloth. $1.50.

The original text of Lempriere has in this edition been carefully revised and amended, and much valuable original matter added. The work is now a complete Bibliotheca Classica, containing in a condensed and readily accessible form all the information required by the student upon the geography, topography, history, literature, and mythology of antiquity and of the ancients, with bibliographical references for such as wish to get fuller information on the subjects treated of.

GROVES'S GREEK DICTIONARY.

A Greek and English Dictionary, comprising all the Words in the writings of the most popular Greek authors, with the difficult inflections in them, and in the Septuagint and New Testament. Designed for the Use of Schools and the Under-Graduate Course of a Collegiate Education. By JOHN GROVES. With corrections and additional matter by the American editor. 8vo. Sheep. $2.25.*

The object of the compiler has been to produce a work which young Greek scholars could use with ease and advantage to themselves, but sufficiently full to be equally serviceable as they advanced.

PICKERING'S GREEK LEXICON.

A Comprehensive Lexicon of the Greek Language, adapted to the Use of Colleges and Schools of the United States. By JOHN PICKERING, LL.D. New Edition, revised and corrected. Large 8vo. Sheep. $5.50.*

This work contains all the words in the Greek language, with their correct interpretation into English, and their different shades of meaning carefully distinguished and illustrated by citations from standard authors.

www.ingramcontent.com/pod-product-compliance
Lightning Source LLC
LaVergne TN
LVHW020106110826
845151LV00001B/74